THE BIG CHANGE
AFTER THE ENVIRONMENTAL REVOLUTION

Also by Max Nicholson

THE SYSTEM: The Misgovernment of Modern Britain
THE ENVIRONMENTAL REVOLUTION:
    A Guide for the New Masters of the Earth

THE BIG CHANGE

Max Nicholson

AFTER THE ENVIRONMENTAL REVOLUTION

McGraw-Hill Book Company
New York   St. Louis   San Francisco   Toronto

Copyright © 1973 by Max Nicholson.
All rights reserved. Printed in the United States of America. No part of this publication may be reproduced, stored in a retrieval system, or transmitted, in any form or by any means, electronic, mechanical, photocopying, recording, or otherwise, without the prior written permission of the publisher.

Library of Congress Cataloging in Publication Data

Nicholson, Max.
    The big change.

    1. Environmental policy.   2. Environmental protection.   I. Title.
HC79.E5N48   301.31   73-5703
ISBN 0-07-046487-1

123456789 BPBP 79876543

A portion of "New Year Letter (January 1, 1940)" from *Collected Longer Poems* by W. H. Auden, copyright © 1941 by W. H. Auden, is reprinted by permission of Random House, Inc.

Contents

Foreword vii

1. *Introductory* 1
2. *The Build-up of the Change* 31
3. *Setting the Requirement* 66
4. *Toward Ecological Humanism* 86
5. *Ways and Means: Direction and Guidance* 116
6. *The Population Explosion* 142
7. *The Prospect of Doomsday* 166
8. *The Quality of Living* 190
9. *People in Society* 206
10. *Change and the Citizen* 231
11. *A Way to Human Survival?* 252
12. *Conclusion* 275

Index 279

Illustrations

Figure 1—Page 18   The Biosphere and the Technosphere

Figure 2—Page 20   The Evolution from the Biosphere, via Man, of the Noosphere and its Extensions Nomosphere and Technosphere

Figure 3—Page 95   Man's Place in the Global Environment

Figure 4—Page 173   Relationship between Human Processes and Structural Levels of the Biosphere

Foreword

So unnatural has been the modern conjunction of traditional institutions and values with vast technological innovations transforming every aspect of human life that something has had to give. Immense and complex stresses of a seismic character threaten the social foundations of our contemporary order, or disorder.

Countless possible solutions, policies, and programs of remedy have been advanced, many within the limits of traditional thought, and many more outside the limits of realistic options for the future. It is only as the beginnings of the great grinding process become traceable that the situation can be reappraised in some depth and the irrelevance of so many well-meant interpretations and propositions can be discerned.

As our inherited fabric of partial world order disintegrates before our eyes, it is blindingly evident that any tolerable successor to it must be far more comprehensive, more universal, and more readily acceptable on a basis of free choice by educated communities. It has for generations been apparent that the scientific method alone could provide the necessary basis for a new order.

Unfortunately, modern science has been too fragmented, too timidly reluctant to approach the fundamentals, and too largely enslaved to the military-industrial complex, to be able to face the responsibilities which science has engendered. In the face of this impotence, combined with the lost credibility of familiar religions, political creeds, and social institutions, the present chaotic and tense stalemate has been created for the world.

This stalemate has many varied potential outcomes, some catastrophic, some merely violent, others conceivably peaceable. Only in the past few years has any new factor emerged which could give a clue to the way through the woods. This book explores the possibility that the worldwide surge of concern for the welfare of man's physical environment, reviewed in its predecessor *The Environmental Revolution,* may point the way, and, if its lessons are vigorously applied, enable the stalemate to be broken.

That is not to say that ecology, even in the loose sense now in vogue, can itself provide the answer. Rather, it seems that the broad and deep impact of second-hand ecological principles on our lives, and the illumination which they have thrown on current dissatisfaction with prevalent values and institutions, is creating a new stable surface on which fresh attitudes, principles, concepts, policies, and programs can be built up, first supplementing and eventually largely superseding those which have become manifestly obsolete.

This book therefore is not yet another presentation of the ecological dilemma of mankind. It starts from the point where such presentations have hitherto ended and seeks to answer the question how and where a world which has absorbed that message can consciously undertake to redirect its social evolution so as to integrate ecological considerations. It is written for those who, being more or less convinced of the case for far-reaching change and of the relevance of ecology to pursuing it, now look for something more concrete and constructive about where we go from here.

Such a bridging work at this pioneering stage demands both an extensive experience in public affairs and administration and long familiarity with ecological principles and their application in conservation and management. Given the small existing population of ecologists and the remoteness of most of them until very lately from public affairs, I am among the few who are at home in both these worlds.

Forty-five years ago I opened my book *How Birds Live* with the words, then strange to most readers, "There is a flourishing science, Ecology..." and I went on to review its application to understanding the way of life of birds and their relation to their environment. My membership in the British Ecological Society is of forty years standing. Sixteen years ago, I organized, presided over, and contributed to the Edinburgh (6th) Technical Meeting of the International Union for the Conservation of Nature and Natural Resources, which first brought scientists, managers, and public administrators together to discuss internationally and in depth such questions as the relation of ecology to landscape planning and the rehabilitation of areas devastated by human interference.

After studying public affairs widely and deeply as General Secretary of the research group named Political and Economic Planning (PEP), I gained extensive practical experience during World War II as a senior official of the Combined Shipping Adjustment Board and later in Whitehall as head of the Office of the Lord President of the Council (who was also then Deputy Prime Minister). It would be wearisome to recite at length the dual qualifications which have gone to the making of this book and which have been referred to in *The Environmental Revolution* and elsewhere.

It is important, however, to bear in mind that propositions in the realm of public affairs, unlike propositions in the realm of science, cannot be tested experimentally or measured and followed through accurately so as to analyze the roles of the many variables involved. That, however, by no means rules out the scientific approach as irrelevant or ineffectual for public affairs.

Especially in the all-important area of constructing hypotheses and model-making, it is already possible to provide a scientific basis at least for the earlier stages of decision-making, even if at later stages a choice between the remaining possibilities must rest on largely subjective judgments. In the present immature state of the social sciences, ecology and other branches of biology have an important part to play here.

This book accordingly represents an attempt to interpret, in the light of ecological principles and knowledge, the relevance of recent advances in environmental conservation to the hitherto unsolved problems of conscious and accelerated human social evolution over the foreseeable future. It is based on experience in successfully applying these principles in a wide range of cases, not only to management of land and natural resources but to the creation of an effective series of national and international institutions and programs for developing public interventions in the interests of environment. It seems legitimate to assume that these same principles, interpreted with wide knowledge of both ecology and public affairs, can offer a promising approach to the creation of a new structure for concerted advances towards the guidance and furtherance of human evolution during the next decades or generations. That such a structure must be created if catastrophe is to be avoided, and that it must be created so far as practicable on a broadly scientific basis, are assumptions which should now command general acceptance.

On such a foundation this book can offer neither the confident dogmatism and simplistic persuasiveness which might appeal better to some readers, nor the massively underpinned and exhaustively documented deployment of facts which might be more congenial to others. Fortunately, the range of material on which all workers in this wide realm must draw is becoming increasingly well known in outline to serious readers, and much of it can be readily traced. This book can, therefore, be kept within such limits of length and technicality as will enable it to be readily understood by general readers having a sufficiently serious interest in the problem of mankind's survival through the years ahead.

In ending this foreword, I feel bound to point out that the nature of the subject and the difficulties of reaching forward to meet the future are such that an effort of mind-stretching is called for on the part of the reader. Those who are unable or unwilling to entertain the idea of stretching their minds are advised to avoid vexation by putting the book down before going any further.

A growing number of thoughtful people are coming to experience the satisfaction of participating in a serious effort to understand the nature of the contemporary human predicament, and how this affects them personally, and to determine what adjustments they feel moved to make in their own attitudes and activities.

There are also immense numbers of people who still do not know what all the fuss is about, and who are fully content either to paddle along as they are or to confine their ideas of necessary change to gradual and minor adaptations in the patterns familiar to them from past years. Those who belong in this second category will win little joy from embarking on *The Big Change*. To them it must seem utopian and far out. Others who are unlikely to find it rewarding are those whose religious, political, or economic preconceptions are so fixed as to pre-empt their approach to the future in favor of some narrowly formulated creed or theory.

This work is addressed to the open-minded. Fortunately, there is every indication that here the ranks are at last growing quite rapidly, and that the long reign of the closed and half-closed minds is slowly ending. New ideas, new knowledge, new aspirations, and new sensibilities are on the move, and it is with these that the following review tries to deal.

It takes its place as a sequel to the important but now largely played-out debate on the environmental consequences of modern technology and of its accompanying attitudes and practices. That debate has cleared the way for a shift of thinking toward the restructuring of human society, the reshaping of prevailing attitudes, and the evolution of new policies, programs, and priorities.

1

INTRODUCTORY

A Big Change is bearing down upon us all. There can be few thoughtful men and women who do not yet sense it. Their dawning awareness, however grudging and qualified, is no less significant than the change itself. Evolution transforms other species in spite of themselves. Human evolution has to be a creative blend of external imperatives and of some groping conscious effort to discover and to pursue what must be. Both these essentials are now manifest. Whether we like it or not, whether we speak and think of it or not, the Big Change is on its way. For good or ill, human life, human institutions, and man's view of his own identity can never be the same again, unless some stupendous catastrophe brings a relapse to illiterate barbarism.

Yet this profound and overwhelming event, the greatest for

many centuries or even millennia, is allowed to be swamped by countless trendy trivialities, which are accorded infinitely more resources, time, and attention. What little heed it receives is largely pre-empted by special facets which are treated as self-contained subjects rather than as inseparable manifestations of the Big Change. We seem to find it embarrassing, even baffling, to approach openly a problem so complex and cosmic, in which our own inhibitions and feelings are so inextricably involved. Its brooding presence bothers us not merely in itself but as an unpalatable reminder of our incapacity to measure up to the true status of Man.

Understandable as such aversion is, it cannot be persisted in without leading to unimaginable disasters. We must face the Big Change in its entirety with courage, understanding, and a common resolve to make the best of so immense an opportunity. The swollen human race now musters close on four billion members, but their fate depends upon the vision, the capability, and the devotion to posterity of a tiny fraction of that multitude. Only if enough of these can now acquit themselves as men will there be grounds for hope that man may yet survive and prosper on this earth.

The awakening efforts of this fraction are witnessed by a fast-expanding flow of writings, speeches, plays, films, and other treatments of parts of the problem. Varying as these do in tone, in scope, in angle of approach, and in originality they still converge encouragingly toward tackling the next stage of human evolution.

Much of the impetus toward new awareness of the plight and the potential of mankind has come from ecologists and other students of nature. Somehow their message has been attentively heard, while other more insistent voices have been ignored. Ecologists alone, however, cannot provide a new pattern for human evolution. This book, based on an ecological approach, aims to promote a wider program of acceptable action for tackling the next series of intellectual, ethical, and institutional gaps within the social and economic fields and for harnessing to such a program much effort which might otherwise run to waste.

This objective demands a highly extensive and therefore often superficial treatment of a wide range of problems. It precludes much discussion in depth, and many qualifications and cautions which would have been desirable had space permitted them. It assumes, however, that those readers who are seriously interested will also refer to at least some of the valuable and relevant works which are cited, and others which may have been overlooked. Unless that happens, the value of this work as a catalyst and as a handbook to constructive action will be largely lost. If a means of shaping human evolution is to be fashioned it must be the converging work of many minds, using ecological principles not as fetters to restrict the human handling of human problems, but as a basis for progress.

Agonizing as the prospect is, some encouraging things have happened during the past five or six years. The tedious and distasteful task of stripping away the cloak of bogus respectability from many inherited but shoddy idea-systems and institutions can now be left to complete itself with the momentum it has already gained. Attention can be concentrated on more forward-looking and constructive tasks, with confidence that reasonable approaches and practical proposals will no longer be ignored, or frustrated for the better part of a lifetime before being considered on their merits. The rigidity, the complacency, the authority, and the inner self-confidence which held each country in thrall to its own variant of the System are crumbling away.

Demolition is an essential, if unpalatable, early stage of reconstruction. It can, however, prove worse than useless unless there is promptly made ready a sound and acceptable set of principles on which satisfactory reconstruction can smoothly follow. Here the issue remains open and obscure.

One salutary gain over some past situations is worth noting. The same processes which have undermined the credibility of the inherited order have revealed as equally insolvent the stale doctrines and programs of revolutionary or reformist groups wedded to particular dogmas. These have in some cases been waiting in the wings for decades to profit by some convenient and possibly manipulated breakdown of an existing regime. Conventional Marxism of all brands, fascism, and other shop-soiled isms are inhibited from exploiting the situation not only because their old-fashioned idea-systems appeal to few but professional conspirators and their usually callow dupes, but also because they cannot and will not honestly obtain democratic acceptance. Even liberalism, socialism, conservatism, and nationalism can rarely command more than minority and tepid loyalties. Whatever great moving and unifying principles and causes the future may hold, they will be not be those of the recent past, or of any of its jaded crusaders. Whoever may be the intended manipulators, and whatever virtues they may claim, people are no longer content to be manipulated in such ways. They want something better.

Conditioned as we have become to changes brought about with excessive publicity through wars, revolutions, demonstrations, or long-winded political debates, we may fail to recognize the full significance of tacit abandonments of past majority views through incessant exposure to contrary opinions diffused by mass media. It is even easier to be misled by recessions in intensity of commitment to attitudes still nominally held, but now so feebly that when it comes to the crunch they no longer prevail over underrated opposing positions.

Perhaps the greatest change of all is in attitudes to change itself. The concept that change is not something to be dreaded and resisted as such, but is often a natural and welcome process, has bitten in deeply to western culture, with particular encouragement from the United States. Psychologically, however, overrapid change, without adequate guidance and sense of direction, is increasingly felt to be generating insecurity, frustration, and even violence. It is clearly beyond our powers to put the clock back, or even to check or retard the process in which we are currently being swept along. The only constructive course is to view inevitable change in the light of a much more extended time scale. We must learn to perceive and to determine our direction in terms of at least the next three or four decades, instead of the hitherto customary three or four years.

We are coming to realize that although intentions and ideals translated immediately into action programs may make good drama, they are doomed to frustration if they do not relate to what people feel they need. To bring about effective action on fundamentals it is necessary first to establish the right psychological and intellectual basis, in the light of the limits imposed by social, political, economic, and technological conditions prevailing at the time and place.

The occurrence of change depends on readiness for change. Despite the earnest writings of revolutionaries we remain ignorant of the processes which bring about this readiness—above all a readiness for general acceptance of change in a certain direction and at a certain pace. Few aspects of public affairs are less seriously studied and more carelessly mishandled than the intricate and delicate operations concerned with the management of change. Plainly it involves a subtle interplay between personal and social aspirations and frustrations, with a progressive erosion of constraints and build-up of positive pressures. But how and at what stage is action triggered and its course set?

Change is accelerated today partly because education and communications are widening and lengthening the channels which lead up to it. The steps toward decision-making, and the interlocking of policies and options, involve wider and more continuous consultation or monitoring of public opinion, and more complex professional surveys and advice. Sudden changes of direction, whether constitutional or revolutionary, become more difficult and more often illusory. Past changes increasingly dictate both present and future courses. Both the ballot box and the barricade are farther down the line than they used to be.

Paradoxically the plane of ideas is now where the action is. The freedom of choice remaining up to the conventional last moment shrinks as the choice between options at that level becomes increasingly predetermined. It is no longer good enough to ask ourselves what we ought to *do* now. A much more serious question is what we ought to be worrying about now in order to make it possible for men and women thirty years hence still to have sensible and tolerable options to choose between. If, and only if, we look after the thinking properly will the action take care of itself. The right choice of agenda now is an essential step toward the right decisions later.

People in large numbers amount to no more than ineffective or dangerous rabbles unless they are given coherence and harmony by an acceptable set of ideas and beliefs, operating through a familiar and congenial structure of institutions, law, custom, and up-to-date practice. The people lean upon the institutions, and the institutions lean upon the ideas which prop them up. If and when these ideas become discredited and untenable it is only a matter of time before the institutions decay and collapse, leaving the people naked and bewildered. When that stage arrives, as it is now arriving almost throughout the world, the only alternative to chaos is to rethink the basic ideas in such terms that a compatible fresh institutional structure can be devised and can be progressively adopted by general consent. But new ideas can express themselves convincingly only through new types of people, vividly aware of their common predicament and eager to share their common vision.

The all-important factor here is time. Some wake up early but others sleep late. If the early risers are too hasty in launching an effort to transform society they will find the still redoubtable resistance of entrenched supporters of the conventional System reinforced by the mass inertia of prostrate hosts of slumberers. They will also run the risk of misconceiving the full extent of the requirements, through premature crystalization of ideas still needing to be adapted to new psychological or technical factors which would emerge at a later stage.

On the other hand the main effort for change must not be

too long delayed. In that case the atmosphere will be soured, and confidence undermined through a sense of helplessness and frustration, due to the manifest incapacity of the outworn System to find out what the real problems are and to frame measures for handling them effectively. Ensuing apathy, sectionalism, disillusionment, and even sheer violence will narrow the scope for wise leadership and may even interpose a long negative and destructive interlude before reconstruction can begin. The first moment that a potentially decisive block of opinion understands the futility of continuing as before is the moment to intervene.

For western civilization, with its patently disintegrating beliefs, ideas, and institutions, the hour is already late. Wherever we look we see the red lights flashing like countless bush fires in the dry season across Africa. It is arguable that the Aztecs and the Incas were in important respects still in better shape than ourselves up to a few months before their civilizations were consigned to the pages of history. Yet until the end of the sixties our own threatened and virtually doomed society devoted next to no resources to exploring how to insure that it has a future.

If there are signs of awakening they are still alarmingly feeble and dangerously dispersed. Clear formulation and vigorous dissemination of the necessary guidance seem to lag behind the quite widespread awareness of the lateness of the hour. A small number of writers, largely of scientific background, have come forward with stimulating analyses covering various aspects of the problems we are facing. The world's appointed leaders, however, still find it more convenient to lead from the rear.

Such thoughts, hovering between hope and gloom, beset those who doggedly cling to a belief in the evolution of man in the future as in the past, and who feel committed to assist in getting him through the agonizingly perilous pass to which he has managed to bring himself. By concentrating on that exacting task we may at least hope to mitigate the sense of cosmic vertigo as we shuffle awkwardly along the rim of the abyss.

For all its apparent complexity the task is in essence a fairly straightforward one of higher administration. The mess into which the affairs of the global village have been allowed to drift by its elders is different mainly in scale from those all too familiar in cozier little parishes.

As I have tried to show in *The Environmental Revolution,* the recent successful transformation of a number of earnest splinter groups of nature-lovers and conservationists into a worldwide movement of commanding influence has been due largely to a particular mix of scientific research and extensive amateur observation, of voluntary effort combined with the effort of official agencies, of fierce local pride and care for particular types of heritage acting in conjunction with a global sense of trusteeship and resolution to work together on the part of men and women scattered over many countries but dedicated to similar ideals. The blending of these and other elements has generated an almost irresistible dynamic force, by comparison with which the support of other equally good causes tends often to look tepid and disintegrated. Moreover, far from having reached its peak, this dynamism of the environmental movement is still firmly set on its upward path, with every promise of widening and deepening its influence at least well into the seventies. Perhaps the main threat at the moment is that of internal dissensions due to the conflicts generated by newcomers in a hurry, who disregard the principles whose success has attracted them.

Reflecting on such achievements, we are led to wonder whether a comparably intelligent and concerted effort might not go some way toward doing for the conservation and further evolution of mankind what is being done, so far as human misbehavior permits, for the survival of nature. As I expressed it in *The Environmental Revolution:*

> It seems clear that in order to live through this phase successfully it will be necessary to develop something fresh, parallel to the conservation movement in its recently broadened form. A kind of human conservation movement seems

to be called for, which can study, analyse, devise remedies for and tackle the self-defeating and self-destructive tendencies of mankind, in the light of modern science and independently of the dogmas and retrograde patterns of churches, political parties and other conservatively-minded and out-of-touch institutions. Urbanism, delinquency, racialism, commercialism, bureaucracy, dogmatic politics, pop culture and social satisfactions will be among the central preoccupations of such a new approach.

... Eventually a time must come when through fusion of ideas, through reappraisal and shaking out of values, and through the removal of obstacles to intercommunication between what are now separate worlds of discourse, it will become impossible in current practice to make the kinds of distinction which unfortunately still need making now between ecology, conservation, and environmental aspects on the one hand and education, religion, prevailing cultural patterns and public affairs on the other. A new ecologically-oriented culture will find it hard to imagine how people of our times could ever have supposed that any other approach made sense. ...

That passage foreshadows the function of this book, which is to consider how the principles and approaches developed for harmonizing Man with nature might also be effectually applied to harmonizing men with Man, and people with one another. Whenever a public meeting on the environment closes with general discussion there is usually some kind of demand voiced to that effect. Time and circumstances have often prevented me from responding to such pleas. This book provides an opportunity to offer an explanation.

It is already evident that recent progress in such studies as ecology, ethology, and social anthropology will have repercussions upon western culture comparable with those of Darwinism a century earlier. Students of the realms of animals and plants in nature are inexorably being compelled to turn their minds inward toward the situation of man.

As early as 1950 Dr. Niko Tinbergen concluded his important work on *The Study of Instinct* with a section beginning "Man is an animal" in which he followed up some earlier contributions by Konrad Lorenz, and criticized "the almost universal misconception that the causes of man's behaviour are qualitatively different from the causes of animal behaviour." This misconception has of course been resolutely fostered by the churches. During the past decade essays aimed at bridging this supposed gap have become more frequent and have attracted increasing notice by a wide public.

Ecologists have matched this trend with essays on human ecology, while a leading plant geneticist, Dr. C. D. Darlington, has surveyed the whole prehistory and history of mankind from a genetic standpoint in his *Evolution of Man and Society*. In contrast to most of the work of sociologists, these contributions have thrown real light upon those elements in human nature and in human history which are relevant to the present need for a fundamental reappraisal. A very few economists, notably Professor J. K. Galbraith, have also made significant contributions. It is from such sources, duly synthesized and evaluated, that a solidly based new knowledge and new outlook begins to emerge, perhaps comparable in importance with that earlier big change which afterwards came to be known as the Renaissance.

It is useful to bear in mind the historical parallel of the Renaissance. It had been preceded by a period of vigorous growth which included the construction of a vast network of cathedrals, abbeys, and churches, the establishment of flourishing cities and trade routes, of ecclesiastical and secular administrations, laws and courts of justice, and the first universities and centers of free scholarship. The contemplation of such achievements, and dissatisfaction with their limitations, led to a conviction that man could not be merely what the theologians and rulers of Christendom assumed him to be. Artists, scholars, poets, inventors, early scientists, and explorers attracted keen interest and lavish patronage in their successful search for a new image and concept of man. That image strained and eventually broke inherited conceptual and institutional patterns, and released a new surge of creative energy. Our problem today is similar. However, in the absence of any serious hope of constructive leadership from the current artistic and literary world it is to the ecologists, the ethologists, and the still lagging social sciences that we must look for the intellectual foundation of the Big Change. It is their task to hold up a bright new mirror in which twenty-first-century man will be able to see his likeness with a shock of belated recognition, and perceive what he has to do by observing who he really is.

As in the Renaissance, a fresh dynamic is arising partly from the revolt of individuals against laws, rules, and conventions which they have come to view as infringing on the fulfillment of their personalities; partly also from disillusionment and contempt at the manifest gulf between the lofty pretensions of established institutions and their sordid conduct and results; and partly from a sense of intellectual claustrophobia induced by the cramping and suffocating influence of stale and outworn assumptions and concepts which go on being disseminated long after they have ceased to be relevant or credible. Such reactions, not only among the young, are a necessary and healthy first stage, but only a first stage, toward cultural renewal in the form of a more aware, more flexible, less hierarchical and compartmented world society, reshaped in conformity with what we are coming to know. Yesterday's heresy gives rise to today's bewilderment and to tomorrow's orthodoxy. In the process we are faced with some revolting paradoxes. Self-styled champions of human rights shout down and assault others seeking to exercise these same rights. Communities ostensibly dedicated to love indulge in murder for kicks. Emancipated critics of Man's exploitation of Man adopt the exploitation of their more settled fellows as a way of life. Ideals, impulses, aspirations can soon become a mockery in the absence of a code of social conduct responsibly embraced.

If such unworthy excesses are to be put in their place as the acts of a lunatic fringe, or of evil manipulators, it is essential without further delay to build up an intellectually and emotionally satisfying core structure upon which a worthier culture can grow. Without that, appeals to law and order cannot avail.

Fortunately the study of animal behavior, which we call ethology—a term not yet included in this sense in most dictionaries—has come to our rescue. It has shown that many kinds of animals have elaborate patterns of conduct in relation to one another which bear marked similarities to certain types of human behavior. Aggression, sexuality, the formation of pair-bonds, the creation of an accepted pecking order between more and less dominant individuals, and social releasers or displacement activities are examples which have become widely familiar. Originating largely from ornithology this new and illuminating study has shifted its focus to mammals, including man as well as other primates. Its concepts, based upon intensive field observation as well as on laboratory experiment, have thrown a fresh light on the springs of human actions and on the evolutionary struggle through which Man has painfully and precariously reached a plane of reasonable and moral conduct.

From this new vantage point, and from those simultaneously reached by palaeontology and archaeology, we can not only dimly perceive the route by which man has arrived at his present awkward transitional state, but can begin to understand how and why he is still subject to such disgraceful relapses, and which way he must shape his course in order to overcome, if not the tendency, at any rate the conditions in which they can seize command of him. The way is thus opened to a dispassionate pragmatic treatment of man's age-old burden of sin and guilt in terms linked with medicine, education, and environmental design rather than with fire and brimstone. A particularly important aspect of this advance is that it is not biased toward pinning "guilt" upon individuals, groups, or social conditions. It leans first toward understanding and diagnosis, as the first steps toward prevention and cure.

The application and dissemination of this new knowledge on the human plane began less than two decades ago. It is a vast task, especially since it enjoys as yet something under one-millionth of the resources which it clearly merits, and which are essential if it is to be pressed through in time to avert incalculable and needless further human misery and waste. Yet at least we have now seen it launched. It will gather strength, and it will prevail, but how slowly, and with how many losses and setbacks?

At the present stage one of our most pressing strategic tasks is to link together the principles derived from ethology, and from related studies concerning man's evolution and potential, with those emerging from the even more fashionable science of ecology. Once linked, and buttressed by computer power, the two will provide for the first time a fully respectable and effective foundation for the lagging and hitherto largely abortive social sciences, whose contribution so far has hardly ever failed to disappoint. Unfortunately both ecology and ethology must mature much further before their stimulus can be transformed into a firm foundation. The special versions of these new disciplines now in vogue may well prove ephemeral.

A main contribution of ecology is that it makes us think in terms of the healthy interplay of Man and his total environment. What are the limits, quantitative and qualitative, within which we can interfere with our inherited natural environment without dire consequences? How far can these safe limits eventually be stretched, given more knowledge and understanding, and more time? What are the penalties of overstepping them, as we have and will, and how can these be mitigated and injuries checked or healed? What is the relation between pressure of human population and the carrying capacity of the earth? How far can practicable corrections of the needless extravagances and wastes of our present economy and technology contribute toward a new equilibrium?

Such quantitative and as it were negative questions can be matched with others of a more qualitative and constructive nature. Given that so much of human development has hitherto been based on the subjugation and exploitation of nature, how is it possible to switch our energies toward the opposite aim of achieving harmony with nature in every sense and at every level? Can such a switch prove an adequate substitute in terms of human psychological needs? Can Adam put away his ax and contentedly revert to being a gardener? Can Cain satisfy his bloodthirsty instincts as a game warden? What kind and scale of conservation, urban as well as rural, would be required to provide opportunities of environmental fulfillment for all? What corresponding satisfactions at other levels are needed in order to yield a stable and balanced way of life? What kinds of education and training, of economic and social provision, are required to attain or approach fulfillment for a human society making use of the principles contributed by ethology and ecology?

In this introductory chapter these questions must suffice to indicate the scope of the present review, and the lines along which it will seek to explore the problem of utilizing ethology and ecology as a new alternative basis for the development of human societies. Without such a fundamental new basis, elaborated, understood, and eventually universally accepted, all other efforts will fail. Thought is the better part of action. But that is true only when thought is concentrated upon the areas where fuller knowledge will lead toward right action, and when action is recognized as the eager henchman of thought. The enfeebling divorce between thought and action is a key defect of our times. For a leader to say that he had no time to think is the ultimate admission of incompetence: those who have no time to think should quickly learn to think in no time, or they should resign.

We are just emerging from the long night of materialism,

during which the range of possible patterns of living has been made to seem far narrower than in fact it is. The spontaneous mass reaction toward what we call a permissive society and the visible recoil from the slavery of the ratrace are natural and up to a point healthy preparatory moves toward a more worthy conception of the way to human fulfillment. It is not, however, at all creditable to the present generation of intellectual, artistic, and moral leaders that mankind should be left to grope so blindly toward a set of positive principles and objectives which might give a little more coherence, direction, and pace to a movement much clearer about what it rejects than about what it wants, and what it is ready to do for the love of it. Much more could and should be done, and quickly, to make good the arrears of imaginative thinking and disciplined foresight. The crude limitations and distortions of current essays in futurism starkly expose our collective cultural impoverishment.

The general recognition that our inherited culture is dying and can no longer be serviceable to us, and the dawning hunger for something radically new and acceptable to our altered selves, will have to be met by much serious and solid work. This must be based upon the range of scientific knowledge which we are now acquiring about the fundamental nature of Man. Basically what is most frightening about the plight of modern Man is not the imminent possibility of his utter destruction by nuclear war, or by senseless injury to his habitat, but his acquiescence in drifting rudderless through perils which he could quickly make less serious by the conscientious use of available charts to select a more sensible course. We are the prisoners of a frivolous and selfish refusal to take the fate of mankind seriously.

Fifty years ago Pierre Teilhard de Chardin wrote in *The Phenomenon of Man:*

> Geologists have for long agreed in admitting the zonal composition of our planet... the barysphere, central and metallic, surrounded by the rocky lithosphere that in turn is

> surrounded by the fluid layers of the hydrosphere and the atmosphere ... science has rightly become accustomed to add another to these four concentric layers, the living membrane composed of the fauna and flora of the globe, the biosphere ... instead of representing a more or less vague grouping it forms a single piece, the very tissue of the genetic relations which delineate the tree of life.
>
> The recognition and isolation of a new era in evolution, the era of noogenesis, challenges us to distinguish ... yet another membrane in the majestic assembly of telluric layers. A glow ripples outward from the first spark of conscious reflection. ... Much more coherent and just as extensive as any preceding layer, it is really a new layer, the "thinking layer" which, since its germination at the end of the Tertiary Period, has spread over the world of plants and animals. In other words, outside and above the biosphere there is the noosphere.

Recently it has proved necessary to supplement these terms by expanding the scope of the term biosphere to cover the influences upon fauna and flora of the lithosphere, hydrosphere, and atmosphere, and by adding the concept of the technosphere. This latter concept,* adds the now necessary distinctions between Man's natural environment, Man's inherent beliefs, experience, and knowledge, and Man's inflated and now semiautonomous technology. Concerning the interplay of the biosphere and the technosphere I wrote,†

> These two terms are used to indicate that the total activities of nature and of man respectively are being viewed

---

* As proposed in my article and diagram in the *Geographical Magazine* of January 1970, and more fully defined in my paper, "International Economic Development and the Environment," for the Columbia University Conference of February 1970 (*Journal of International Affairs*, 1970, pp. 272–287).

† In my Columbia paper, p. 273.

specifically in terms of the physical processes involved in their operation, divested of any philosophical, ethical, economic, social, aesthetic, or value judgments. The biosphere converts solar radiation and inorganic elements into a world of living matter or biomass, maintained by continuous processes of biological productivity. It is primarily responsible for the creation of vegetable matter and secondarily, through vegetation, for growth of animal matter. The technosphere extracts from, or crops, the biosphere by mining, farming, fishing, hunting, and other methods, to acquire elements which are processed into "usable" products. Most of these are immediately distributed to human consumers or users, while a few, such as pesticides and fertilizers, are channeled back into the biosphere by being spread on the land. In addition to these "usable" products, however, vast quantities of wastes, effluents, and gases are either leaked or dumped back into the biosphere. These latter processes, like extraction and cropping, convert the land and natural resources affected from a natural into a humanly modified environment. [See Fig. 1.]

Even more recently clear analysis has begun to point to a further realm. From his evolutionary standpoint Teilhard rightly laid primary emphasis on the noosphere as the "thinking layer." He had no reason to be concerned from that standpoint and at that period with the possibility, which has only subsequently become a visible fact, that the noosphere would [hive] off from itself in two opposite directions great and complex organisms which would proliferate on a global scale and begin to obey laws and to establish a momentum of their own making, no longer readily amenable to the supervision and control of Man their creator. In addition to the *technosphere* already outlined we therefore have also to distinguish the opposite extension from the *noosphere,* emerging as a system of laws, institutions, accepted values, and established practices which may be termed the *nomosphere,* or

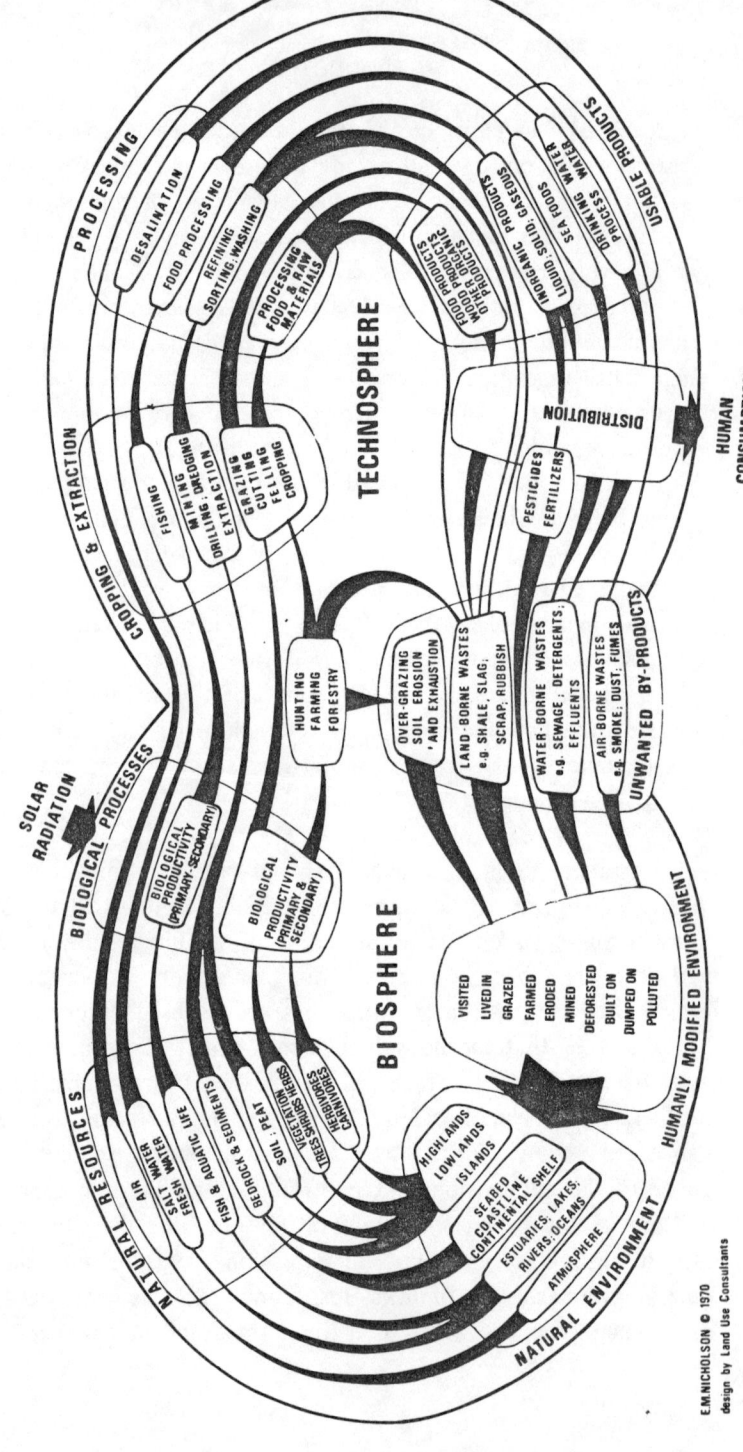

FIG. 1
THE BIOSPHERE AND THE TECHNOSPHERE

the realm of law. This forms the intangible semiautonomous counterpart of the highly tangible and also semiautonomous *technosphere*.

Like the technosphere, the nomosphere is characterized by the fact that, once brought into existence and launched, it embarks upon a course of development extending far beyond the human generation which thoughtlessly created it for immediate ends. This development arises from its own inherent logic and impetus—often neither understood nor effectively controllable by generations which subsequently inherit it, and who may come despairingly to feel themselves no longer its master but its slave.

By being tempted in recent decades to pour such immense resources into overhasty development of the technosphere, with its consequently dizzy acceleration of the pace of global integration of human activities, modern Man has immensely aggravated the problem of adapting, and retaining mastery of, the increasingly inhibiting and obsolescent pattern in which the nomosphere has for the time being been permitted to crystalize. To cap these follies, modern Man has elected largely to ignore and to starve of resources just those higher studies which could have thrown light upon the central issues of the human predicament. His punishment is to wander the earth as a blind, bewildered, unhappy giant, having conquered nature only to exchange for its beneficent rules of life a frustrating subservience to mindless and impersonal mechanisms, which he knew how to establish but not how to adapt or control.

Only superficially can modern Man be described as the creature of an urban environment. Without a complete sustaining relationship all around there can be no true environment. Modern urbanism is not so much an environment as a shifting and shoddy chaos, reflecting the blind interplay of the still disjointed technosphere and the currently obsolete phase of the nomosphere. These, until they can be mastered, must inevitably work to dehumanize and sterilize Man himself, as well as what he desperately tries to conserve as an environment to protect him against them

FIG. 2
THE EVOLUTION FROM THE BIOSPHERE, VIA MAN, OF THE NOOSPHERE AND ITS EXTENSIONS NOMOSPHERE AND TECHNOSPHERE

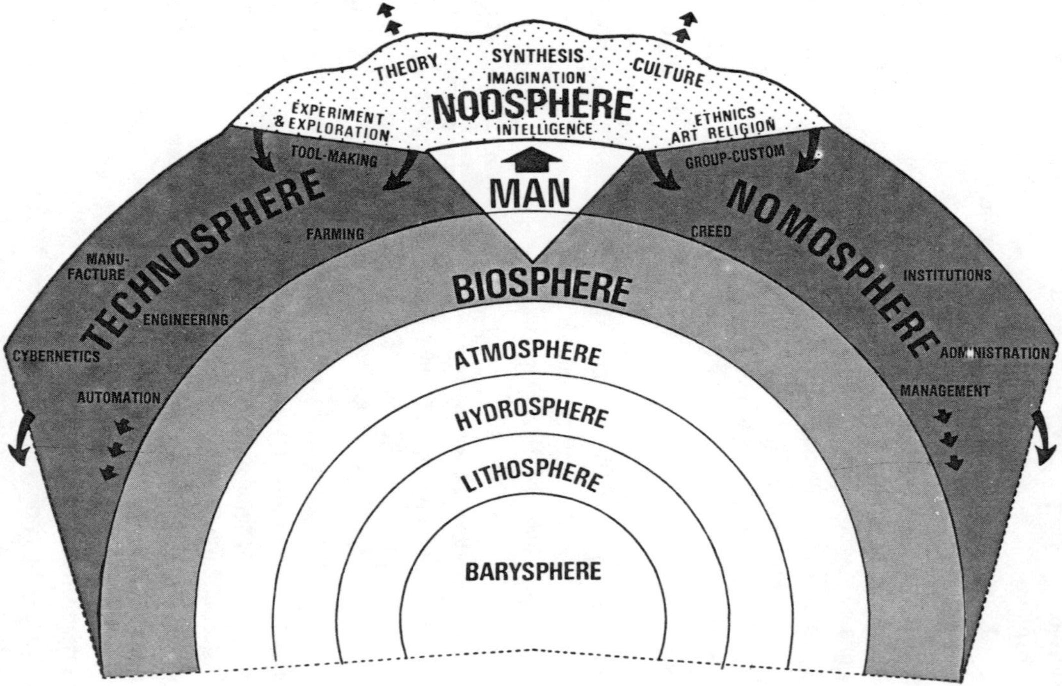

both. It should by now be plain enough that there is no future in that course, which merely fritters away time in fighting symptoms rather than causes.

Even though some may find these concepts unduly abstruse and theoretical, it is impossible to overstate the importance of achieving a sound and workable fundamental model, roughly corresponding to the situation in which we find ourselves. Without such a model we are lost. In order to avert unprofitable argument between those interested in different approaches it may be best not to insist that the technosphere and the nomosphere be accepted as additional layers to the noosphere, but rather to treat them as offshoots and extensions of it, in process of acquiring an autonomous existence and role. Metaphorically the noosphere may be regarded as the central incandescent nucleus of a human layer, which on one side relapses into a viscous cooler and visibly patterned form as the nomosphere, and on the other into a hard, obtrusive, mechanistic, material system as the technosphere. (See Fig. 2.)

In brief, after originating in the biosphere, human evolution has taken a course involving the emergence of a triple specifically human layer of first-rate importance for the planet. The central part, the noosphere, emerges from Man's revolutionary development of conscious thought, and the power to confer immortality through successive human generations on the ideas and knowledge which it accumulates through sustained cooperation across frontiers and across centuries. The second, the technosphere, grows from Man's incessant urge for tool-making, and the resulting vast complex of processes for manipulating material resources. These tend to become too complex and powerful to remain readily amenable to intelligent and effective human control, even when they lead to consequences which were never intended by the innovators and which are intensely displeasing to those exposed to them. The third, the nomosphere, is more akin to the noosphere in its abstract nature but can be related to the technosphere in the cumulative and often unintended tyranny which it exerts over peoples' lives. Although invisible, its fetters and sanctions are keenly felt by mankind, and they can certainly hurt both Man and his environment.

In considering the long-term requirements of mankind it is of immense importance to grasp the new dilemma of reconciling Man's conflicting interests in the biosphere, the noosphere, the nomosphere, and the technosphere. In the background of our gravest problems loom these four huge, grotesque, and shadowy figures: Man the runaway ape, led astray by ambitions above his station; Man the mad toolmaker, awakening like the sorcerer's apprentice to the horror of what he has let loose but cannot control; Man the superstitious lawmaker and ruler, helplessly cocooned in stupid and cruel ancestral institutions and beliefs; and Man the failed would-be rational being, who stumbled into the noosphere, as it were absentmindedly, and who faces the idiocy and guilt of having to become a drop-out from it.

In terms of human life and aims the key to reasserting control over the technosphere, and ending its tyranny over Man as well as over nature, is to modernize and reinforce the obsolete and neglected framework developed by our predecessors in the nomosphere, and above all to revive and intensify our feeble and half-hearted communications with the noosphere, which should be the supreme value and source of guidance for all mankind. In this perspective the modern worship of the technosphere is an unworthy retrogression, and indeed merely a variant upon the ancient worship of the Golden Calf. Where the claims of the technosphere conflict with those of the noosphere or of the biosphere it is the technocratic claims which must be made to yield.

A common feature of the noosphere, the nomosphere, and the technosphere is that their influence on Man occurs at any or all of three levels. Simply by virtue of being there, they all set bounds and open opportunities which place human life on a different plane from the animal. They are as much a part of Man's environment as any other, even if particular individuals or groups ignore and keep clear of one or more of them so far as possible. Beyond this, each is open freely to human entry, and the man who becomes busy in, for example, the technosphere can tap and be influenced by its stored resources even if he contributes nothing to them and hardly understands how they work.

Yet each of these great products of cumulative human social effort over the centuries resembles a coral reef, in that a great mass of new inert material supports at its top and on its flanks a living element which is busily expanding it, and without which the rest would have no function and no defense. Only in the case of the technosphere have the much publicized discoveries of scientists and inventors made public opinion aware of this vital process of renewed growth, and of the requirements for sustaining it. The corresponding requirements of the noosphere and the nomosphere have been ignored, cold-shouldered, or left to chance.

Underlying all policies and all deployment of resources, whether we recognize it or not, there are all-important issues of the respective shares which are to go to renewal and expansion within the noosphere, the nomosphere, and the technosphere. During at least the remainder of this century the vital question is how to wrest from the technosphere the grossly excessive share of manpower and other resources which it has come to monopolize, and reallocate these fruitfully and effectively within the noosphere and the nomosphere. Once the implications of this are followed through in detail it will very soon be seen that they are anything but theoretical and remote from practical affairs.

Vast as are the problems which we face in the biosphere, the technosphere, and the nomosphere, it is in the noosphere that the main strategic theater lies. If Man can become securely established in that still unknown land of opportunity, his capacity to do the right thing in the biosphere, the nomosphere, and the technosphere will become secure as well. The crux of the matter is therefore to explore the noosphere with at worst no less devotion, ingenuity, and resources than we dedicate to exploring the moon. In exploring it we must learn how to become at home and at ease in its thrilling but rarefied atmosphere, and how to establish and sustain in it organized settlements which can harvest its potential and can channel some of this harvest back to the everyday world in the form of a higher quality of living.

In principle our organisms of higher learning, including research institutions, universities, and learned societies, have to be regarded as equivalent to missions of exploration and development in the noosphere, however ill equipped, clumsily led, and ineffective some of them may seem to be. Some indeed appear to be perpetually en route to the noosphere without ever managing to set foot in it, while others get bogged down in its fringing morasses or suffer crippling accidents before thrusting far in.

From the standpoint of human evolution it is sobering to reflect how small a fraction of mankind has hitherto become equipped to appreciate the rewards or even the existence of the noosphere. It is possible to be born and live as a man without participating to any significant extent in the greatest creative achievement which distinguishes Man from the many other admirable animals with whom he shares this earth. Indeed this is the fate of the great majority of our predecessors and our contemporaries. Terminating illiteracy is all very well, but does it make sense to conduct human affairs so that the mass pursuit of such an abysmally low ideal absorbs so much more care and effort than the advancement of Man's highest capabilities?

Even given that there can be no sound progress without such a reconstructed intellectual foundation, far more will need to be done before any remaining hats can be thrown in the air. Deprived of the consolation of being watched over by Divine Providence, contemporary world society has come to regard itself as a bewildered patient having to administer self-treatment in the absence of a doctor. Or, perhaps more aptly, as a family of self-willed children, some infants and some teenagers, who have rejected and absconded from their unworthy parents and are learning the hard way that it takes something more than that repudiation to become really grown up. Lacking self-knowledge, or a trained appreciation of ways of adapting to life's realities and opportunities, our society throws itself obsessively into oversimplified tasks such as the pursuit of higher G.N.P., or into crude exercises in escapism, or even into infantile gestures and tantrums leading to violence.

A new social fabric is needed which will fulfill the role of an intelligent and understanding parent, especially toward the weaker members of the human family and will seek progressively to encourage and assist every individual to share this parental type of role and responsibility at every possible level. It must be borne in mind that deprivation of such enlightened parental care, especially during the earlier stages of life, has been a main factor in the widespread growth of misbehavior of all kinds, including crime. Such deprivation is quite largely due to mistaken political attitudes and decisions regarding the role of force in this world, and also the extent to which welfare responsibilities can successfully be assumed by a bureaucracy. One of the great merits of adopting a comprehensive science-based approach to an accepted goal of promoting human fulfillment in every sense is that it provides the necessary authority and integration for the recast institutions and processes through which society will have to function, as the only feasible middle course between totalitarianism and anarchy. Another is that it promotes a more open-minded, less defensive, and more sympathetic style. One of the worst aspects of our present culture is its disgracefully poor style.

Such a maternal and healing style of society will provide a gentle continuous background ambience and active presence to mediate between the humane philosophy of promoting human fulfillment and the sensibilities of those who, in seeking it, encounter all kinds of obstacles, difficulties, and deficiencies. Society can offer them understanding, encouragement, and assistance without encroaching on their own personal responsibilities, freedom, and right to pursue diverse ends by diverse means, provided that they do not prejudice the rights of their fellows to do likewise.

A combination of wrong ideas, beliefs, and requirements, aggravated by wrong treatment of the governed by governments, has brought about a sick society. Its maladies are too many and manifest to be denied, or to be explained away by any of the traditional excuses and myths of those who have led us to this pass. One of the main areas which must be closely studied and monitored is the process of revival of healthy communities, in which the symptoms of stress can cease to multiply and gradually be reduced, both at social and individual levels. Just as our environment is dangerously polluted by misguided technology, so our culture and ways of life are polluted and distorted by misgovernment and misdirection. The places where this evil shows can be identified, and the incidence of the trouble charted year by year, in much the same way as air pollution. A system which is accompanied by more and more mental breakdowns, more lawlessness, more escapist efforts to contract out, more industrial friction and more ill-health traceable to psychological stress stands convicted as unworthy and untenable. Such results equally condemn those who have presided over it.

All that remains is to devise better means of measuring its evil consequences, and carrying through the necessary drastic changes to arrest and reverse them. In terms of modern technical, administrative, and political capabilities there is nothing particularly difficult about such a task, except that it will take a long time, even if it is undertaken with a will, a clearness of thinking and a commitment of resources which are currently conspicuous by their absence. A healthy community, soundly based upon contemporary knowledge of what Man is and what he might become must however be the objective. The sooner it is converted from vague generalities into terms of practical realization the better.

One area urgently demanding reexamination is the pattern of resource allocation. It has very gradually become recognized that the prevailing distribution of income between inhabitants of developed and developing countries, between warlike and peaceful activities and between supporting increased numbers or improving the lot of existing populations makes no sense, and cannot be morally justified. Yet years of international pursuit of disarmament, and of programs for improving the lot of the developing countries, have led to a situation in which the world is burdened with more costly, more lethal, and more widely distributed modern arms than ever. The gulf between the more affluent and the poorer countries has never been so broad and intractable. The only sane conclusion to be drawn from this discreditable situation is that we are trying to deal with symptoms, even if they are symptoms on a grand scale, without tackling the underlying social causes.

The most alarming aspect is that the population explosion and the threat of worldwide lethal pollution, which we are just beginning to get to grips with, show signs of falling within the same category. If they do, the early possibility of partial or entire destruction of civilization, and even of mankind, from some blend of these explosive elements cannot be dismissed. The one slender ground for hope is that the new recognition of the futility of conventional half-hearted approaches may achieve fundamental changes within society which no one threat could have brought about alone.

Our traditional education and training lead us to define our activities and problems under vague, often misleading labels. We readily succumb to the fallacy that because we choose to allot them different compartments in our minds they somehow become separate entities, amenable to being independently handled regardless of the fact that they form facets of a single whole. When the ineffectiveness of this approach builds up too much head of criticism we naïvely or cynically reshuffle the pack of government departments and change their names. Subconsciously admitting the futility of such treatment as we are ready to apply, we hope that by changing the names of intractable problems we may somehow magically induce them to go away. This is a gambit far older than civilization.

It is as if no one suspected or would admit that what is really wrong is the fundamental failure to study and treat our problems of adjustment to our environment and to one another as parts of a whole, which is resistant to piecemeal and half-baked initiatives. We are slow to recognize that modern communications and technology have not only vastly accelerated rates of change but have knit together innumerable groups and situations which until recently could think and act or be handled independently. Above all, we are oblivious of the hierarchical and sequential connections which render it strategically essential to tackle the various aspects of a complex of problems not merely together but in the right order. It is basically this incapacity to analyze and resolve complex moving situations which leads to such abject failures as in the struggle against inflation by means of prices and incomes policy.

Having got ourselves into such a global mess, so far in advance of the necessary education and training to handle its complexities, it would be idle to expect any simple or palatable answer to appear in the short run. Perhaps the most promising approach, which at least has the merit of posing clear-cut issues and enabling its results to be traced in some detail, would be in terms of resource allocations.

There is a growing mass of evidence that the relatively easy expansion of Gross National Product and of consumption which has characterized the past two decades is tending to level off. In any case, the increasing demands which it makes upon natural resources, not to speak of the accompanying pollution, will enforce a halt, and quite probably a substantial cutback, during the coming decades. No one, and least of all the economist, has so far got around to calculating in sufficient technical detail the scale of human use of resources which is consistent with a sustained offtake over a century or more ahead. There is strong reason to suspect, however, that in terms of conventional resources exploited by any presently foreseeable technology we are already close to, or may even have overshot, the highest acceptable rates of usage. And this at a time when we are all set to add a further two billion consumers by the end of this century, and when the majority of the present world population are disgracefully short of many simple necessities, including foodstuffs.

It thus seems overdue to start studying the implications of a zero economic growth rate for countries with a per capita G.N.P. of above, say, $1000 annually. These include North America, all northern and western Europe except Ireland; Italy, Czechoslovakia and East Germany, Japan, Israel, Kuwait, Libya, Puerto Rico, and Australasia. A main object of such a standstill would be to slow the draft on world natural resources until the implications for the long term could be thoroughly appraised, while enabling the many countries which are still at between a twentieth and a tenth of that level to narrow the hitherto widening gulf.

Such a standstill on indiscriminate economic expansion of the "have" countries may soon be just within the bounds of practical politics. The arguments for calling a halt to the ever more perilous division between affluent and penurious peoples are not confined to ethics. Peace, health, and economic stability could well be rendered untenable by continuance of current trends.

Moreover, the ending of prospects of financing reckless expenditure by boosting present income at the expense of the future would at once introduce into politics and economics a welcome note of sanity. Who, on such terms, would wish to sacrifice to armaments or space travel all hope of finding additional funds for highly desirable projects nearer home? Simultaneous pressures for a reallocation of resources from state to community and individual programs could do more than all the pious resolutions passed round conference tables to bring about effective action. If such a reallocation were accompanied by a critical scrutiny of those current activities involving the most extravagant use of natural resources and the highest pollution hazards it might also be possible to secure a high standard of living no longer synonymous with a high standard of wasteful consumption of material things. The mix to which we have become accustomed between material and nonmaterial components is far from being the only possible one. Nor are the technological methods currently in operation remotely defensible in terms of economy of resource use. It is arguable that a truly high standard of life would not only be consistent with, but would require, lower consumption in many areas, such as energy, paper, packing, drugs, and even steel.

Closely related to it is the question of how our modern command of technology can be intelligently utilized to cut back on the rat-race, and to encourage and enable people to follow the principle that *life is for living*. Two immense human groups, young people and women, are rightly showing increasing impatience at the absurdly elaborated compulsions which make a mockery of promises about increasing leisure and improved quality of life. Grown men, as the drafted habitual runners in the ratrace, have every incentive to join them, but through sheer force of habit and lack of spare energy have on the whole preferred to keep their gaze fixed narrowly on the rats immediately ahead of them. One of the items on the agenda for this book is to pay some attention to the desirability and possibility of encouraging such popular deviation from the dogma of keeping up with the Joneses. The part which it might play in enabling more energy to be devoted to human evolution, and the contribution it might make toward a less hectic, more smoothly running economy, with corresponding relaxation of social stress, deserves some notice.

Such examples should be enough to set the scene for what follows. The Big Change is necessary, it is possible, and in one form or another it is coming, whether anyone likes it or not. The all-important question now is what form it is tending to take, and how by forethought and resolution we can help to shape it.

2

THE BUILD-UP OF THE CHANGE

The proposition that a Big Change is in progress may appear self-evident and even platitudinous. To accept it as an assumption without further discussion may nevertheless be undesirable. Some analysis of its main elements and trends is necessary, both to validate the theory behind the argument and to illuminate aspects of the change which will need to be kept in mind later.

Such an analysis demands some consideration of the nature and the dynamic role of change in human affairs, of its evolutionary, cultural, and historical significance, and of the criteria to be applied. We need to define and distinguish examples of those kinds of change which represent something more than trivial, fluctuating, or cyclical deviations from a trend which at the grand strategic level may be virtually unmodified.

Each kind of change, in order to merit consideration, should be illustrated by one or more examples. Some rough classification should be possible to test the practicability of showing which changes may be linked with which, and what criteria should be applied in the search for valid examples. Consideration should then follow of the nature, scale, and manifestations of the supposed change. Its incidence, geographically and at different social, economic, and cultural levels, and its status in relation to both national, local, age, and sex differences call for attention. Its results and its impacts on different human groups are no less important. By applying, even in summary outline, such a range of tests we may hope to obtain a clearer picture of current workings of the process, and thus to find a better basis for considering problems of change in the future.

Evolution is change, but it is change of a particular sort, promoted and guided gradually over long periods by natural selection. Being part of an evolutionary system, and claiming to represent its highest flowering, Man must perforce accept as a fundamental the kind of change through which evolution works. Room for serious argument appears to be confined to three issues:

(1) How far is it desirable to submit human evolution to the processes of natural evolution, as they have operated in the past and as Man is slowly coming to understand them?

(2) How far is it desirable, and permanently practicable, to maintain an alternative system to natural selection, permitting or ensuring the survival, reproduction, and social status of human beings whom natural selection would have eliminated at an early stage?

(3) How far is it desirable and practicable, especially on the plane of the noosphere (which is presumably still too young to have developed its own means of natural selection) to complement preexisting evolutionary processes by new continuous interventions guided by conscious human research and design?

THE BUILD-UP OF THE CHANGE

While the challenge implied in these questions must be made at the outset it would be rash at this stage to attempt to answer any of them. Awareness that sometime, somewhere, somehow they will have to be answered is as far as we can go just now.

It follows that consideration of change must have reference to the evolutionary process. That in itself forms a revolutionary change from historical eras in which either total resistance to perceived change, or the fostering of change on lines demonstrably inconsistent in method and aim with evolution, have both been conspicuous and often dominant. It must also be noted that the handling of change upon lines inconsistent with evolutionary processes is a basic objective of a number of currently important institutions and movements, political, religious, and economic. Problems and stresses are clearly inevitable here. Even among those who fully accept the basic proposition there is plenty of room for disagreement over its application.

Probably all cultural, social, and political institutions developed by Man enshrine some sort of compromise or attempted settlement between the need for stability on the one hand and for progressive change on the other. Until recently the need for stability has often been accepted as overriding. This may be attributable to three factors.

First, the traditional religious and historical nature of the main background sanctions necessitated the inculcation, often by fear and by force, of an exaggerated attachment and loyalty not only to the principles but to the forms and accredited custodians of creeds and sovereign institutions, with their many ancillaries. Loyalty to a changing pattern or creed is a more sophisticated requirement. Secondly, the technological, scientific, exploratory, and economic impact upon society was until recently insufficient to stimulate and support change. This favored the stand-pat maintenance *en bloc* of existing institutions, customs, and methods. Thirdly, and perhaps most important of all, change was associated mainly with national defeat or with internal rebellion, and there was a lack of knowledge, experience, and capability concerning the promotion of systematic voluntary change by gradual, peaceful, and effective means.

The briefest reflection will show that the entire balance of forces and considerations affecting the relative desirability of change versus perpetuation of what exists has now been reversed. For that reason alone we must expect at least a longish period during which rapid, fundamental, and deliberately guided change will prevail. If change there must be, it would be incompatible with the modern outlook not to attempt to shape it.

In terms of social evolution, however, there can be no greater contrast in selective bias than between a basically traditional, hierarchically structured society and one which is future-oriented, experimental, and consequently innovating and tolerant. The two require for their management not only differing but largely opposite human types. It can therefore be said with confidence that the Big Change will be accompanied not just by general changes in outlook but by substitution for the hitherto established ruling types (and also their political opponents) of a series of sharply differentiated new men.

Comparison with previous administrative and managerial generations in the United Kingdom, for example, in terms of social origins, school education, later training, and preferred qualities indicates that such a change is already well advanced. The recent wave of executive-level redundancies in the United States, and to a less extent in Britain, and the setback in demand for graduate recruits of various descriptions, suggest that the change may well be accelerated by a process of unnatural selection.

For the first time sophisticated large employers are beginning to be able to look more coolly and scientifically at the entire flow process of their personnel from education and recruitment through various levels of responsibility to retirement. They are acquiring a much more precise capacity to specify which types and backgrounds they want and which they will not take. As such organizations operate increasingly in an international area of competition and comparison it appears that many men of types strongly represented even in controlling positions in the recent past will be effectively disfavored by future personnel selection. Insofar as prevailing values, attitudes, priorities, and possibilities emanate from top management, and from ruling circles, rapid and drastic changes are to be expected on this account alone. If long sustained these trends would also imply genetic consequences.

In generalized terms, therefore, we can discern three powerful driving forces, over and above those arising from technology, economics, and demography, which operate to generate rapid and drastic change. These are the necessity for replacing a preevolutionary by an evolutionary philosophy and approach, the reversal of the advantages until recently held by perpetuation of existing patterns over change, and the resulting clearance of the way to the top for new men whose different social origins, training, interests, and attitudes will inevitably alter the whole decision-making process, and therefore the decisions reached.

Important as these forces are they go only part of the way to indicating what kinds of change are probable. For this purpose we need to look more concretely at given areas where significant change may be expected. These include intellectual structures of idea-systems (such as the concepts of fair play, a growth economy, or a welfare state) which have hierarchical importance in shaping public opinion and attitudes. Pressures or shifts leading to the modification of centrally significant institutions, policies, or customs are at least as important as are new movements of concentrated linear pattern, intensifying and spreading through society in one direction, or movements which score in their emotional intensity and capability for winning loyalty even though intellectually or practically they may show serious weaknesses.

It is necessary always to look for similarities with, or differences from, analogous past movements which have proved effective in bringing changes, making full allowance for differing background conditions. A further type of criterion is the presence of a common factor between various examples of change, especially if drawn from different fields, which show a pattern of espousing certain aims or preferences, and rejecting or declining to give adequate support to certain others. Such criteria can prove helpful in discriminating between passing vogues or trivial and superficial changes and those which contribute to shaping the future.

Since it is not very helpful to assemble a ragbag of assorted examples of change without being able to assess their relevance or relationships, it is also necessary to devise some kind of classification. Unfortunately a truly taxonomic classification, which would link together those from a common parent stem, is impracticable. In any case it might be misleading, when what we want to know is rather which changes are most symptomatic of the main trends and most likely to reinforce one another in promoting recognizable new developments.

It seems that at this primitive stage the best rough tool of analysis is the categorization of those examples which pass the tests of significance already indicated, according to three pairs of characteristics: whether they are "soft" or "hard," whether they are positive or negative, and whether they are active or passive. By way of explanation it may be added that "soft" changes are those occurring on the planes of thought or feeling, while "hard" changes are crystalized in some structure or action, such as a new or reformed institution, a law, or a deployment of resources. Positive changes emanate from the application of free energy to objectives or projects which have hitherto been neglected, or have not become practicable earlier. Negative changes represent a reaction against, or a compensation for, conditions or demands which have become irksome or inacceptable, and therefore usually contain an element of direct substitution of something new for something older. Active changes contain some built-in dynamic element, such as a supporting group or a responsible agency, which seeks to further and extend them. Passive changes, on the other hand, are mainly a result of the release of pent-up energy stored in consequence of shifts in the relationship of their underlying masses. In the physical world an earthquake is the classic example of such a passive change: it looks and feels formidable at the time but there is no future in it; once the earth's surface layer has been forcibly adjusted to accumulated pressures in the lower rocks its force is spent and a period of quiescence follows. By contrast active changes are more akin to a river shifting over to a new course or a break-in of the sea through an eroded dune system: here the initial change makes way for a follow-up process which may be powerful, far-reaching, and long sustained.

To mention a few examples, a typical "soft" change is the spread of a permissive attitude toward personal conduct, while a typical "hard" change is comprehensive legislation establishing a welfare state, or nationalization of industries. A typical positive change is the collective urge toward space travel, while its negative counterpart would be the campaign against pollution, or against race discrimination. A good example of active change might be the growth of international tourism, while passive change might be exemplified by the transformation of the British Empire into a loose and nebulous commonwealth, circumscribed in its activities within narrow limits.

It would be wrong to ascribe undue significance to such a system of classification, however. Its main utility is as a safeguard against being misled into assuming that because something is listed as a "change" it has more in common with other "changes" than is actually the case.

It is no less essential to bear constantly in mind the inadequacies of our semantic and analytical tools for such a task. Different authors may with equal justification make quite different lists of changes which appear to them significant. They may describe what is essentially the same change in widely different terms under different names. Some may distinguish between changes which others lump together, and vice versa. Some may treat as universal changes which are in fact traceable only in limited areas or in limited social or economic groups; others may confuse the ephemeral with continuing and cumulatively influential developments. Such cautions do not invalidate the broad lines of argument, but they do underline the need for critical reserve in regard to most of the specific examples which are quoted for the sake of greater concreteness in discussion.

One further warning is necessary in relation to the dynamics of social change, about which we still know little. It is already clear that to speak of accelerating change is an oversimplification. As change accelerates, on an ever broader front, change itself changes. It not only moves faster but the greater frequency of repercussions modifies its direction and character, and gives rise to chain reactions, fusions and fissions which make the problems of nuclear physics look comparatively straightforward. Even, therefore, if we can correctly identify a fair number of significant components of the Big Change, we still lack a sound theoretical basis for predicting where their interaction with others yet unrecognized will take us. Prophecy of the resulting future trends and events therefore remains beyond us. Taking the exercise as far as we can should, however, at least enable us to observe more accurately and to reach sound judgments more quickly, as year by year these processes come to fruition before our eyes. If we cannot rightly predict the future we need not at least mistake a distorted view of the recent past for a true picture of where we are today. Closer study of the ball which is in play before our eyes may tell us more than gazing at the crystal ball, valuable as that can be in moderation.

With this introduction the time has come to review very summarily a series of contemporary examples of change which appear significant in relation to the Big Change, and may form parts of it. For convenience the list begins with those classed as soft and ends with those classed as hard; in each of these classes the positive are reviewed before the negative and the active before the passive.

Among the wide choice offered by changes which may be classed as soft, positive, and active, that which most clamors for precedence is the population explosion. Being the unplanned, unanticipated, and now widely undesired consequence of medical, technical, and economic developments, it is undoubtedly soft, even though such international and governmental efforts as are made to counter it must qualify as hard. Its status as positive is somewhat arguable, since the energy released in it may be held to have changed much less over the years than might be supposed from its spectacular consequences, which derive largely from the sudden removal of preexisting checks. Nevertheless, as one of the most literal and impressive exhibitions of human creative urge, it must qualify as active.

As later discussion will show, the population explosion is by no means so simple or so directly manageable a problem as is often assumed. Its relevance here is as perhaps the most significant reminder that the immense flow of biological energy now channeled through the human species can quickly assume a different role and acquire an impact of quite different magnitude as a result of the changing context which modern science and technology have created. Instinctive urges and deep-rooted social attitudes which were well adapted to earlier human living conditions can suddenly become disastrous when stresses and difficulties which they were adapted to meet are removed, or are taken care of by other means. When the locked door is suddenly opened Man falls flat on his face. Suddenly freed from plague and famine, men and women find themselves over-reproducing and overeating. The need to cut down is hard to face, either way.

The unexpected necessity to move human reproduction over from the instinctive and even subconscious to the conscious and planned area of human activity has unluckily coincided not only with hasty economic and technological development but with a worldwide crisis in relationships between government and governed. Even those who think seriously about such problems have been caught in some confusion between an approach to the population explosion based upon national policies and international planning, and an approach based upon making efficient and economical means of birth control generally available and relying on people to make adequate use of them in the context of changing outlooks and standards of living. It is not enough to argue that a blend of both approaches is needed. Much more thorough study and discussion is required of the nature of such a blend and the methods of realizing it in practice.

The issue will be treated more fully in a later chapter. Here it must suffice to note that the population explosion is not only one of the vastest components of the Big Change, and one of the most vivid demonstrations of the changing nature of change, but is also one of the most powerful engines propelling many other types of change through human society. For all these reasons it needs to be constantly borne in mind.

Another facet of the Big Change, which already ranks not far in importance behind the population explosion, and in the long run could have even greater significance for human evolution, is the changing pattern and scale of gene flow. This fortunately has been recently reviewed at length with great authority and skill by Dr. C. D. Darlington in his *Evolution of Man and Society*. So many previously impossible new combinations of human genes have recently been created by the intimate cooperation of men and women of different races and social groups that the whole context of human evolution is bound to be modified as a result, in view of the very large scale of multiplication and the high rates of survival now prevalent. Most of the current preoccupation with problems of race relations, for example, is in terms of immediate complications, but it would possibly make more sense to concentrate greater study on the likely outcome of these and other new departures on a long-term genetic basis.

In his final summary Darlington outlines developments in thought following Darwin's demonstration that man as an animal is subject to the principles of natural selection, with all its special forms of sexual selection, artificial selection, and unconscious selection. Intelligence—its measurement, its inheritance, its evolution, and its diversity concerns those mental faculties which have increased the chances of survival in our own kind of society. The idea of intelligence is itself undergoing evolution. Carr-Saunders showed that human societies, like animal societies, regulate their reproduction by reducing competition and avoiding conflict, but the process may be distorted in deference to religious teachers. The stratified societies of cities were derived from cooperation of different races. A new civilization is conditioned by an immigration of a different people and a mixture of two different stocks. Human evolution is governed by the interplay of inbreeding and outbreeding, mediated through religious, social, and racial barriers, and their breakdown from time to time. In certain forms of social environment, determined by the genetic character of a particular society, the principle of deference to superiors and of subservience to a moral environment created by them assume a temporary dominance. A further factor of decisive significance has been the development of agriculture, and its invariable consequences in damage to the environment and destruction of habitat, limiting potential resources and closing options for posterity.

The possibilities for a unified history of Man have been transformed in the last twenty years by the sudden complementary development of archeology and genetics. Some major uncertainties nevertheless remain. Until lately it appeared to be established that the whole of Old World agriculture and civilization spread from a nucleus in the ancient East, through movements of people whose breeding created the nations of mankind. Recent joint use of carbon-dating and dendrochronology, however, indicates that the megalithic cultures of Europe and the Middle East may well have developed independently, and that the priority of Egyptian and Minoan cultures cannot be taken for granted: agriculture arose separately and with different crops in the New World.

To trace the spread of cultures is to trace the movements of society and the factors associated with its growth and decay. The evolution of Man and society arises from what individual men and women do, and from their purposes and character, which are conditioned by genetic processes. These, we now know, are entirely at the mercy of the system of breeding, swinging between the opposite poles of inbreeding and outbreeding.

> ... with inbreeding heredity is all-powerful; determination is absolute; the group, the population, the caste or the race are invariable; they can be destroyed or removed but if they remain nothing can change them. With outbreeding heredity disintegrates; recombination produces unpredictable variability, endless innovation. Uncertainty, organized uncertainty, dominates not the organism but the population; determination in controlling evolution is transferred to the selective power of the environment.

Darlington's masterly analysis, here very briefly and inadequately summarized, throws much light on the underlying reasons for the emergence just now of the Big Change, and for the course which it is taking. It also emphasizes that the belated arousal of informed opinion to the sheer quantitative menace of the population explosion could easily lead to a disastrously distorted and misconceived approach being adopted to the problem of the rational adaptation of human breeding systems, which may be even more significant in the long run. These matters will be further discussed later.

In the foreground of such vast universal processes, whose recent upheavals so largely condition our present situation, there are certain more immediate and limited phenomena which need reference here in order to illustrate the role of the soft elements in the Big Change. First to be mentioned is the rise of what Michael Young has named the meritocracy—the new administrative, managerial, and technical group formed by modern schools and universities from recruits of much wider and more diverse class origins, and much more fluid and nontraditional backgrounds than its predecessors in the seats of power. While the character and progress of the meritocracy vary somewhat from country to country, and its local impact depends on what came before, and on the persistence or vanishing of preexisting interest groups and attitudes, the phenomenon of the meritocracy is now virtually worldwide, through developing as well as advanced countries. While its early effects are plainly visible in the organization and practice of international and national agencies, official and unofficial, its consequences in terms of new values and attitudes, new breeding systems, and social stratification can hardly yet be discerned. Undoubtedly, however, they will be deep and far-reaching. That the meritocracy will provide the bulk of future rulers seems virtually beyond doubt, but will these rulers also develop some equivalent of a priesthood, and if so, of what kind, and with what success and sanction?

The new and increasingly pervasive organs of the United Nations and its associated agencies, together with supranational or cooperative intergovernmental bodies and international business firms, provide an outstanding range of opportunities for able meritocrats liberated from social, religious, and nationalist ties to outflank and dominate the survivors among earlier ruling circles, power groupings, and priesthoods. Judging by what we have already seen in the earliest days of these new organisms their power and authority is likely to develop at an accelerating pace, and they seem destined to play a major role in developing the "hard" elements in the Big Change. It is true that their advance is in important respects still inhibited by sets of ideas, beliefs and values inherited from the past, but the further life expectation of these does not seem to amount to much. As a factor the meritocracy clearly ranks as soft, positive, and active, with most of its development potential still ahead.

The meritocracy, however, has not sprung fully armed out of nowhere. It is the offspring of an equally significant new global phenomenon, the complex of expanding and diversifying educational institutions, from nursery and primary schools to polytechnics, universities, and higher vocational training colleges of many kinds, and thence onward through postgraduate and advanced institutes to staff colleges, organized seminars, and think-tanks.

Historically several of the greatest forward steps in civilization have been associated with a timely conjunction between political and technical expansion and a fresh impetus to higher learning. In post-Roman days this was true of the absorption by the conquering Arabs of Persian and other intellectual resources, and by their adversary Charlemagne of the manuscripts and scholarship of Celtic and Byzantine Christianity at the school directed by Alcuin of York at Aachen. The pattern was repeated for twelfth-century Christendom by the cultural spoils of the Crusades, and the establishment of embryonic universities north of the Alps, especially at Paris and Oxford. It was repeated again for the high Renaissance three centuries later by the new schools, from Ferrara to Eton, and by the impact of the dispersion of scholars through the fall of Constantinople to the Turks.

Today's multiplication and enlargement of centers of learning is far more vast, more comprehensive, more lavishly and popularly supported, and more intimately and influentially linked with the shaping of political, social, and economic institutions than any of its predecessors. Apart from the often-quoted fact that more than ninety percent of the scientists who have ever existed are now alive, account must be taken of the enormously increased proportion of citizens in many countries who have had a higher education, and the more general acceptance of education as a passport to status and authority. This proportion is however still much lower in age groups above than below forty, so that its main impact at the top levels of authority is still to come. Changes in structure and curricula, moreover, intensify this effect in terms of the relative numbers trained in natural and social sciences and in other modern studies, and the extent of acceptance of continuous or periodic retraining and refresher courses, as against standing on the position that education finishes on graduating or on leaving school.

In considering the Big Change we need to bear ever in mind the close link between the takeover of power by the meritocracy and the emergence of the educational and research establishment as inheritor of the kind of role earlier held by the church. Through these twin channels new sources of genes are matched with new knowledge, new ideas, and new values in the higher reaches of control over human institutions. This fact alone would point decisively to the imminence of change on the largest scale. It would be contrary to all that human history teaches us to regard such developments as in any way compatible with a mere modification or extrapolation of preexisting trends.

In contrast to the mushroom growth of the meritocracy and the world of learning, as we see it in the seventies, there is reason to question whether the element of science and technology, which has spellbound and elevated recent generations, may not now have passed its peak as a direct contributor to change. Whatever the eventual outcome it is possible to list several important inhibiting factors here. Merely in terms of share of Gross National Product technology and some leading branches of science have come to demand more resources than can readily be found, and to prove more of a gamble than alternative strong candidates for investment funds. The budgets and rests of military aviation and rocketry, of space exploration and supersonic civil transport, and of other high technology supported for prestige reasons are inducing a visible adverse reaction, reinforced by environmental considerations. In some important fields diminishing returns appear to be setting in, while elsewhere the headlong pursuit of new medical techniques affecting sensitive areas for human integrity is threatening to outstrip the ability of society to devise and enforce acceptable ground rules for application. The fairly widespread reluctance of young people to commit their careers to disciplines subject to such doubts and objections, and the growing insistence upon social responsibilities of science and upon the quality of living point in the same direction.

While the flow of scientific discovery will no doubt go on unabated it may be expected that the split between traditional and scientific culture will gradually give way to an integrated new culture in which both these elements and others will be combined and cut down to size. The quasimagical prestige of science in the eyes of nonscientists may be expected to fade away. Scientists will expect and be expected to give much more attention to the social implications and responsibilities of their researches, and to the task of reconciling their results with other findings and considerations. In this the growth of mixed teams from various disciplines and of complex computer programs may assist. The apartness and mystique of science may thus be exorcised, with the aid of a jury of informed opinion no longer so scientifically illiterate as to be susceptible to veering between credulous overvaluations and prejudiced inhibitions.

The role of science in the Big Change has however to be examined at several different levels of focus, from the most specific and mundane to the most cosmic and fundamental. At that end of the spectrum it may be contended that possibly the greatest and most menacing of all the built-in stresses and contradictions of modern civilization is that between a still basically prescientific, or even antiscientific, culture and social system, on the one hand, and a mushrooming science and technology, which is bearing it rapidly farther and farther away from its roots and its field of understanding. Logically and practically such a combination cannot be other than ephemeral.

Sooner rather than later either the scientific approach must capture and remold the culture, or the culture must reject and try to break away from its scientific excrescence. Evidently we are well past the point where the latter course might have been practicable. That point might perhaps be dated soon after June 22, 1633, when it became obvious that compelling Galileo to recant his scientific theories was to prove an abortive exercise. For the following three hundred and forty years, however, the most powerfully entrenched interests in the western world have continued to hold attitudes which would only make sense if the Inquisition was right and Galileo Galilei had been wrong. Gradually these interests have replaced the persecution and neglect of science by the attempt to convert it into a pet, and at the same time to contain its influence within a compartment walled off from the innermost centers of power and belief.

During the middle years of this century it seemed that the new generation and the new men in public life must side with science and insure the rejection of the traditional values and their upholders. It now begins to look, however, as if something different and more complex is happening. By going in for overdevelopment of high technology, and by creating massive new problems which can be plausibly blamed upon science and technology, while resisting the infiltration of the scientific approach into the strongholds of politics, education, religion, and organized society, the System has promoted a widespread questioning of the values and trustworthiness of the scientific community, and even an irritable reaction against it. This has been unintentionally assisted by the naïveté and insensibility of a number of leading scientists, whose public pronouncements have not always been calculated to allay such suspicions.

It cannot therefore be assumed that time is on the side of the advance of the scientific approach over the many sectors of civilization which have hitherto held out against it. On the contrary, unless a much more effective and better led campaign can be developed, with far more serious support from scientists themselves, the possibility of a setback equivalent to a counterreformation can by no means be ruled out. Scientists already ruefully concede that the golden age of almost limitless additional resources for scientific growth ended during the past decade. If that downturn in financial support is not to be followed by a growing alienation from science on the part of the public there is a clear need for scientists to do more homework on the problem, and to show more activity in collaborating with their natural fellow-travelers than they have hitherto contemplated.

The character and speed of change through the meritocracy and the new world of learning will be greatly influenced by the growing sophistication and coverage of the mass media of communication. Instant news reports, critical commentary, and subsequent inquests and reappraisals not only inform public opinion much better about the course of public affairs, but inoculate a great many against becoming easy prey to propaganda or to inherited or fashionable assumptions and attitudes. By such means public opinion is more quickly and more decisively crystalized and is enabled to influence policy and practice more effectively. Moreover, people are thus enabled to judge the character and motives of public men and women, and to see as in a mirror the faults and limitations of public opinion itself. It is not merely a question of expediting and spreading more widely the flow of information, but of creating a network of challenges and responses which progressively adapt, in the direction of greater sophistication, the relationship between governed and government and between originators and receivers of news. Here again is a factor of comparatively recent growth which is soft, positive, and active and is manifestly transforming the climate of public affairs.

Nevertheless, despite all these changes on demographic, genetic, sociopolitical, educational, and communications levels, the broad and strong currents of daily energies expended through society remain channeled within the age-old framework of a drive to master the natural environment, and to turn its resources to account for immediate human requirements. The immense inherited inertia and impetus toward an exploitative and unbalanced pattern of living is set against the new overriding demands to restrain human multiplication and greed and to work toward some kind of harmonious equilibrium with nature. The widening unconformity between these two directions is near the heart of our current world dilemma. Like a giant tanker which needs many miles to change course or to come to a standstill once it is moving at cruising speed, our civilization is caught unprepared by the unexpected sighting of large rocks ahead.

These two problems of changing course and of reducing speed are quite distinct. Difficult as the first is, the second is even more intractable, because it demands a change of attitudes and ideas in much wider circles. While it is important always to bear in mind the great distinction between structural change and change in the volume, speed, and direction of flows of energy through whatever structure exists, we are very far from being able to measure even the orders of magnitude involved. We only know that structural change is unlikely to be highly significant unless it is accompanied by effective measures to change in kind and in degree the human energy which continues to flow through various parts of the structure.

Change in the structure itself does not necessarily contribute to this, and may well set up additional stresses unless the altered structure is well adapted to the flows. Such flows presumably can be corrected or redirected by changes in the underlying idea-systems, by changes in intensity of motivation, and by shifts in the means of pursuing some or all of the chosen objectives. For example, if enough people become convinced that the present kind of pursuit of economic growth does not lead to happiness, or to an assured future for younger generations, the political pressure for such policies would correspondingly diminish and redirection into alternative channels of effort toward a higher quality of life would become practicable.

It is still to early to judge whether this example is merely theoretical, or whether it corresponds to a real shift in energy flow. At the moment the signs point toward the latter alternative. Clearly much will depend on the weight of opinion presented through the mass media, and on the degree to which the new meritocracy, as heir to a technocratic new order, will be prepared to swing in deeds as well as in words against the fashion of according top priority to high technology.

Close attention to this issue during the early seventies will probably provide some dependable clues to the outcome. In common with conservationists generally, I for one am opposed to a continuance of *present* policies for economic growth. Like many others I conclude that the particular patterns of growth and of distributing the resulting product call urgently for such drastic revisions that it would be wiser to supersede our current cult for indiscriminate "growth" by new concepts of reshaping the rate, direction, and composition of the modern economy. But whatever one may believe, it is important not to underrate the magnitude of the issue, or the difficulty of the processes by which it will be determined. While overt policies for promoting rapid economic growth are new, the motivation and attitudes behind them go back much farther than civilization, and will be correspondingly resistant to change.

The affluent society, which is the glittering goal of all this effort, is becoming quickly tarnished. It looked good in prospect to the long-deprived and aspiring masses, but its manifest tendencies to bring more and bigger problems and stresses and less happiness are encouraging many, especially among the young, to take a cool and critical look at it. The inability of its leaders and apologists to provide any credible and acceptable answer to the question "where do we go from here?" is adding to the danger of a crisis of confidence, in which a strong reaction of public opinion could occur.

The build-up, at this precise moment, of widespread concern about pollution and the future of the environment provides a possible vehicle for a successful challenge to the whole philosophy of the materialist culture, which has recently carried all before it. The course of public dialogue on such issues as the authorization of the Concorde and other SSTs, the Alaska Pipeline, and a third London airport show clearly that the proponents of more and bigger technology have failed to recognize until very late the need for a more serious and fundamental justification of the policies which they have hitherto taken for granted.

Currently they are clearly losing the initiative with public opinion, and although leading industrialists on both sides of the Atlantic are now well aware of the problem, and are making enlightened and sincere efforts to meet particular lines of objection, the debate on a more philosophic level remains one-sided. A particularly ominous feature is the scarcity of economists of the caliber of Dr. J. K. Galbraith to reply with authority to the arguments in this sense with which he has supported the cause of the environment. On present form the probability is that informed public opinion will become increasingly alienated from the materialism which has dominated the West for well over a century.

Turning now from soft positive to soft negative factors, it is easy to list a number of strong impulses contributing toward organized reaction against the conspicuous features of our civilization. Propelled by the inspired efforts of novelists, dramatists, and film directors during the first half of the twentieth century, the most obvious headway has been made by the countermovement against all forms of Puritan and authoritarian restraints on personal morality, which has become labeled as the permissive society. Reflection on the familiar course of this movement shows clearly how the daring and conventionally repudiated standards of a bold minority have become spread through the various subcultures at higher and lower social levels and have eventually resulted in corresponding hard change in laws concerning divorce, birth control, homosexuality, and so forth.

Matters hitherto unspeakable gain a place in public discussion and representation; matters hitherto dictated by church and state are shifted over to the realm of personal conduct where they belong; and consequently the status of the citizen, woman as well as man, is advanced and the usurped authority of churches and governments is clipped. The fact that two full generations were needed between initiation and general acceptance is a measure both of the deep-seated resistances involved and of the slow tempo even now of cultural change.

We may be sure that the repercussions of this salutary demonstration will become evident soon in many other fields. The divine right of the state, and the mystique of organized religion, still seem to exercise through custom and inertia a role which they have already in substance forfeited, and of which time will inevitably strip them. Appeals to authority, to tradition, to dogma, and to values which are sloppily assumed to be true without good supporting evidence have all been rendered indefensible by the rigid and inconsiderate attitudes adopted in such matters, and are now no longer seriously upheld.

One of the most far-reaching confrontations of the fifties and sixties has been between the new social forces and the backers of the armed sovereign state, especially among the so-called Great Powers. The aftermath of World War II would in any event have led to a strong reaction against mass slaughter and waste which many who watched it coming, as I did, held and still hold to have been entirely unnecessary, given reasonable foresight and firmness during the thirties.

The arrival of the nuclear bomb as a bolt from the blue, and the evident intent of governments to handle this staggering mischievous device in a crazy cloak-and-dagger power game led to the first great organized nonpolitical revolt, in the nuclear disarmament movement. Although unsuccessful in banning the bomb this movement did bring about a worldwide sobering up of governments, both in relation to control of the spread and use of nuclear devices and to their reckless and indiscriminate testing. Nevertheless the immense prestige and resources of the military-political authorities and their commercial backers and dependents, with the continuing endorsement of churches and schools, maintain almost unimpaired the capacity for mischief on an international scale, as was tragically and ludicrously demonstrated by the Anglo-French Suez adventure in 1956. Our Bourbons in modern dress then proved how little they had forgotten and how little they remembered or had learned about the contemporary world. How much have they even learned since?

The United States authorities, who had, as much by good luck as by good management, steered clear of Suez proceeded in the early sixties to engulf themselves in the greater and much more agonizingly protracted folly of Vietnam. The spectacle of the world's chief military power being permanently defied with success by the twelfth most populous state in Asia proved as widely disillusioning as the deceits, crimes, and inhumanities which were shown to have been committed in the name of democracy and freedom.

The Pentagon Papers have demonstrated, perhaps more plainly than ever, how the giving of warlike equipment and privileges to a professionally interested group almost inevitably leads to the search for outlets and means to play with those dangerous toys.

The pressure of the draft system of recruitment inevitably led to a confrontation between the United States military-political establishment and the youth of the nation, with traumatic and obviously irreversible results. Very belatedly the message was received and partly acted upon in Washington, but not before it had left a profound psychological imprint on the citizens of all advanced nations. The right to declare war, or to embark on undeclared war, and consequently the justification for levying heavy taxes to maintain huge and threatening armaments, has begun to be effectively called in question.

The limits within which any government can unleash its military forces with any assurance that its orders will be loyally obeyed are manifestly narrowing. The whole logic of the modern world implies that the Big Change will bring with it some kind of formal drawing of the teeth of the sovereign state in respect to international violence. While the unwisdom of recent uses of the war-making prerogative have done more to bring this near than the somewhat ineffective efforts to achieve disarmament, it would be rash to count upon an early solution, which indeed might be indefinitely postponed by the outbreak of some uncontrollable conflict meanwhile.

Looking at the recent pattern, however, some slight encouragement may be found. Europe, historically the great fount of conflict, appears more firmly inoculated than ever before against warlike adventures. Overt international conflict in recent years has been concentrated mainly along two narrow zones of politically seismic instability. The first, in the Far East, runs from the Amur frontier of China through Korea and Vietnam to Indonesia. The second runs from the Baltic through Poland and Czechoslovakia to Greece, Cyprus, Palestine, and the Red Sea. Secondary regions of more localized tension and instability run along the Himalayas to the Bay of Bengal, up the Andes to the Caribbean, and across Africa from Nigeria to Rhodesia and the Cape.

Although hostilities have been chronic in parts of these regions they have tended to mimic civil rather than classic interstate wars. The expression "mimic" is used advisedly, since the genuine strictly domestic civil war has at least temporarily become almost as rare as the classical encounter between national armies and navies. In most recent cases of armed confrontation some external party, not always a Great Power, has played a decisive role either in fomenting the conflict or in keeping it at boiling point, often by supplying weapons and training to one side, and by covert diplomatic or open publicity maneuvers. This was true even of the Six-Day War between Israel and Egypt, although it at first simulated the ideal military conflict in appearing to produce a quick, decisive, and elegant solution. In fact it proved to be merely a brief episode in a long-drawn-out struggle partly manipulated by other powers.

From our immediate standpoint it is relevant to note the cumulative experience which has compelled the major military powers to refrain from overt and direct armed clashes. At first it was thought sufficient to avoid shooting between the Great Powers themselves, but since Vietnam and Czechoslovakia it has become evident that even armed intervention by a Great Power against small fry can be perilously counterproductive in terms of world strategy and diplomacy. Such anachronistic outbursts can be indulged with relative impunity only by states so small and already isolated that they have little to lose in terms of worldwide interests and are correspondingly more difficult to discipline by limited types of pressure.

Dangerous and precarious as this situation is, it is already a great advance on that of the thirties. No substantial nation can any longer look to armed aggression as a road to aggrandizement or to the easy solution of domestic strains, nor is there any dictator left who finds it expedient to adopt a saber-rattling attitude toward neighbors. Even the devious and covert methods of applying force which have been tried since 1950 have with hardly any exceptions produced a final balance sheet decisively unfavorable to their promoters. A most striking feature has been the dropping of the *Lebensraum* argument so stridently voiced by Hitler, Mussolini, and the Japanese forty years ago. Objectively the pressure of population on the land is now far greater than during the thirties. Yet no nation any longer claims that it cannot live within its existing national limits. Here is a classic example of myth parading as policy only so long as particular myth-makers stayed in power.

Contrary to the predictions of prophets such as George Orwell, the apparently limitless potential for the exercise of totalitarian authority and control has proved impossible to exploit successfully, except in very localized and ephemeral situations. In the long run people simply will not have it. Those who saw the future in terms of the defeat of big capitalism by Marxist dictatorship, or vice versa, have proved just as wrong as medieval contemporaries who looked for an eternal hegemony of the Pope over the Holy Roman Emperor, or of the Emperor over the Pope. An evolutionary approach to these matters shows beyond doubt that even the most apparently irresistible political institutions can crumble with remarkable alacrity and thoroughness when exposed to major underlying change at the human level. It is to the correct diagnosis of those human undercurrents that we must look in order to shed light on the life expectations of the various institutions, beliefs, and systems which dominate world affairs today. Above all, the changing capability of people, individually and collectively, for understanding their wants and for making these known to those in authority either by positive or by negative means is a factor of revolutionary force.

Not only has modern technology made war intolerably costly and destructive. It has also deprived those making it of nearly all the deep and strong primitive outlets and satisfactions which have hitherto maintained large groups basically well-disposed toward war in advanced nations. The disbandment of the cavalry was symbolic of this deprivation. To mount horses and to charge with sword or lance was a psychological release of a different order from push-button warfare against unseen adversaries. At the same time economic consequences, as the then British government quickly learned in 1956 in Suez, render modern warfare suicidal to the national interest of countries which still have much to lose elsewhere. Perhaps the greatest remaining obstacle to disarmament is to be found in the vast vested interests of the military-industrial complex, which has proved easier to build up than to disband. Having failed to maintain its active pace-setting role it has settled down to a more passive posture of great inherent strength. Indeed, there is no easy answer to the question how to dismantle it quickly without dire economic repercussions.

If this diagnosis is at all well founded, however, a new and more serious drive involving major disarmament measures must be looked for by the middle seventies. There is a huge unconformity meanwhile between the persisting apparatus of military power politics and the lessons which have apparently been painfully learned at last both by the governed and governments. But for the East–West confrontation, surviving in a rigid and perhaps moribund form, the existing contradictions could not have endured so long. All that we find and learn indicates that the maintenance or abandonment of war as an instrument of national policy is a decisive issue for human evolution. At the same time our new understanding of the roots of human behavior and of the interrelations between war and the dominant idea-systems of modern civilization enable us to appreciate better the reasons for the failures which have resulted from all efforts at disarmament so far. Disarmament will be easy once the required deeper adaptations have been made—until then it will stay impossible.

Several other significant changes are linked in the same series. Modern warfare, involving the sustained application of immense economic resources backed by willing and disciplined effort, has relied heavily upon the success of the sovereign state in welding together close-knit blocks of manpower united above all by a mystical patriotic devotion to particular nationalist groupings. In most cases such groupings have pretended to be more unitary and more deeply integrated than they actually are. Recent history has once more demonstrated that the devotion of the Basques to Spain, the Bretons to France, or the people of Quebec to Canada is at least qualified, while the Scots, Welsh, and Irish Catholic partners in the United Kingdom, the Italians of the Mezzogiorno and of Sicily, the Nagas in India, and the Bengalis formerly in East Pakistan have proved resistant to being lumped together indiscriminately with alien majorities sharing common citizenship. The spread of an intense form of splinter nationalism, often linked with a yearning for linguistic and other forms of autonomy, is a widespread phenomenon which contradicts the oversimplified claims of many governments to express the principle of national self-determination. The growth of supranational institutions and commitments appears to favor this trend, and to handicap the conventional national governments in pressing too hard on awkward minorities. Both developments combine to deflate the naïve and blinkered patriotism on which the effective working of sovereign nationalistic states so much depended.

At the same time the former convenient fit between national economic resources and the requirements of effective war machines has suddenly vanished. Fewer and fewer sovereign states can create and maintain a credibly adequate range of modern armaments on any terms which preserve their sovereignty. Dependence on imported armaments exposes national governments to international pressures and hazards and to severe pressures on foreign exchange. The whole concept of "national defense" rings hollow in face of the military realities of today. The tacit abandonment of civil defense as a serious organized activity is a clear admission that Defense forces can no longer defend, and are therefore, on that ground at least, themselves indefensible.

At the same time more positive forces are equally active in undermining the nationalist-military-patriotic-political complexes. On the "hard" level the worldwide network of airlines is building up highly influential populations of well-seasoned travelers who are no longer dependent on secondhand channels for getting to know what is being done, thought, and felt in countries other than their own. The speed, frequency, and scale of such contacts has changed the context of national separatism, not only in degree but in kind. It plays a major part in eroding the authority of localized national myths and pretensions, and in creating a more integrated and comprehensive international public opinion, which even the most stubbornly retrograde governments find it increasingly troublesome and unrewarding to go openly against. Nevertheless many policies, laws, and institutions today continue to function on the basis of concepts of sovereignty and of nationalism which will not bear critical examination. That is true at the level of political theory, and it also applies with great frequency where concepts of nationalism and sovereignty are mistakenly adopted, either explicitly or implicitly, in institutions to which they are improper or irrelevant.

At a different level the expanding student population of the world is rapidly emancipating itself from the inherited myths of nationalism, although the myths with which its more colorful and articulate leaders seek to saddle their unfortunate contemporaries are equally stale and irrelevant to the emerging world. The extravagances of the late sixties, like those of 1848, are probably significant less for what they explicitly claimed than as cries of pain and as danger signals, which authorities both in the state and in universities have been compelled to respond to with reforms which were badly overdue. A most important aspect of the mushroom growth of student population is that it siphons off the very age group whose enthusiasm, or at worst acquiescence, is essential for warlike adventures, and places them in a strongly organized posture to determine as a generation whether they will or will not cooperate. Both negatively in this way and positively

THE BUILD-UP OF THE CHANGE 59

as a committed body of support for supranationalism, the modern student body is assuming a decisive role in vetoing the persistence of conventional power politics between national governments. Perhaps later this limited and negative function may through wiser and more constructive leadership be developed into a more creditable effort by young people to actually participate in building the new institutions and new environment in which their lives must be led.

Cries of pain and protest are also multiplying from that even larger justifiably disgruntled element of mankind, the adult women. Insofar as political, economic, and social development has hitherto been virtually a male monopoly any substantial injection of a feminine viewpoint and any considerable female infiltration into decision-making levels must be reckoned with as a factor in the Big Change. Its complexities and its potential are discussed later.

Another immense group exposed to severe strain by the Big Change is formed by the urban proletariat, which was built up by demands of the Industrial Revolution. New sources of power and mechanization then needed to be complemented by immense inputs of low-grade human labor, partly in terms of muscle power and partly of subordinate control and sorting operations and simple material processes. Recent technology has made it possible, and recent increases in real wages have made it necessary, to supersede most of these labor inputs by mechanization and automation. So far this drastic changeover has been carried forward without impossible social stresses, owing to the coincidental expansion of employment in services, to redundancy payments and retraining opportunities, and to an inflationary situation which has enabled trade unions to enforce heavy overmanning in certain industries in the countries most affected.

In the long run however the unpleasant fact remains that the human breeding systems hitherto fostered by western society in the joint interests of a cheap expanding labor force and of ample military manpower reserves have now become incompatible with the modern requirement for more trained heads and fewer busy hands. Humanity demands that this awkward and politically delicate transition problem should not be left simply to the rough interplay of economic forces. Wisdom and commonsense equally require that it should be fully studied and frankly faced as an essential stage in human evolution toward a society based on the possibility of true human fulfillment through a higher quality of living.

The inflationary pressures and tightly supported industrial action recently becoming epidemic throughout the new affluent societies in part reflect the instinctive closing of ranks among those who see the economic justification for their existence becoming inexorably eroded by technology. A kind of defensive tribal loyalty deepens into a conscious and deliberate posture of alienation from society. On the other wing those meritocrats who feel entitled to benefit by the enhanced demand for their abilities become equally restive as they find their rewards nullified by the thrusts of inflation and by leveling up of pay and conditions enforced through strike action. Where these differentially affected interest groups happen to be made clearly identifiable by differences in the color of their skins, the stresses are further aggravated by temptations to racial friction. The simultaneous introduction of computerized control systems, favoring vast business mergers and demanding awkward adjustments by Man to the way that computers like him to behave, add to these complex strains in employment and in everyday life. The new managerial classes, often wielding powers beyond the dreams of their capitalist predecessors, again find themselves deprived by inflation and by punitive taxation of the recompense which they feel is their due. At the same time the ever-increasing problems of staying in line with others, both nationally and internationally, deprive them of the sense of opportunity and of having elbow room which used to be a compensation for burdens of responsibility.

In such discussion of change there is inevitably a bias toward focusing on the conditions close at hand and underrating the extent of variation in other cultures. There are still scattered over the world smallish human populations untouched not only by the current Big Change but by virtually all other substantial changes of the past ten thousand years. Some Arctic Eskimo, some Amazonian tribes of American Indians, some forest pygmies, desert nomads, Australian aborigines, and natives of large remote islands between Australia and Malaya still maintain a human relict existence of great significance to science in enabling primitive ways of life and genetic inheritances to be studied as a going concern. People from these groups can often be contrasted with others of the same stock who have become culturally contaminated by western influences, such as the Eskimo inhabitants of that most squalid of earthly cities, Barrow in Alaska. Sometimes too there is available for comparison a third group, such as the Eskimo of Greenland, who under two centuries of enlightened Danish administration have been enabled to absorb some of the most valuable elements of western technology and culture, while being shielded from its worst horrors.

From such groups, and from growing archeological and anthropological knowledge, we can see more clearly how people of much the same physical and mental capacities as ourselves can be held environmentally in cultural levels which may seem to us in many ways much inferior to our own. We can also observe the often surprisingly quick and successful adaptability they exhibit when faced with the necessity to integrate themselves in an alien culture, and on the other hand the price they have to pay in terms of stress and schizophrenia and of making do with the gross social inadequacies which offset the technical and economic advantages of western ways of life. In observing how these often gifted "primitive peoples" face the most far-reaching and demanding types of change we can perhaps learn something about what is in store even for western man as the Big Change rolls on. Such observation raises the question whether we can any longer justify distinguishing some peoples as "advanced" and others as "primitive." It might be truer to think in terms of only two main groups, both of primitive peoples, the first still living by traditional means while the second is equipped with advanced technology. Genuinely advanced peoples have still to emerge. To evolve some should be our supreme aim.

Such relict and lately primitive peoples, however, amount to well under one ten-thousandth of mankind. They are greatly outnumbered by the poor peasant folk who have been forced off the land in India, Brazil, and many other countries by overpopulation, and who create a new subculture in the squalid urban *favellas,* or even the streets of overgrown urban centers. These are essentially passive human flotsam for whom virtually no choice of options exists, and who are singularly ill equipped to take initiative to master new patterns of living in replacement of those which first produced and then rejected them. Even to provide them with decent dwellings and basic services is a colossal and ever-growing task; to enable them in addition to acquire a new status and a new resource base for their lives, and to adapt to the new environment in which their lot is cast, calls for a degree of understanding of the nature of change and the ways of managing it which is still beyond us.

Alarmingly numerous as they are becoming, these displaced persons are greatly outnumbered by peasant populations still clinging to the land. Indeed it is the ratio of rural to urban population, together with the percentage of admitted illiteracy, which most clearly differentiates the great mass of human beings who are still somewhere between the Neolithic and the Industrial revolutions from those who, having passed beyond those stages, are now fully caught up in the Big Change. The zone of illiteracy embracing over eighty percent of a country's inhabitants still covers all Africa, except parts of its northern and southern extremities, and virtually all Asia between the Red Sea and the Yellow Sea, as well as much of the East Indies and New Guinea and some regions of the Andes and of Central America.

It has been estimated that in about 1750 the proportion of the world's active population engaged in agriculture was above

80 percent; by 1950 it had fallen to around 59 percent. North America (13 percent), Oceania (17 percent) and North and West Europe (20 percent) led in this area, Great Britain having actually got below 10 percent by 1900. By contrast such countries as China, India, and Africa and Southeast Asia as a whole remained above 70 percent, with individual levels as high as 86 percent in Thailand and Turkey.

Such yardsticks show that for very large regions of the world the Big Change remains more an indirect than an immediate influence, since they have not yet sufficiently caught up with earlier changes to become susceptible to it, except in isolated urban communities. There are a few maverick territories which, while fundamentally still in this group, have suddenly through some windfall such as oil leapt up to a level of per capita Gross National Product comparable with the more mature advanced nations. Kuwait and other Arabian oil states. Libya, and curiosities such as Nauru in the Pacific and Grand Cayman in the Caribbean belong to this newly rich group. Libya, for example, has now overtaken the Republic of Ireland, and more than doubled the level of Portugal. The pace, nature, and management of change in such territories would be an unusually rewarding field for study.

Even among the most mature countries the base level for embarking on the Big Change varies greatly. Italy, for example, although in G.N.P. still behind the countries of northern and western Europe (except Ireland), now matches Czechoslovakia and surpasses all others in eastern and northern Europe except the German Democratic Republic. Yet if north Italy were shown separately it would take an even higher place, possibly above the United Kingdom, which in any case now ranks below Sweden, Switzerland, Luxembourg, France, Denmark, Norway, Federal Germany, and Belgium. These, with the United States, Canada, Australia, and New Zealand are the rich and technologically advanced nations for whom the Big Change is already a reality. For some its most troublesome impact relates to industrial modernization or to the redeployment and retraining of labor. For others it means finding an entirely new political role and drastically recasting their institutional structure. For others again it hits at the traditional stratification and interrelations within society, or the basis of educational and religious values. These and other different kinds of impact may become blended together, or they may occur in successive phases, perhaps being felt earlier or even exclusively in certain regions or in certain social or economic strata. No doubt when the Big Change has run its course, sociologists wise after the event will be able to demonstrate the rules governing the incidence of its various manifestations on different human societies. Meanwhile if a little more serious attention could be given to this neglected subject it should not be difficult even now to acquire a good deal of understanding which would help to mitigate strain and suffering.

In this highly condensed and necessarily superficial outline of some of the main aspects of the Big Change certain common threads can be traced. The human population of the earth means something quite different now from what it meant only twenty years ago. Its numbers multiply, its average age falls, its standards of living diverge ever more sharply between the advanced and developing territories. Its long-established rigidly channeled breeding systems dissolve into new melting pots between regions and classes and between nationalities and races. An immense unconformity emerges between the new types of people, living new kinds of lives with a new degree of knowledge and awareness about themselves and about one another, and the entire obsolescent structure of institutions and systems of ideas and values against which different interest groups find themselves impelled to struggle. The bewildered and increasingly demoralized upholders of the established System tinker with successive reformist expedients without understanding what is going on, and without being able to gain the strategic initiative in guiding change. Irremediable breakdown or blowup is averted less by their bungling statesmanship than by their unfailing timidity, which at least leads them to forget about face-saving and to turn hastily to doing the opposite of their previous policies whenever their antennae tell them that the game is nearly up.

The kind of analysis crudely suggested in this chapter needs to be pursued with a thoroughness and on a scale clearly indicated by the importance of reaching a sound and acceptable view of where we stand and what are our future options. It would thus be possible to move over from our present blind, piecemeal, and tense approach to the future, and to replace it by a more confident, understanding, tolerant, and progressive posture. To accept the fact of the Big Change, to analyze all its components, to monitor its development, to cushion its harsher impacts, to align it with the needs of human evolution toward a state of wider human fulfillment—this surely is a worthy main item for the agenda of what is left of this sorry century.

3
SETTING THE REQUIREMENT

Historians in possession of all available evidence for the beginning, the entire course, and the outcome of a period or aspect of history still have immense difficulty in satisfying themselves about the truth of what happened. To satisfy their fellow historians is often impossible.

How much more forbidding is the task of those who are persuaded not only rashly to assess the significance of changes still in progress but to look forward to what the future may or may not unfold. Refraining so far as possible from prophecy, as the most gratuitous form of error, the task of defining possible lines of advance may be approached by several alternative methods.

The first and simplest is to try to extrapolate what has happened so far, on the assumption that no dominant new factor or unforeseen change of trend will cause things to turn out differently. At some periods this approach could have yielded reasonably good results, but the period of the Big Change is not one of these, and for obvious reasons it must therefore be discarded.

A second, representing a more sophisticated variant of the first, is to use extrapolation as a basis, but to modify it by bringing in new or altered factors wherever grounds for doing so are found. If the object of the exercise is mainly to forecast impending technological change, and to assume that any other forms of change will be governed by it, such an approach may appear reasonable, although experience shows it to be hazardous. But, as has been shown, the fundamental assumption that technology will go on dominating mankind as much in the next half-century as in that just past is open to serious question. Insofar as it is not justified this second approach also fails to qualify.

A third frankly subjective approach may be labeled the utopian. It involves formulating a series of ideal goals, adding up to a model of what is held to be a desirable future state and discussing some of the implications. Among the fundamental objections to this approach are that it can neither allow for taking up options according to circumstances and tastes, nor can it envisage an indefinite period of evolution after, as well as before, the attainment of the postulated utopia. To assume that evolution will be halted at some future date is no less fallacious than ignoring the extent of evolution occurring before our eyes.

Having rejected these approaches it is proposed here to follow a fourth which, although by no means free from disadvantages, at least has the merits of assuming and providing for continuous evolution, of being relatively independent of extrapolation, of involving a precise date sequence, and of assuming both the desirability and the probability of a course of events which will provide for diversity and the holding open of a wide range of options.

This fourth approach rests on an analysis and continuing refinement and revision of the requirements for a future stage of human evolution. That stage must not be so distant as to be utterly nebulous, nor too close to serve as a rough model indicating how to progress toward it from where we now are. This, after all, is analogous to the method which would be used in briefing the designers of a required new airliner or spacecraft, or a new system of meeting needs for energy. There are many possible ways of satisfying the need, and many alternative techniques and principles for developing competing designs, but at the end of the day certain plain requirements must be met in terms of performance, including cost, payload, endurance, speed, mechanical efficiency, and so forth. By analogy, among all the possible futures for mankind those which can be viable and tolerable must fall within certain limits of "performance" which can be analyzed and determined in the form of a set of requirements.

Given these requirements, study can be applied to the scale, character, and timing of the means which their achievement would call for, and to the solution of those problems arising which remain to be tackled effectively. Similarly technologists might be set the task of finding metals capable of withstanding higher temperatures or stresses within certain limits of weight, or of overcoming inacceptable risks or nuisances in terms of noise or other pollution. It is here contended that the development of such a combination of requirements for an acceptable next stage of human evolution represents both a practical and an essential tool for civilized society, and a yardstick for testing the validity and priority of proposed political and economic policies. It would be far too much to hope that this chapter should actually provide such a statement of requirement; all it can do is to furnish an outline, and an illustration of what should be developed.

Human evolution is about the improvement of people, so that they can both stretch their potential further and at the same time realize more of the immense unrealized or partly realized potential already in their possession. The requirement must therefore be focused on that plane. It includes numbers as well as capabilities.

It implies conscious effort toward the evolution of the noosphere, that universal and perpetual common intellectual and psychological heritage which forms the only demonstrably immortal and transcendental part of man. The general recognition of the sacred role of the noosphere, and of the need for enhancing the value of what is in it, and of giving free access to it for everyone, is the central issue here.

It also concerns standards of life, not merely in material terms but in terms of the quality of living and the relation of people to environment. The choices here are between different patterns of life, and the balancing of their rewards against the costs, sacrifices, and disadvantages which they bring in the short, medium, and long term.

Consequently there are institutional implications, and structural requirements for a less primitive form of human society than ours. We barbarians of today will not live to see such a society, but we can at least shed our mental sloth and restrain our inherited prejudices and cravings sufficiently to clear the way forward for our ill-starred offspring.

On such a basis of long-term evolutionary requirements, to be modified and elaborated as a continuous process, the way will be cleared for discussion of the problems of ways and means involved in going forward from *here* toward *there*. We must never forget that *there* may never be reached, at any rate in the form which it seems to present itself to us through the mists of distance, yet the conscious effort to reach it will bring its own reward.

It is unnecessary, even if it were possible, to construct a model of a future state of mankind which is at all accurate and reliable, but it should not be impossible quite soon to devise a series of parameters indicating approximately within what limits any acceptable state must lie. Far from being disappointed with such an indefinite and sketchy outline of our goal we should rejoice that we are able to work out such a series of guidelines. They are not only much better than nothing but are actually preferable to any more cut-and-dried blueprint of a future which by its nature demands to remain fluid. A plan may prove all the better for being pursued but never finally fulfilled.

There are many advantages in developing a comprehensive series of requirements which can be formulated, revised as often as necessary in the light of new knowledge, and gradually translated from generalized to detailed terms. In principle it can cover all the needs of all mankind, but in practice an infinity of variations, of additions, and of omissions can enable its application to be tailored to every circumstance and to all tastes. It is far better to admit even inconsistencies and lapses, where local conditions so dictate, than to insist on lip service to standards which are not believed in, or which people are not prepared to strive after. The frequent discussion, review, testing, and monitoring of standards, year after year, will gradually indicate the validity of differences in approach, and the significance of variations in performance, enabling each human group to educate itself as to its relation to others and its success in fulfilling its own values and aims.

Nor is it necessary that all should participate at the outset, or even ever. A fair sample either of entire nations or of other regional or interest groups collaborating in different continents would suffice to set up international yardsticks and to enable the educational and participatory benefits to be demonstrated. The choice of the original and of later additional subjects to be covered, the gathering of information concerning current conditions in each for all the interested territories, the framing of precise criteria, definitions, and methods of measurement or assessment, and the provision of examples and guidelines would prove a large but constructive and absorbing task for the kind of organizations outlined in Chapter Five. There is plenty of material available, and the task itself presents no worse inherent difficulties than several which the international conservation movement has already successfully undertaken.

Beginning with people and fulfillment of their potential the natural starting point is physique and health. According to our present state of knowledge recent progress in this field has been remarkable. Average weight and height have risen in many human groups, expectation of life has greatly increased, many (but by no means all) of the more serious diseases and bodily defects have been much reduced and locally eliminated, and physical performance, as measured in terms of athletic timings and distances, and of endurance tests, has steadily improved.

In terms of requirements the first point to be made is the wide and apparently growing gulf between the physique and performance of a picked minority, especially of athletes and sportsmen, and the lower, often wretchedly poor standards of the majority. Many of these cannot reach the minimum levels demanded for entry into an occupation where physique is significant to efficiency. Whatever value may be attached to the superb performances of outstanding champions it can afford little consolation for a low and declining capability on the part of the vast majority of mankind.

Athleticism and high physique may be inessential to human fulfillment, but there are minimum levels below which physical health and attainment become incompatible with the minimum standards for human self-respect. The elimination of such incompatibility, and the universal realization of a decent minimum standard, however that may best be defined, must be included among future requirements. At the present time preoccupation with living patterns which inevitably lead to extreme physical unfitness, and the formation of breeding systems on that basis, must add to the concern created by the dysgenic tendencies of modern ghetto urbanism, and of the increasingly soft self-indulgence of an affluent overweight society. A systematic monitoring of prevailing standards of physical fitness would almost certainly result in findings highly disturbing for the fitness and physique of our posterity.

A second disturbing feature relates to disease and death control. During the past quarter of a century preventive medicine has enjoyed a windfall of wonder drugs and of antibiotics which have been so unwisely exploited, through ignorance and commercialism, that several of them are rapidly losing their powers. Getting the upper hand of many diseases, notably venereal diseases and lung cancer, is fundamentally a matter of education and exercising self-control. In its place the false doctrine has been propagated that people can count upon science and modern medicine to save them, in some magic, painless, and cost-free manner, from the results of their own selfishness and folly. Requirements for the limitation of disease will need to be framed on the basis of necessary changes in attitude and effort, and not only on that of miracles being invoked for the undeserving and the irresponsible.

The need for plainly stated and accepted requirements extends far beyond conventional targets for the elimination of traditional scourges to human health and mortality. It is widely realized now that the development of novel means of prolonging life by transplants of organs, and by costly injections and so forth, raises issues of ethics and equity of unprecedented delicacy. Have certain human beings a right to prolong their lives indefinitely, far beyond the hitherto normal span, if they can find the resources and techniques to do so? If so, is this right to be exercisable only by the rich who can alone afford it? If not, how is equity as between the eligible old persons and as between them and the young to be maintained? What principles of ethics should guide the doctors concerned, and whom should they consult and follow? If there is to be a right to prolong life artificially, is there equally to be a right to determine it at will?

If the young demand unlimited breeding and the old indefinite prolongation of life while the environment is already burdened in excess of its carrying power, something clearly has to give. On what principles is this to be decided? Legalized abortion and other recent developments have already strained the Hippocratic oath. The impending developments will clearly entitle and require doctors to have the benefit of some plain and universally accepted guidance concerning their duties to mankind, which they themselves will feel ready to observe with a clear conscience and without conflict of loyalties.

Mental health is another area in which crisis is impending. Inadequate research, parsimonious allocations, old-fashioned and sometimes even barbarous attitudes, and a lack of liaison between medicine and the social sciences and social services have led to the cumulative growth of an immense problem, still largely underrated and evaded. The fact that mass mental illness is a major regular element in the Gross National Products of western states is still conveniently ignored, and its victims are shuffled away as secretively as possible. Yet we still do not even know what mental illness is. Sixty years after C. G. Jung and others showed the way we are content to leave the subject in a mess. What is a reasonable percentage of the citizens of an advanced civilization to be put away in mental hospitals at any one time? No one can say, but it may be suspected that, whatever the justifiable level is, it must be far below that now prevailing.

Similar considerations apply to juvenile delinquency and adult criminality. Does the elimination of illiteracy and of smallpox really outweigh a doubling of mental certification and of indictable offenses? While we are contemplating pollution, ought not acceptable standards to be set, monitored, and realized for maximum tolerable levels of pollution of society by mental disease, offenses against the person, and offenses against property? The analogy with pollution, however, can only be valid if it leads to a scientific tracing of the origins and flow processes of these social ills throughout society.

It is widely understood that a complete rethinking is needed in regard to differences of status, function, and education between males and females, and for the increasingly protracted and indefinite transition period from child to adult. Here again is a promising area for the setting of generalized standards, a subject which will be discussed more fully later.

One of the most vital requirements in regard to human

evolution is that levels of intelligence, that most precious and distinctive of human attributes, should not be allowed to decline. Unfortunately, after a too confident start in the nineteenth century, recent research has left us in some doubt what intelligence is, whether there is any meaningful definition of it applicable to all cultures, and how to measure it reliably. These difficulties are associated with the fact that attempts to define, measure, and understand intelligence have been made only on a relatively small scale and with limited scientific resources. There is no reason to believe that satisfactory results could not be achieved if these problems were assigned a priority commensurate with their importance. The truth or otherwise of assertions that levels of intelligence are declining in certain populations is a matter of the utmost moment. To maintain intelligence at the highest levels which people are able to reach is in a literal sense vital to the future of mankind. It is discreditable to our civilization that we seem neither to know nor to care which way the trend is going.

Here, again, there is a further underlying issue of critical importance. For generations we have been busy breaking up long-established breeding systems which have helped to produce our existing reserves of intelligence. Whether or not the process is proving an aid or a menace to maintaining the level, or possibly a mixture of the two, it has been occurring unseen, unconsidered, unmonitored, and uncontrolled. This situation is unlikely to continue indefinitely.

Previous human history suggests that the current melting pot, especially at higher levels, must in time give place to a new swing in the direction of inbreeding, which may or may not be advantageous. A highly probable new factor in the near future is the emergence of new techniques for modifying breeding systems which will move the burden of choice from the unconscious to the conscious sphere. As such options open, responsible parents may be expected to take a much deeper interest in the eugenic implications of their breeding practices, and to look for some scientifically sound and humanly acceptable body of guidance to which they can turn before making up their minds. In such obvious cases as hemophilia this is already usual.

It is hardly far-fetched to envisage a future in which it will become common practice, before engaging in reproduction, to obtain background information and advice on the likely outcome, correct to a degree of sophistication and detail still beyond the imagination of most people. Before that stage could be reached, however, vastly increased research and recording of reproduction and inheritance will be necessary.

Whatever may be sought on the plane of genetic inheritance, the goal of human evolution demands also a new emphasis on the responsibility and function of parenthood. It is a sad reflection that many of our contemporaries who preach the sacredness of human life are perfectly content to encourage and drive countless couples into procreating children in conditions when their realistic prospects include neither enough food for their proper nutrition, enough individual attention and education to develop such talents and qualities as they may possess, nor enough employability to be able to look forward to any worthwhile kind of job.

If human evolution to a higher state means anything, and if we care at all for the future quality and survival of life, it is most urgently necessary to establish a generally accepted requirement that procreation of children shall be accompanied by a solemn dedication to secure them a worthwhile future in a world composed of wanted children brought up with far greater care and parental service and aid than all but the luckiest enjoy today. Far from lazily envisaging the transfer of such responsibilities to a welfare state, they should be placed squarely upon those who choose—as all can now choose—whether or not to bring children into this world. In a recent celebrated case in England a family planning clinic had to bring proceedings on grounds of professional misconduct against a family doctor who abused the confidence of a girl patient to inform her father that she was taking "the pill," which the doctor dogmatically pronounced to be contrary to God's will. This episode illustrates the big leap which has to be made from a culture which persecutes and bullies those who wish to fulfill their human responsibility not to bring unwanted children into the world. The weight of public disapproval should be felt not only by those who actually behave irresponsibly in such matters but by all those interfering bigots who constantly, by word and deed, conspire to encourage such behavior by others. It is these false guides who have been tolerated too easily and too long and who, by their bitter and incessant persecution of unfortunates, have contributed so much to the sum of human misery. If they will not learn better they should be shown how it feels to be at the receiving end of the social disapproval which they have so long abused to further their narrow prejudices. To express any sincerely held view is one thing, but to misuse social positions to impose it is another.

It is at this pivotal point that the key issue of human fulfillment through a higher quality of living is linked with the other key issue of checking and reversing the population explosion. It is a fallacy to suppose that this immense and catastrophic event, so deeply rooted in so many varied defects of our modern culture, can be successfully neutralized merely by passing around a few thousand million contraceptive devices and persuading people to have fewer children out of wedlock and smaller families. It demands nothing less fundamental than a far-reaching modification of every aspect of civilization contributing to the trouble, reinforced by a thorough audit of the future carrying capacity of the planet for a new civilization worthier of that name, and equipped with a full range of institutional, medical, and social devices for the efficient voluntary regulation and reduction of birth rates.

The necessary steps and tools for this purpose include the definition and monitoring of standards for raising the quality of living, the scientific assessment of the global carrying capacity for human population on a sustained yield basis, with full assurance of maintenance of the health and quality of the environment, and the intensification and large-scale expansion of existing efforts for family planning, birth control, and related objectives.

There is of course nothing new about setting standards for raising the quality of living. Environmental health measures, such as supplies of pure (or at least safe) drinking water, public refuse collection, mass inoculation against diseases, and public educational provisions designed to reduce illiteracy to an insignificant percentage are familiar examples of the elementary stages. The task now is to proceed to much more advanced, sophisticated, and therefore expensive levels. In this task the new public awareness of environment, and keenness on reducing its pollution, is no more than an earnest of readiness to face the deeper challenge. While quality of living cannot be directly defined or measured, the relevant actions and goals can often be indirectly quantified in such a way that directions and rates of progress can be set and monitored. Insofar as it is true, where quality of living is concerned, that the more people claim a share, the smaller each share must be, there is a direct relation here to the control of numbers.

It seems probable that the outcome of such scientific examinations will be to indicate a need for the most rapid practicable reduction of world population after it has climbed from its present level of 3.8 billion to its inevitable peak above some eight billion early next century. Once we begin thinking in terms of quality of living, arguments concerning the ultimate limits of standing room for people, or even the maximum number who can somehow be fed become irrelevant.

Population levels which do not safeguard against future collapse of the carrying capacity of the environment must be dismissed as equally puerile. Perhaps less clearly unacceptable, but also inconsistent with any worthwhile quality of living, are densities which allow too little for living space, for amenities, and for freedom of movement or choice of location. To close such options for our descendants is something which no one has any right to do.

Both directly and indirectly availability of sufficient space is one of the first prerequisites for liberty to enjoy a high quality of living, and for security to go on enjoying it. Conventional standards for dwellings per acre, for persons per room and for open space per thousand persons merely scratch the surface of the problem. Much more comprehensive and exacting standards will be needed, and they will be quite incompatible with the insane and indiscriminate multiplication in which mankind continues to indulge, with the encouragement or acquiescence of many who ought to know better.

An elementary requirement for advance must surely be to carry on much farther and faster the recent great expansion in higher education. It should not prove impossible, within the next half-century, to bring the majority of the population in the West at least up to present university entry standards, and to raise at least one third to present postgraduate standard. In other parts of the world a proportionate gain on present levels could well be sought.

Whatever view may be taken of the relative significance of genetic inheritance, environment, and education, nothing that we know now could indicate any insuperable obstacle to raising a great many people to much higher standards of intellectual attainment, if all available techniques and resources are enlisted. The fact that finding the necessary resources will inevitably call for big cuts in alternative forms of expenditure such as "defense" is a further reason in its favor. It must however be stressed that such a course has little in common with the recent twisted aim to "produce" more scientists and technologists in order that they may the better serve big organizations in expanded programs of national aggrandizement or material affluence. It means education in order to build up an educated community, and to serve whatever needs such a community may express, as it struggles to outgrow the legacy of twentieth-century vulgarity.

In the long run a section of the population will almost inevitably exhibit an incapacity, and probably also an unwillingness, to adapt to the demands of higher education and training and of a less crude pattern of mass entertainment and unskilled employment. As often in the past, such changing standards and social opportunities will have to be met by changing breeding systems in a progressively more eugenic direction. It is all important that this delicate problem should not be rushed, or tackled with overtones of politics or pressure. If adequate research and study is conducted with timeliness and good judgment, and is well publicized when, and only when, it gives clear results, any necessary adaptation should occur gradually and spontaneously. Given the knowledge and the effective choice few parents want to produce children who are unlikely to be able to hold their own in life. The bogey of "problem families" recklessly outbreeding and swamping the rest of society need not be taken too seriously.

It goes without saying that a massive increase in the proportion of the population reaching or approaching the plane of higher education will carry with it immense and salutary changes in values and discrimination right across the board of public and consumer demand. Such a trend has already been recorded in such different activities as outdoor recreation and leisure pursuits in North America and the relative circulation trends of "class" and "popular" newspapers in Britain. (In the ensuing paragraphs the situation will be outlined in terms of the British problem, which, although peculiar, has an obvious relevance for other nations.)

Historically the first big expansion of popular buying power for nonessentials in Britain during the opening third of this century was dominated by the tastes and trivialities of such commercial forces as the Northcliffe press and the early multiple stores, appealing largely to an ex–elementary school market. This power, as Lord Salisbury cynically put it, was divided between those who could read but not think and those who could see but not read.

Between the two world wars secondary school types began to come to the fore. These formed the backbone of the Royal Air

Force and indeed of the 1939–1945 British resistance to Hitler, which was much less U in its social-class composition than the leadership of 1914–1918. Whereas the latter had been so heavily massacred in Flanders their more fortunate successors largely survived to take their part in postwar Britain, where they were no longer blocked from doing so by the earlier strength of the System. They were accorded, however, no more than a short inning before feeling the impact on the employment field of the growing army of new graduates and postgraduates from the expanding and multiplying universities. These inexorably narrowed the opportunities alike for the Gentlemen, who took pride in their amateurism, and the early Players, who had to make do with no more than a routine school education and then to learn on the job.

Unfortunately the bewildering and prolonged process of handover from each of these classes to the next, and the accompanying alienation and passive resistance of the still very numerous proletariat, placed Britain at a severe disadvantage against competing countries. Their newly rebuilt economies often came from the outset under the uncontested control of well-educated new men, whose talents and energies were spared such social distractions, and who overwhelmingly belonged to the modern age, having known no other. This obvious explanation, however, remains virtually incomprehensible to the leaders of Britain.

Prolonged and agonizing though the process in Britain may seem it is inherently transitional. As it draws to an end, the freshly reoriented nation under its new style of leadership may be expected to join effectively with others in the immense task of seeing through to success the Big Change. Meanwhile its example most plainly illustrates the genetic, social, educational, and economic adaptations which must underlie that change.

All great new departures in human evolution are based upon a similarly complex structural renewal, the need for which must therefore rank high in our list of requirements for future advance. Only along that path can civilization shed the clutter of accumulated falsehoods, *Kitsch,* evasions, pretensions and pretenses, myths, and political tribalism which have distracted and inhibited its recent custodians from following their clear duty to posterity. It is unnecessary, and in the highest degree undesirable, that they should go as a result of blind violence and of a mindless urge toward something ostensibly new and wonderful, but actually very old, negative, and sordid.

Fortunately, in Britain the old order is at last so decisively outflanked, and its morale so deeply undermined, that a comparatively orderly and peaceful transition seems fairly well assured. Such an unexpectedly and perhaps undeservedly fortunate respite must not deceive men of goodwill into neglecting the immense urgency of the need to recognize that somehow, in Britain as elsewhere, something different must rapidly begin to jell to fill the present moral, political, and psychological vacuum. If this something is not a coherently worked-out approach on the basis of evolutionary requirements it is only too likely to be some half-baked or retrograde philosophy, capable of putting the clock back with a grave risk of catastrophic consequences. In considering the setting of requirements we are therefore not indulging in an intellectual game or fantasy, but dealing with some of the means of handling what may well prove to be a last chance of avoiding catastrophe for mankind.

As world citizens, we are compelled to embark at this late hour on problems of cosmic magnitude and complexity which will take much time to solve, and more to explain to everyone concerned. We are also greatly handicapped by obsolete and irrelevant attitudes, values, and ways of thought, by lack of essential data, and by inexperience and lack of expertise in gathering and evaluating such data and using such techniques and equipment as exist. For example, as indicated by the preliminary work of Professor Jay Forrester and Professor Dennis L. Meadows of M.I.T., there is little doubt that even the primitive computers now available could do much more to facilitate the tasks of adapting our society and economy, if it were possible to find the resources for this purpose and to learn the art of using them.

This sketchy outline of the problem of setting requirements has shown something of its nature and scale, and of the central role which it might assume. The task of replacing the collapsing beliefs of the past by a set of long-term goals might unite people of goodwill in all countries, including many of those who themselves continue at least partially loyal to earlier creeds and ethics. Everyone in possession of a live mind must recognize that a continuance of the current crumbling of beliefs and values without some acceptable replacement, at least for what is evidently lost beyond recall, is likely to prove disastrous. Some kind of united effort to avert disaster must be in the interests of every group, except those who hope to profit by fishing in troubled waters.

Requirements can be considered on different planes, and no attempt has been made here to go beyond the most fundamental and generalized. That will be tried to some extent in later chapters.

The conclusion at this point is that our newly won perspective of the story and nature of man and of his place within the known universe now enables us to define for practical purposes how far he has traveled along the path which his potential marks out for him, and in which direction he has to proceed as he emerges from the phase of unconscious to conscious evolution. In earlier times initiatives toward this end have had to be undertaken in the dark by individuals or small groups of believers. They have usually been on a mystical and never on a scientific plane, and have inevitably relied upon sectional proselytism rather than on agreed and concerted use of available human institutions ripe for the Big Change. We are thus faced with a mutation from unconscious to conscious evolution, from mysticism and abstract philosophy to science-based and media-borne new approaches, and from inherited misfit institutions to a restructured society and economy. Modern circumstances require that these shall be shaped in conformity with the wishes and wants of the members of society, and with practical possibilities opened out by research, technology, and a disciplined use of trained imagination.

We are challenged to establish harmonious relations between Man and the biosphere, the technosphere, the nomosphere and the noosphere. The problem of reconciling modern science with Man's abiding religious and ethical needs, and of stopping the rot which is currently eroding the morale and authority of civilization, calls for a new intellectual and moral approach based on Man's enduring need to vindicate and advance his development of the noosphere. Human misery is caused neither by necessity nor by fate or divine will, nor by political distortions, but above all by the universal failure to adapt outlooks and ways of life to the actual options and constraints within which people must in practice live together. All are guilty here and all have to make a new effort, especially the young.

As a leading means of realizing this objective the intensive further expansion and improvement of education at all levels up to the highest must be accorded high priority. From this will flow many changes in standards of living, in consumer choice and taste, in use of leisure, and in patterns of life generally, making possible an abatement of crude materialism and a switch toward less greedy and wasteful demands upon resources.

Underlying and accompanying these changes we must expect large shifts in the distribution of power and influence in favor of groups of new men. These shifts will be magnified in their effects through a crumbling of the base of the preexisting social pyramid and a drastic restructuring of institutions, bringing changes of policies, and programs and practices to correspond with new circumstances. Not only the magnitude but the suddenness and speed of these changes will put them in a class by themselves historically and will intensify the resulting strains and the urgency of achieving psychological adjustments.

Traditional centers of guidance such as churches, political parties, and conventional voluntary movements with roots in the past will find great difficulty in keeping abreast, and in continuing to play anything like their customary roles. There will consequently be a great need for improvising a broad new alliance of progressive bodies and individuals, ready to collaborate in exerting a stimulating and at the same time stabilizing and reassuring influence during the transition period, which may be expected to extend into the twenty-first century.

Without such a broad alliance there is little prospect of carrying through the necessary concerted program for acceptable and coherent change. Conversely, without a new evolutionary-based set of principles to be applied to a concrete series of requirements for progress there will not be sufficient common ground to hold such an alliance together and to keep it on the move.

There is nothing revolutionary in the concept of a requirement-oriented program in social and economic policy. Slum clearance, elimination of infectious diseases, nationwide literacy and many other successful examples come readily to mind. All that is new in the present proposals is their comprehensiveness, their emphasis upon scientific measurement of human potential and of the means of more nearly approaching it, and their focus less upon means and more upon ends in the sense of ultimate human performance and welfare. Our society has seen too much go wrong with too many ostensible ends which proved to be only means incapable of yielding the hoped for results. Affluence, the welfare state, the United Nations, universal education, and many other rosy ideals have brought disillusionment as soon as they were attained. People now are less ready to be fobbed off with such unreal substitutes, and more able to tell the difference between them and the genuine condition which was sought. It is therefore appropriate to start thinking in terms of setting and monitoring standards of progress independent of the mere passing of laws or organizing of services, which may of may not achieve what they purport to.

Nevertheless we must not underrate the difficulty and complexity of moving over from programs of half-baked and crudely improvised political and administrative expedients to the setting and fulfillment of genuine standards of performance and of quality. Even to ventilate the subject, and to devise a preparatory set of requirements capable of being put into practice, can hardly take less than a decade, and it could take two or more. Worldwide application of such an approach, if attained at all, must be a task for the twenty-first century. By that time, no doubt, such progress as may be made in certain directions will be heavily offset by enforced retreats and shortfalls in others, under pressure of the great bulge of people. Yet even on such terms the existence of clear objective standards of what might be will prove a great asset; indeed without them there will be a danger either of permanent acceptance of the second and third best or of a spread of defeatism and despair. A comprehensive, realistic, and widely acceptable series of requirements for the next stage of human evolution can in fact fill the role of war aims for the battle which the twenty-first century must unhappily fight to vanquish the legacy of twentieth-century folly.

4

TOWARD ECOLOGICAL HUMANISM

As we learn more of the astonishing acceleration of human evolution during recent millennia, and especially during the last fifty or so centuries, we are compelled to recognize the extra leverage exerted once Man's generalized intellectual capacities became reinforced by specific practical advances in tool-making, in writing and speech, and in organization and management. Until these came along man's heritage in the noosphere lay unclaimed. Genesis has misled us. Far from having begun in the Garden of Eden, and been cast out of it, Man was permitted only distant tantalizing glimpses of the guilt-free paradise of the noosphere and is still fitfully groping to find a way of becoming at home in it. Far also from having lost possession of paradise through Woman, Man is never going to attain it without first enabling Woman, with her healing feminine principle, to take her equal share in creating its human and mature ambience. Only with such drastic amendments can the tale of Adam and Eve be safely accepted. So far we have only had Cain.

Prehistory and history confirm the dynamic strength of Man's myth-making faculties. Trading in goods, as well as military struggles, has reshaped events and relationships in the short and medium term. In the long term few things have proved so decisive as the making and swapping of myths. (The word is used here for all widely held beliefs serving an explanatory or justifying role in a culture, without necessarily implying that their content is baseless or fictitious.) Cultural and national groups owe their cohesion and permanence largely to commonly shared and binding myths. Conversely the defeat and destruction of vital myths can carry with it the collapse of a culture beyond all hope of revival. Is it purely coincidental that American Indians, living even on the sites of the great Inca and Aztec cultures of less than five centuries back, persist in a sullen apathy without a flicker of evidence of the great talents presumably latent in them? The races survive but the all-powerful myths which sustained them were shattered by the *conquistadores*. Since World War II we have seen a far less traumatic, and indeed seemingly not unwelcome, collapse of the myth of British imperial status. That myth however was no more than a late excrescence upon British culture, and it never really impinged on the majority of the nation. Amid the lamentations of the few they bore its loss with equanimity.

In order to appraise a culture, including our own, we need to consider the coverage, the authority, and the vitality of its principal myths. In highly simplified terms the cultural authority of myths can be viewed as passing through four main phases. In the earliest the myths are shaped, nursed, and disseminated by some kind of priesthood, often utilizing a formalized ritual and a sacred hierarchy localized in some kind of temple or holy place. In the second phase the myth is in addition written and pictured in ways which enable it to become more widely and continuously disseminated and to be conveyed in sacred books and taught widely to the young. In the third phase there is a partial dissolution of the links between the myths and their sacred or other custodians. At this stage the myths become fully embodied in popular culture and thus susceptible to its fashions, to its unauthorized reinterpretations and criticisms, and eventually, at the fourth stage, to its rejections and oblivion. This final process can be painless and gradual to the extent that surviving exponents and upholders are not personally or forcibly repudiated but are merely left high and dry. It is, however, painful in its conflicts of loyalties and its demand for conformity to new and hard realities. It is at this point that most of the myths and religious beliefs which have hitherto held together western civilization now find themselves.

What happens next? Can modern Man exist socially without myths? Other gregarious mammals which do not have the problem of retaining and reusing stores of accumulated knowledge and wisdom over successive generations get along through immediate day-to-day contacts. Man cannot function like that. He can only readily tap what he needs from the store of available knowledge by becoming suitably programed. For this he needs to be fitted out with a good serviceable range of myths, or of stereotypes which rapidly come to resemble myths. The more knowledge he has to draw upon, the more myths he will require to help him out. It is wrong to suppose that the more educated a man is the more emancipated he becomes from myth. Basically the converse is true, but higher education does try to develop at the same time some critical apparatus capable of looking a bit quizically at myths, in order to discard the more bogus ones and to take the rest with a grain of salt. When higher education fails in developing such a monitoring mechanism we are coasting down into the myth-ridden culture—a widespread current vice.

Here it is important to emphasize that while a scientific statement is valueless unless it is demonstrably true, a myth can have immense cultural value irrespective of its truth. It only needs to win and hold acceptance as if it were in some sense true and to help to steer its believers in some socially successful direction or to inhibit them from socially unsuitable conduct. It is clear, for example, that whatever may be the objective merits of science and technology the current role accorded to them even in supposedly sophisticated cultures relies less upon these merits than on strong irrational deference to their quasimagical powers. Science is no myth, but its cultural role can be.

However much this popular appetite for myth-making may be disdained and deplored by the rationalist, it is itself a scientific fact and also an essential cement of society. It is reasonable to infer that only by recognizing and going along with it can social cohesion and the willing acceptance of restraints against antisocial conduct be maintained. At any rate that is the assumption adopted here.

If old myths are proving harmful we must find a basis of new myths which can prove constructive at Man's present stage of evolution. That means that the obsolescent or fragmentary elements in our current stock of knowledge and attitudes toward Man and his role in the world need to be consciously and systematically replaced on the basis of what we have now learned. At the same time we must try to become more sophisticatedly aware of the way we use myths and the way they use us, if only in order to be safeguarded against cunning political or commercial manipulators.

On such a view it follows that we have to examine and synthesize modern knowledge about Man's environment, Man's origins and evolution, Man's history and achievements in civilization, about the principles of science and the highest contributions to ethics and religious values, and finally about Man's current situation, problems and prospects. Such a stock-taking and appraisal may well be justified on merits as a basic work of reference, but its main essential function is educational and cultural. If ordinary people are no longer expected to believe in the truth and authority of the Bible, the Koran, and other traditional works there is an imperative need to put something in their place which is internationally and scientifically acceptable, and is at least as widely accessible.

Such a conclusion was reached early in this century by the far-seeing writer H. G. Wells, who produced in 1920 his *Outline of History*. More recently Julian Huxley, who had collaborated with Wells in the companion *Science of Life,* was instrumental in initiating through UNESCO (of which he was the first Director-General) a six-volume *History of Mankind: Scientific and Cultural Development*. This global production, planned and written from an international standpoint by experts of worldwide reputation, shows in words and pictures the ways people lived, developed their customs and arts, borrowed from each other and are held to have diffused their respective cultures. The continuous evolution from prehistory to the atomic period is reviewed against the background of religion, politics, economics, and historical events.

Evidently, in undertaking such a novel and formidable task, immense difficulties arose in reconciling different approaches from different parts of the world and in achieving a satisfying perspective and sense of proportion. Among the criticisms to which the work is open, it was unfortunately written too early to appreciate the now widely recognized significance of ecology, and it thus shares the blind spot of its time regarding Man's relation to his environment. Nevertheless, as a pioneering effort it fully establishes the practicability and value of treating the history of human thought, culture, and actions from the standpoint of all mankind. With its aid a very much better and, it is to be hoped, more widely read and appreciated successor will be possible before long, in the light of many new discoveries.

Is there not already a need for the preparation, with full international resources, and under United Nations auspices, of a comprehensive and authoritative Book of Man, to be reissued every decade in revised and wherever necessary rewritten form? Although probably best planned and organized by a standing international commission of scholars, and frequently renewed and updated, this great work might invite volunteered contributions from authorities of different countries and on different subjects, as well as using commissioned material. In certain cases the inclusion of two differing versions covering the same ground might help to counteract tendencies to embrace or encourage a narrow orthodoxy. Seminars might be arranged to help toward balanced coverage of difficult topics. Since the main work would necessarily consist of a number of volumes, a single-volume compressed version would be highly desirable. This might be prepared in as many languages as possible by outstanding writers for use in universities, schools, and libraries and for the widest possible dissemination. The aim might well be that within every library, public or private, large or small, at least the one-volume version of the Book of Man would be found.

It is out of the question here to go beyond a very tentative and imperfect indication of possible contents. The Book of Man would be extraordinary in its status and function rather than in its content. Being planned and prepared internationally, and circulated officially throughout all countries, it would belong to all mankind as no other book could. It would carry through successive editions the best attainable presentation at that time of Man's environment, his identity and achievements, his inheritance, and the challenges confronting him. Countless other presentations, through all kinds of media, would pivot upon it and amplify or extend its message in terms of particular cultures, subjects, and levels of appeal. It would not however claim any supernatural, infallible, or overriding authority for its contents, which would be plainly indicated as intended for periodic correction, amplification, and improvement in the light of fuller knowledge.

It would thus express the common experience, knowledge, and continuing mission of mankind toward higher evolution, in contrast to any divine revelation or asserted superior authority, and would form the current apex of the ever-growing structure of international scholarship in many cooperating disciplines. Gaps and problems encountered in writing and revising would, it may be hoped, attract special attention and resources in order to enable a more satisfactory and complete version to be produced on the next occasion. A constant feedback of criticisms and suggestions from scholars and users would assist the editors in their unceasing task. National academies and scientific institutions would be encouraged to participate, and teachers and educators would have a voice in its presentation.

On such a basis, a Book of Man could safely be accorded a central role in educational curricula. So far as it went it would be up to date, authoritative, unbiased, and informative, especially on the nature of Man and the basis of his life on earth. Other subjects and other sources would thus naturally fall into place around it. All educated men and women everywhere would in time come to share it as a common foundation and inheritance, enabling them to communicate and work together with ease, understanding, and confidence. Since the Bible ceased to be the unquestioned linchpin and arbiter of belief and conduct in the Protestant West there has been no work which could fulfill such a role of unifying guidance. In this role the Book of Man would be a powerful contributor toward world unity and toward stable progress, not excluding a healthy skepticism wherever this might be felt to be justified. That at least would be far preferable to any undue and unjustified deference being paid to what would be no more than an instrument and a symbol of a common human will to replace ignorance and distortion by knowledge and by a single perspective of mankind for mankind.

Instead therefore of the impossible task of trying to sort out countless conflicting and fragmentary bits and pieces into an acceptable integrated approach, students would start with the aid of an untainted, up to date, critical basis put forward on behalf of mankind and would be able to start questioning, probing and supplementing it according to taste. Exponents of traditional national and religious interpretations would be encouraged to clarify their different standpoints in relation to the Book of Man. It might well be useful to circulate to teachers a rather full summary of the queries and issues which arose in preparing the published version, as a further aid to scrutinizing the final product, and to appreciating the eternal vigilance which is the price of truth as of liberty.

The proposal to open with Man's environment is made with several considerations in mind. Men have for so long regarded their environment as of little worth, and as readily expendable, that for several decades at least a strong corrective emphasis will be necessary, in order to create a basis for harmony between Man and nature. As the concept of a supernatural deity recedes from the cosmic scene it is also most important to avoid giving the impression that Man himself can henceforward occupy that niche. By introducing Man after and within his planetary environment the limitations and necessary restraints on his arbitrary conduct are established at the outset and the external challenge to his heart and mind is clearly expressed. Moreover, insofar as ecology and ethology are coming to be seen as basic to human society and economics this approach establishes the right sequence.

Recent discoveries in paleontology, archaeology, prehistory, and anthropology lead readily and naturally to the dovetailing in of human origins and evolution and of the birth of civilization within a natural cradle. These in turn lead to treatment of the outline of human history as a whole, not distorted by the perspective of some particular nation or creed, and to a broad appraisal of human achievements in the social and economic fields and in the arts and sciences and elsewhere. The principles, approaches, and standards resulting from these achievements would call for special and extended handling. Problems of today and challenges of tomorrow would come next as the conclusion.

It would seem natural to open a Book of Man with the remote view of this Blue Planet seen with fresh eyes by astronauts journeying from the moon. Such a beginning would stress the arrival of Man at a new stage of evolution through voyages of discovery in space and would unfold the new perspective on his cosmic and planetary environment enforced by this addition to his earlier voyages of discovery by land and sea.

Modern America emerged when the experience of pushing forward the open frontier and of possessing vast new natural resources transformed the stiff ex-European colonists into a new type of plastic man with new values and a new inner drive. Gradually part of this acquired make-up flowed back to Europe and led to changes in European outlook too.

Today's new global frontier is the freshly unfolding environment. The new frontiersmen are the ecologists and conservationists who pioneer a new living relationship between that environment and Man. In consequence Man has to adapt his great inheritance from the past to the new tasks which face his new self.

The physical universe as it is yet known, and the origins and composition of our own planet, lead naturally to considerations of the processes by which continents have drifted apart, and seismic, volcanic, and erosive forces have operated, in conjunction with hydrological and climatic influences, to bring about the global conditions in the management of which Man is now presuming to claim a share.

Hitherto in the evolution of the biosphere the stuff of life has been molded by these conditions and by natural selection into a vast range of animal and plant species, adapted to living together on the earth as it was before Man's impact was felt. Through the dynamics of biological productivity and the processes of ecological equilibrium existing patterns of population have arisen (Fig. 3). It is perfectly possible, and essential to a sound education, that the basic elements of recently acquired knowledge about both the inorganic and the organic elements in Man's environment should be authoritatively reviewed and effectively presented both at a learned and a layman's level of understanding. Biology and other aspects of environment will increasingly condition human ways of living. The low valuation hitherto placed on these subjects in

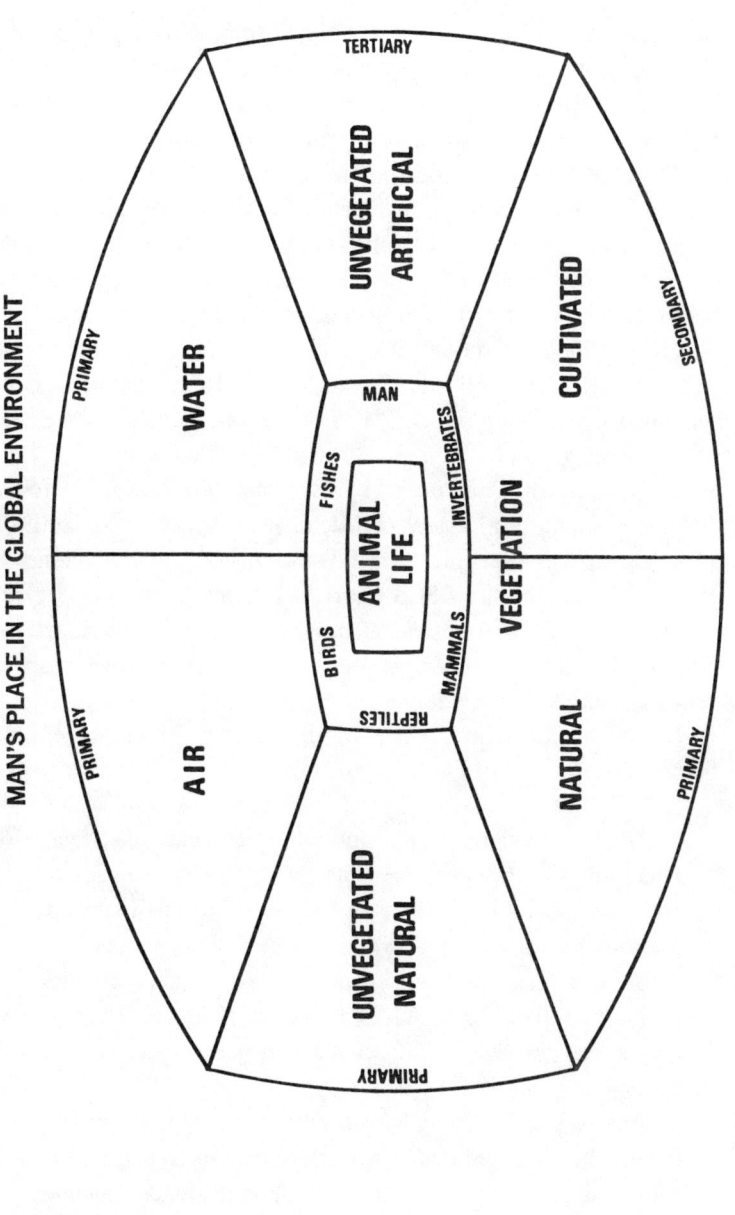

FIG. 3
MAN'S PLACE IN THE GLOBAL ENVIRONMENT

education simply will not do for the future. No single measure could do more to redress the balance than making these subjects the opening part of an international Book of Man. This part might well close with an analysis of Man's influence on nature and of nature's contribution to Man's economy and welfare.

Much of the necessary spadework for the biological treatment has already been excellently done on an international scale by the American Biological Sciences Curriculum Study, especially in its *Green Version* which lays special stress on the ecological approach to biology, although it retains as its main title the simple label "high school biology." This textbook for students is complemented by a *Teacher's Guide to the Green Version,* which explains its background.

Initiated in the late fifties by Dr. Marston Bates, Professor of Zoology at the University of Michigan, to provide an authoritative ecological viewpoint for advanced biological teaching in schools this part of the BSCS effort has in one giant stride given students not only in America but now in many other countries—including Britain—a truly up-to-date and comprehensive basis of knowledge and understanding.

To quote from the preface of the second American edition (thirteenth printing) of December 1969:

> There are two major aims in studying any natural science. One aim is to become acquainted with scientific facts and with the general ideas that are built upon them. These are ideas that have greatly altered our views of man's place in nature and that have tremendously enlarged human abilities to use the forces and resources of nature. These are the ideas that make our lives today so different from those of our ancestors.
>
> The second aim in studying a natural science is even more important: to understand what science *is*—to recognize its spirit and to appreciate its methods. Upon this understanding

depends our ability to participate intelligently in the life of our scientific age.

If most citizens in a democracy think of science as a kind of magic, our scientific civilization will certainly not endure. For science is not magic. Science is a complex process by which we can arrive at reliable knowledge of our surroundings. It is compounded of curiosity, observation and thought.... It is a social undertaking, depending on accurate and free communication. It is a progressive activity, each generation building on the accumulated knowledge of the past.

Science, then, is a human activity, without any element of magic about it. If science is to flourish, the whole community must understand to some degree its aims, its methods and its consequences.

In my foreword to the British edition of this great work, entitled *Biology: An Environmental Approach* (1972), I have referred to the significant historical point that the impetus for this whole concerted large-scale effort to modernize and improve science teaching in American schools resulted from the shock of recognition, when the USSR launched the first Sputnik in October 1957, that more serious and systematic approaches to education in science could give superior results. The scale and quality of the American response, the excellence of the organization created, with the full participation of scientists, teachers, and educators, the thoroughness and two-way communication of the repeated revisions, and the generosity with which other nations have been admitted to share the experience and its benefits, make this one of the grandest and most inspiring cultural achievements of our time. It is all the more discreditable that so many of the ostensible leaders of western culture have virtually ignored it.

Part Two appropriately concerns itself with the knowledge, much of it also newly won, of Man's remoter evolutionary origins and relationships, and of the prolonged shaping and building up of Man's mental and moral powers in a successful struggle to become free from utter subservience to natural forces. The genetic, ethological, and ecological factors involved during the immense stretches of prehistory are coming to be sufficiently understood to make possible some appreciation of the ways in which Man acquired the kind and degree of endowments which he began turning to good purpose during what is more commonly thought of as prehistoric time. One great benefit of such a treatment would be to make people generally aware of the importance of physical and psychological traits which are of prerational origin but which continue to play an active role in modern cultures despite being neglected, repressed, or misunderstood. Here, again, is a capital defect in modern education, in failing to enlighten the student on matters so essential to self-knowledge.

This introduction would lead naturally to a coherent account of the making and diffusion of all kinds of human discoveries, such as fire, the wheel, the plow, domestication of animals, pottery, weapons, language and writing, navigation, irrigation, urbanism, mathematics, ritual, social organization and government, harnessing of power, printing, factory production, engineering, chemistry, medicine, law, banking, and such modern additions as computers, aviation, and space travel. By handling on a worldwide scale the successive decisive inventions and their spread much might be done to put in true perspective the contributions of different peoples and continents, and the surprising blind spots to which Man as toolmaker has always been liable. The contemporary technological hegemony of the West would look less overpowering to the peoples of developing nations in such a context, while the coming generations in the West would be freed from the unpleasant species of technological chauvinism and vanity which has recently swayed and deceived them into costly follies in the name of prestige.

Having thus explored the natural and the technical basis of Man's rise to hegemony it would be an appropriate role for Part

Three to recount the history (including the verifiable prehistory) of the earth's peoples and the unhappy tale of their mutual relations. History as learned by most schoolchildren in most countries has been notoriously biased toward accounts of battles and allegedly heroic or patriotic figures. While something has been done to eliminate the worst features, there is still a severe lack of perspective. Among the most important things to be learned from history is the sheer futility and wastefulness of many policies and projects on which great resources have been lavished or lives and property sacrificed. Another is the endless human capacity for saying and perhaps even believing in something but doing something else quite different and incompatible with it.

A true history of Man would trace the courses and consequences of excessive emotional concentrations upon divisive, retrogressive, or irrelevant loyalties, policies and projects, and the resulting losses and setbacks to mankind. Such a history would assist its students to develop a critical faculty toward current propaganda and errors and to recognize mass self-deception when they encounter it. A main source of mistrust of adults by the young is the suspicion that they cannot or will not face an honest retelling of history or permit critical reassessments of cherished beliefs and interpretations. If this breach is to be healed the record must be set straight. Without belittling the stimulus and benefits of true patriotism, and of legitimate national pride in a common heritage, a Book of Man could assist the peacemakers by enabling the many to share a realism and a healthy disenchantment which is still the privilege of a few. Demagogy, irredentism, and extremism feed on the shallow and romanticized view of history. If the advanced countries are to enjoy the benefits of reducing such sources of friction and conflict they themselves must set a better example, and must support the creation of a fair and objective world history, not least by teaching it in all their own schools.

Fortunately in the realm of the arts, sciences, and culture most people of all nations are ready to recognize a common inheritance. Through a different medium Kenneth Clark's brilliant series of thirteen color television programs on *Civilisation* (also converted into book form) have shown, by their content and their impact in various countries, how an effective stimulus and link can be provided internationally by imaginative use of our knowledge of Man's heritage with the aid of modern media. It has won immense audiences, far beyond the bounds of the educated minority for whom it was originally made. It is a happy accident that the British Broadcasting Corporation should have been ready to venture a scale of resources which it could at the time ill afford in order to present the world with so imaginative and mature a perspective upon important parts of its collective inheritance. Conversely it is shameful that when so much is being squandered upon unneeded and scarcely workable high technology, our generation should not be able to point to many parallel examples of enlightened first-class presentation of the most enduring achievements of mankind.

At least we have here the basis for an inspiring and comprehensive treatment in Part Four of human culture and art, linking together the record of history with that of the aspirations and talents which have produced achievements capable of stimulating and illuminating successive generations of mankind, without regard to any boundaries. At this point we are perhaps closest to being able to appreciate human evolution in its most tangible and also in its loftiest manifestations, without forgetting that in other fields such as science and technology, the development of institutions and laws, and in geographical discovery similar capabilities are at work which are equally the common heritage of mankind.

This part of a Book of Man would lead on naturally in Part Five to a review of his known capabilities and faculties and of his weaknesses and limitations. In which respects is the gap between normal standards and the best performance widest? To what extent does organized appreciation tend to bring higher standards of conception and execution, or conversely how far is progress retarded or inhibited by undue lack of encouragement? What do we know about the forms and techniques of encouraging higher achievement? About the learning process and the alternative approaches to teaching and training? About the areas in which actual achievement seems to have come nearest to fulfilling potential and those in which apparent potential is still far removed from what is attained in practice? In this part also emphasis would be placed upon the gulfs between ideal and practice and the spontaneous undesired outbreaks of aggression, of greed, of evasion, and of perversions to which our species is so addicted. These gulfs would be surveyed and analyzed coolly and dispassionately as black spots for which all must bear some responsibility.

In conclusion there might be a review in Part Six of Man's recent rate of progress and of stagnation or retrogression in different fields, stressing the different time factors. There might be an attempt to define practicable advances for the next two or three decades, in the light of realistic treatment of the difficulties and obstacles and the costs and benefits involved, to provide a basis for worldwide discussion and effort.

The Book of Man as outlined here would therefore fall into six parts:

(1) Man's Environment
(2) Man's Origins and Evolution
(3) Man's history and its implications
(4) Arts, Sciences, and Culture
(5) Man's capabilities and faculties and his weaknesses and limits
(6) Man's recent progress and the unsolved problems and challenges ahead

The attainment of even some modest degree of harmony in human affairs is at best a very long-dated business. What is important is to start ordering things so as to tend toward harmony, just as certain ecological processes tend toward climax without necessarily ever reaching it. A civilization which is consciously harmony-oriented will contain built-in resistances to the distortions, perversions, and neglects which prove often so divisive and negative in human societies. It will equally tend to further and facilitate the social evolution of Man. And as harmony does most to promote harmony it is essential to insure that through general concern and awareness each success contributes toward the next.

Even a loose understanding of this process within public opinion will help to build confidence and to reduce mistrust and friction. New idea-systems must be designed to further change and harmony together, in the knowledge that they will prevail only in so far as they appeal to people and correspond to the facts of the times. Men must learn to observe the progress of Man with something of the tolerant yet discriminating and keenly committed attitude that they might show toward their chosen football team.

Civilization evolves within a changing envelope of ideas which needs to be closely related to emerging aspirations and requirements if people are not to be alienated. The elimination of untenable ideology and its revision and renewal call for continuous vigilance and for alertness to the practical opportunities presented by many changing trends and modes.

There are analogies between an immature although ostensibly advanced society like ours and an infant. In order to become socialized and to gain self-control it needs continuously to encounter some firm but understanding force able to show it the futility of irritably yielding to thoughtless violence or withdrawal. It seeks and deeply needs to learn that its vague probings will disclose firm limits to contain and shape its range of behavior, and to inculcate the deeper satisfactions of attaining more mature and complex channels of expression through character-building. Even at the subadult level outbreaks of sheer bad-tempered infantilism have lately become frequent, occasionally among university students also. At adult levels similar symptoms are widespread in attitudes to acquisition of property or status, achievement of sexual desires, and oneupmanship on the highway.

In coping with such manifestations it is necessary for society to adopt the posture of an intelligent parent.

Many of the most satisfactory homes and the most settled societies have in common a certain background of values, principles, and accepted practices which limit the foreground arena of uncertainty and confusion. A well-integrated and effectively disseminated view of Man and his potential, and of his line of evolution, will do much to defuse the forces making for frustration and conflict, which have been stimulated and multiplied by our chaotic modern culture. That culture has simultaneously run into limits barring its further development and has begun to disintegrate internally.

Every person, as well as society as a whole, has to face the challenge of finding a satisfying mix of social status, security, and freedom giving adequate outlets for psychological and intellectual drives, for balanced personal and sexual relationships, and for giving or responding to leadership. There is an infinity of possible mixes, but societies, like individuals, can let themselves become trapped in a situation which bars access to any acceptable one. Uncritical surrender to high technology, and unthinking pursuit of economic growth regradless of its impact on other values, provide us with examples.

One of the most astonishing blind-spots of our contemporary culture is its failure not only to achieve a satisfactory answer, but even to recognize that this all-important problem exists. As usual the explanation is to be sought in history. During the breathless years between roughly 10,000–1000 B.C., expanding mankind found the need both for a complex social, political, and economic organization and for a series of well-integrated and authoritative systems of ideas and values to provide the necessary dynamism and cohesion. In the absence, for a further three millennia at least, of an adequate scientific knowledge of Man and his environment, and in conformity with the legacy of prejudice and credulity in those times, it was natural that the essential social and religious matrices should have been derived from dogmatic and supernaturally based mystical revelations such as those of Judaism, Christianity, and Islam. These sought with varying success to lock themselves on to political power systems from which they derived a mandatory secular authority. The crusading and missionary zeal generated by these holy-unholy mergers, and the monopoly which they achieved of so many sources of ancient thought and learning, assured them a dominant role in building modern civilization. Nevertheless, their intolerance and narrowness has, at least in Christendom, resulted in some seven centuries of intellectual and ethical rebellion. We have now reached the point where the established orthodoxies are in an insecure and besieged minority, unable to validate or to give credibility to the sweeping claims inherent in their traditions.

Fundamentally human social evolution requires a flexible and tolerant basis of scientific and philosophic beliefs, expressing and adjusting itself to the total experience of mankind at the time. However, many leaders of thought imbued with their own convictions of what man *ought* to be, have erected rigid intellectual and ethical systems, and have even proceeded to reinforce them by mandatory secular authority.

Marxists and others who have seen here an opportunity for some more recently concocted dogma to sweep aside and replace the old are slowly beginning to recognize that the evolution of man is not like that. Neither the current ideological chaos and vacuum, nor the spurious unity presented by the now collapsing partnership between state and established religion, offer any viable or acceptable solution to contemporary scientifically enlightened man.

Indeed, the sad record shows that, when given half a chance, several Christian or ostensibly liberal groupings have been just as apt as the communists and fascists to substitute intellectual and moral tyranny for freedom. Freedom can only become secure if we can learn to feel truly at home within the diverse long-term processes of human evolution. That is where we belong. We should recognize and accept the need and inevitability of continuing change, trying to facilitate it with willing hearts and hands and to harmonize it within ourselves so that we become graceful, aware, and effective participants in the dance of our own evolution. In this way we may acquire that elegant prevailing style which western culture today so crassly lacks.

There should be a coherent and flexible global basis of self-knowledge, personal and social, about the nature and potential of mankind, to be expressed and kept up to date on lines discussed earlier in this chapter. There must also, however, be provision for dedicated and inspired groups, sharing particular beliefs, values and aims, to pursue their own ideals by any means which do not prejudice or threaten the equal rights of others. What is urgently needed is a resolution of the legacy of millennia of muddle and confusion between the purely practical needs and tasks of civil government and manaegment on the one hand and the abstract mental and emotional framework of idea-systems, ethics, and religion on the other. Not only have the dominant personalities and interests in organized religion and ethical movements persisted in unjustified interferences in state matters, and vice versa, but most religious and ethical movements have allowed themselves to become so cluttered up with material concerns and uneasy compromises that their essential spark and light have become hopelessly dimmed.

However complacent may be the attitude of many members of the Christian churches to the current state of accelerating decay and dissolution of their contributions to western culture, it must give concern to many thoughtful non-Christians. Whatever one's beliefs and assessments, it cannot be good for a culture to permit a carpet which has served it for so long to be so precipitately pulled away from under it. To an outside observer the efforts toward ecumenical union of the churches threaten to level down and average out differences in faith and religious attitudes which may be the last element capable of resisting their final enfeeblement and stalemate.

It would seem preferable to seek rather the establishment of one or at most a very few distinct organizations to build and maintain the fabrics of churches, to administer endowments, to raise funds, to take care of relations with secular bodies, such as local authorities and schools, and generally to leave the various groups of believers to concentrate upon realizing their own conceptions of the service of God, free from distractions and interruptions, and sparing others interventions of a semipolitical nature on the secular plane which are inconsistent with the practice of true religion. A trust or trusts for administering the material affairs of the churches, whether combined or not, could for example tackle realistically such problems as redundant churches and their transfer to other suitable uses, or alternatively their maintenance as churches with state aid appropriate to their "museum" qualities and status.

Freed of the fetters of owning and managing property and struggling with similar material problems, the surviving groups of believers could form viable and effective bearers of witness and renderers of particular types of personal service according to their lights. Instead of extinguishing and reducing to the lowest common denominator the enthusiasms and faiths which are the *raison d'être* of religion, such an approach would enable and encourage diversity to flourish, and would carry into the twenty-first century some continuing proof of the nature of Christian tradition, which might otherwise flicker out.

If it is sometimes necessary to attack the established institutions claiming authority in ethics, morals, and religion, this is largely attributable to their having mistaken their true roles, and neglected the essential values with which their founders were generally concerned, in order to take up the role of amateur politicians and pressure groups. Much of the *fundamental* critique and reappraisal of current trends and principles which could usefully be contributed by religious leaders and moralists goes by default, or is conducted upon superficial and obsolete assumptions capable of raising nothing more than a yawn. Yet the argument that stiffening institutions, reflecting outworn views and values, need to be replaced by new models more in keeping with the current stage of human evolution deserves consideration in depth. If the churches give it such consideration while they still retain some prestige and weight in these matters, it is entirely possible for them to lay claim to a significant role in the future structure of human conscious evolution. It was after all a churchman, Pierre Teilhard de Chardin, who with all his shortcomings has contributed most influentially to this reorientation over the past half-century.

If we elaborate his noosphere by the addition of a technosphere representing Man's tool-making capacity in its vast and semiautonomous modern flowering, and also of a nomosphere representing the comparable, largely intangible, institutional, and law-making product of Man's equivalent passion and capacity for devising rules and organizations to fulfill them, we have a trio of fundamental concepts which enable us to study the interplay between mind in its free workings and the tyrannies and prisons which men invent and proliferate to enslave one another and to perpetuate past power relationships.

Today there are unhappily no longer any free men living. Freedom can be regained only by a much more thorough study in depth of the means and strategies by which we have let ourselves be deprived of it. It is above all the organization of mental and moral forces which can count here. Just as we have successfully claimed for the care of environment very much larger resources than the authorities until recently were ready to find, in the same way we have to develop practical programs which will achieve a massive transfer of funds for building up activity in the exploration and development of the noosphere, in the critical survey and replanning of the nomosphere, and in the harmonization of the technosphere with the needs of the environment.

Very early in the national effort in England to build up the Royal Navy, Charles II and his advisers appreciated that more advanced mathematics, systematic astronomical survey and calculation, and the development of accurate chronometers and sextants were essential as a foundation. How can we expect to find our way about the noosphere and to master the nomosphere and the technosphere unless we have the wit and the enterprise to undertake the necessary preliminary steps?

In our slovenliness and ignorance we are content to conduct our thinking and discussion about Man's future in dense and unnecessary darkness. We have come to accept it as natural and inevitable that the body of assumptions and ideas and values on which we mainly rely in decision-making, and in reacting to new situations, should consist largely of an outdated clutter of material, little of which would bear scientific scrutiny. Meanwhile much of our tested and valid stock of scientifically proven principles and findings remains in a kind of limbo, utilized for book-learning and technology but ignored in shaping mankind's course. It is neither possible nor necessary to seek to devise and disseminate a tidy logical set of ideas and values to be embraced by all as a replacement for the current mass of nonsenses and contradictions which form the common intellectual and moral stock in trade of our shoddy culture. What is necessary is that we should cease taking these tattered shreds of moral and intellectual respectability for granted. A bit of demolition and a measure of astringent critical devaluation will go a long way.

There must however be some positive counterpart, and this must center upon a thorough appraisal of modern knowledge, much of it only won or made meaningful during the past couple of decades, so that we have something defensible and relevant to put up as a point of departure for a renewed and revitalized modern culture. Many recent writers have offered interesting and constructive contributions along these lines. The aim of this book is to take the discussion a stage further toward a deeper and broader synthesis, and to show in terms of practical evolution and of higher administration how we can get on with the job less unsteadily and less tardily.

It is to be expected that the 1970s and 1980s will see a great outpouring of works concerned with many aspects of this immense contemporary problem, and that a stage will soon be reached where they begin to take their place in a widely perceived pattern of adaptation to the new realities. Once such a pattern emerges frustrations and bewilderment will begin to recede. Human energies and creative gifts will begin to lend force to the realization of a new dynamic and healing view of mankind, and of Man's relation to his environment and his hitherto misconceived potential.

Those of us who have wrestled over the past quarter-century with the issues of conservation, and who have seen these issues clarified, disseminated, and accepted by decisive elements in informed public opinion, will insist that a similar approach, pursued with similar dedication and capability, should prove adequate to achieve the necessary transformation of public opinion about the conservation and evolution of man himself.

There is nothing abstruse or esoteric about this. It is just a straightforward job to be done in a straightforward way by those who are ready and able to shake off their inherited fetters and to remove the blinkers from their eyes. Given a reasonable number of participants in this movement, and that is already in sight, no one can block or defeat them, for the situation itself works with them, just as the increase in pollution did for the conservationists. All that is needed is a series of successive guides to thought and action concerning the whole problem and its main components, in order to render effective the build-up of opinion, of overt challenge, and of remedial action by those who have the wit to grasp the need.

Any upheaval and reorientation of such magnitude cannot avoid causing pain and grief in some quarters. Such occasions offer a field day for divisive schismatic or power-hungry groups anxious to profit personally from change, and to stoke up violence or extremism. It is important to emphasize that the aim of this book is to point to ways for achieving peaceful change by peaceful means, and to hold open tolerable strategic lines of retreat even to those groups and interests whose mistaken attitudes and policies have hitherto aggravated the problem.

The stress placed upon the central role of ecology is highly relevant to this healing and integrating approach. The processes of ecology are not self-righteous, power-seeking, or absolutist. They take what is as it is and they set it within a dynamic competitive structure which puts to the test all its latent potential and its diverse capabilities of seeking fulfillment by means which will directly or indirectly further fulfillment elsewhere. The ways of ecology are searching, realistic, and ceaselessly constructive, but they are widely tolerant of variety and individuality. They therefore achieve in sum a wisdom and tolerance which has been matched so far by few human cultures. When we reflect upon the fantastic expenditure involved in carrying a few picked specimens of *Homo sapiens* to the moon, to encounter the easily predictable disillusionment with a planet unendowed with ecosystems, we get some insight into the abyssal depths of ecological illiteracy inherent in our current culture, and the colossal leeway which has to be made up in very little time.

One of the greatest obstacles in this task is the development of ecology itself which has so far been fragmentary and grossly inadequate to carry the responsibilities for illuminating the renewal of our enfeebled culture. Having dealt with this in *The Environmental Revolution* (Chapter Ten) there is no need to say more about it here. Thanks largely to the International Biological Program corrective efforts are now being rapidly applied. In any case the most significant needs are shifting; they now lie in analyzing the human cultural scene by the principles and methods of ecology. That scene contains many identifiable elements, often intangibly lodged within the noosphere or the nomosphere, which are playing out their competitive and complementary roles like species of plants or animals, and which are incidentally having their potentials and their viability put to the test day by day.

In politics there are illustrations to be found in the perpetual struggles of the various concepts and applications of socialist or conservative doctrine and the inarticulate, even unobserved, replacement of one by another. This occurs under the stresses of internal partisan advocacy and of external criticism of performance, and in the last resort the silent acquiescence or rejection of public opinion and the electorate. In face of such processes the pattern and vitality of the political vegetation is ever changing, like that of the actual vegetation studied by ecology. In both cases it is easily possible to ignore or to misread changes, and to draw wrong conclusions accordingly.

The big difference involved in applying ecological principles in human affairs is the implication that we must go beyond contenting ourselves with the automatic laissez-faire processes in nature, and must add or superimpose a continuing conscious intellectual monitoring and guidance, coupled with a firm and sympathetic self-restraint. When the Victorians were first confronted with this issue by Darwin it got them into a hopeless mess, partly because the Establishment leaders were irrevocably committed to the concept of an entirely God-oriented and God-managed universe, and partly because their unconscious aggression led them to interpret nature (against Darwin's findings) as "red in tooth and claw" and as resorting to methods and motivations which we now know to be too beastly for any species except *Homo sapiens*. We now need to back-track, and to study with realism and thoroughness the true applications of ecological principles to the human society and economy.

Ecology (or, rather, the processes which it studies in nature) brings all-round growth in environmental quality through fitness and selection, giving scope to the maximum diversity of participants. Many human societies, by contrast, are arbitrarily interventionist against certain social types, attitudes, and ideas, precisely because of fearing their competitive success. They wish to concentrate rewards and privileges within a limited group, buttressed by a hierarchy, or alternatively they yearn to bring everyone up, or in other words down, to a common level. History shows that efforts to achieve the latter tend to lead to fresh, or rather stale, repeats of the former. The monotonous repetition of such patterns even within allegedly egalitarian and fraternal movements and regimes is clear evidence that politicians and political philosophers of all affiliations delude themselves in supposing or claiming that they have any constructive contribution to offer here. They are too imbued with concepts of the dominance of Man over nature to be able to hold back from the inevitable corollaries of dominance of Man over Man, and especially dominance of Man over Woman. Even debates over equality of status are invariably vitiated by the tacit and deep-rooted assumptions of exercise of arbitrary and obsessive power in the background.

Fortunately there are indications that, without as yet possessing any intellectual basis for checking or reversing these tendencies, the younger generation are at least increasingly alert to their indefensible pretensions. Study of ecological principles in a human context, supplemented by the findings of ethology, could do much to bridge this gap, and to provide respectable grounds and effective formulations for an alternative philosophy which is evidently keenly desired by many. Given the present worldwide intellectual climate this task of building up an ecological-ethological view of man's problems of evolution must be regarded as of the highest priority, and as a potential releaser of creative energies of the utmost significance. Here we can see, nearly ready to hand, a tool of fundamental reorientation and renewal which is potentially commensurate with the scale of the vacuum, and the collapse of the moral and intellectual foundations experienced by our inherited institutions and schools of thought. All the earlier shallow-perspective, narrow-perspective, and short-perspective cultures have come to the end of their road, and they must be replaced in the light of the longer and clearer new perspective which is now dawning. Not only ecology and ethology but human genetics, anthropology, social psychology, archaeology, history, comparative geography, oceanography, climatology, biology, and many other branches of learning will need to contribute to this requirement

There is no need to shed any tears over the loss of what has long outlived its usefulness, unless in the spirit of Wordsworth's requiem on the Venetian republic: "men are we and must grieve when even the shade of that which once was great is passed away." For many years the inherited culture has failed to attract fresh genius to enrich and reinvigorate it. The more conventional and unproductive of the elite have clung to it, but, among the more imaginative, culture destruction has far outpaced culture renewal. This adverse balance at the elite level has been aggravated by the regional and local impacts of technology and mobility. Whereas a well-knit human group, composed mostly of people long settled in one locality, must develop at least a folk culture which is fairly comprehensive in respect of its wants and needs, a more restless mobile and rootless population has no automatic defense against finding itself in a state of cultural nakedness. Indeed the widespread revival of national and regional consciousness may be a subconscious admission of that.

The recent splintering of local, regional, and national cultures through successive technological and political revolutions creates a complex need for devising a series of diverse new cultures at different levels. A human conservation movement, closely linked with the environment, may well be able to serve as a catalyst for this. The range of visible growing points, and the whole pattern of activities, outlets, and satisfactions, needs to be considered in order to provide encouragement and stimuli for new and rewarding contributions to a contemporary culture. There must always be a close link between the basic ideas and beliefs which are shared throughout mankind, and the manifestations, activities, and practices which conform to the tastes and needs of particular communities.

The present situation is messy and confused, and its resolution will inevitably be messy too. Individual and group prejudices and the limitations of inherited institutions exert a constant drag, even upon preparatory studies before particular changes are in question. We have a mania for closing our options before even looking at them. People and interests jump to conclusions, not always right, about their needs to bolster up old attitudes or embrace new ones. Such conclusions may prove changeable according to social trends or to strengthening pressures. Many adaptations which may be urgently needed are blocked because essential preconditions are not yet met. New knowledge emerges and is evaluated irregularly in bits and pieces, so that desirable appraisals are frustrated or delayed, and mistaken judgments arrived at. Practical men, in their bewilderment and rudderless drifting, fail to appreciate that it is their withholding of resources for survey and analysis which largely perpetuates the confusion from which they themselves suffer. It is as if a ship's captain who always gets lost sailing without a compass still stubbornly refuses to have one on board.

There is therefore an unprecedented series of unknowns to be faced in tackling the mass and complexity of new inputs, and in adapting ourselves to see with clear and steady vision the mixed flashes and obscurities which illuminate or darken our entry into the new age. The scale, in time and space, of these problems far exceeds that familiar as a result of our previous training and practice within our blinkered and empirical culture. Yet with all these handicaps there is reason to believe that even a quite modest effort now can have disproportionately helpful results.

The timing is right, and the potential effort which can be built up is immense. More and more people appreciate that there is no tolerable alternative to finding a global view of Man's life and function on the earth which will be generally acceptable to people of intelligence and goodwill, whatever extra or qualified interpretations and beliefs they may wish to superimpose on it. It is impressive to see how decades of effort by educators to lend prestige to more and more intensive specialization at higher levels have led to precisely the opposite result. We now witness the unleashing of a hunger for integrated and comprehensive understanding of life on earth, and the rating of narrow specialists and technicians as victims of educational deformity. Modern life is full of such examples of malformation and ill-health, due to striving against, instead of going along with what comes naturally. Just as the ecologist must become accustomed to healing sick lakes and nursing drugged fields back to health so must the human ecologist progressively identify and help others to recognize the symptoms of the long cumulative blight imposed on the health and happiness of mankind by centuries of counterecological management and government. Even to assemble the necessary task force will take a decade or two, but the nature of the requirement can now be perceived. As in the case of conservation, effective action should not be slow to follow, provided that the theoretical analysis is thorough and that it is not allowed to be thrust aside.

5

WAYS AND MEANS: DIRECTION AND GUIDANCE

In previous chapters it has been shown that many apparently unrelated forces and trends are accelerating and converging to demand and to shape a new leap forward in social evolution. In earlier times new developments, especially technological, appeared to strike our society and economy unexpectedly from without. They inflicted wounds or compelled adaptations which produced a distorted blend of traditional and new cultures. As technological and economic expansion gathered pace and scale, outdated laws, customs, education and training, values, and institutions came under increasing pressure. Efforts were made to keep abreast by means of reform and modernization, on an improvised, opportunist basis, responding almost passively to the vaguely perceived challenges confronting a bewildered and reluctant leadership.

As change goes on, it impinges psychologically on people generally in ways which have been well reviewed by Alvin Toffler in his *Future Shock*. The shock effect, however, is essentially transitory. A check or reversal of the main underlying trends is not possible, even if it were desirable. We have no choice but to devise new approaches, attitudes, and institutions, capable of enabling us to escape from our present temporary subordination to forces with which current idea-systems and institutions do not enable us to cope.

Some of the earliest gropings in this direction have been shamelessly escapist, retrogressive, greedy or violent, and have done no credit to our vaunted civilization. Even these crudities, however, at least indicate that the message is being received, and that the way is opening for a more serious and sophisticated response to the challenge of the times. Mankind is at last grasping the impossibility of continuing to cling to the old patterns, and the imperative necessity for something viable and acceptable to replace them. It is only for this reason that the kind of discussion attempted in this book can claim to be realistic rather than (or as well as) visionary.

Its opening argument, which this chapter will round off, is that success in achieving a worthy and acceptable new order depends above all on three things. First there must be a clear appraisal and comprehensive recognition of the nature, scale, and dynamics of the Big Change, along lines sketched in Chapter Two. Second, there must be a scientifically and psychologically sound approach toward setting requirements and objectives for the next stage of human evolution. Some highly generalized and tentative indications of such objectives on a global plane were given in Chapter Three and were set in ecological perspective in Chapter Four. In practice it would be essential to supplement these by many more specific objectives and programs appealing to geographically or functionally linked interest groups, often overlapping, conflicting, or diverging. Among such groups there would be a need for political parties, less obsessed than now with reenacting dead dramas and quaint folklore from the past, and more alert to the difficult choices and efforts of the future. Such rivalry is essential to create a healthy process of competition and debate and to insure continuous attention to the choice of options.

It is with these issues of ways and means, and with the direction and guidance of change, that this chapter seeks to deal. However clearly the character of the Big Change becomes generally recognized, and however plainly the obvious requirements for the next stage of human evolution are stated and accepted, the exercise must be futile unless and until a broad, coherent, and well-led movement emerges to go in and do something about it.

The central problem here is one of institutional creation and renewal. While man as a tool-maker has very lately learned about the importance of encouraging innovation and of heeding obsolescence in technology, the corresponding message has only just begun to get through to those concerned with social tools such as political, economic, professional, educational, and religious institutions, and their practices and programs. Our recognition of the significance of the technosphere is new: our recognition of the corresponding problems of the nomosphere is still virtually nonexistent. Part of the frustration manifest today is due to this fact.

Awareness among people of all kinds about the urgency for recasting institutions is only feebly shared by the people who run them. Most of these are committed to uphold and operate bits of the now dissolving old order, and are unable to function except on its assumptions, within its limits and according to its rules. Such partial exceptions as exist are mainly concerned with pressing for some limited and often obsolescent reform, without understanding the new context within which it must fit. Many well-intentioned efforts at modernization are distorted by the influence of fashionable nostrums whose popularity may be due as much to desire to compensate for past errors in an opposite direction as to a genuine understanding of modern needs.

Our civilization is thus confronted with dangerous strains not only at the interface between its technological growth and its inherited institutions but also at that between these institutions and the mass of human beings on whose confidence and support their successful functioning depends. The remedy for both these strains must lie with institutions, but they must acquire a new perspective before they can move.

It will be immensely difficult to blend the adaptation of the old and the creation and build-up of the new. The difficulty is aggravated by the fact that the Big Change is catching almost every type of existing institution unprepared, not only practically but psychologically. It seems that salvation for those institutions already in being can only come through drastic infusion of new men and women into controlling positions. History gives little ground for hope that sitting incumbents will prove either willing or able to respond unaided to the kinds and pace of adjustment demanded.

On a smaller scale a comparable type of situation has already been successfully faced by international conservationists. In view of the poverty of relevant up-to-date material from other fields no apology is made for treating the principles, methods, and experience learned in that field as relevant to the problems of creating a constructive form of stimulus and guidance in relation to the Big Change.

As lately as twenty years ago conservationists outside U.S.A. could muster only a sprinkling of small, feeble, impractical, and dispirited splinter groups. The American movement, although greater, was bitterly divided and largely obsolescent in outlook and methods. A profound and detached new look had to be taken at the whole range of problems and the realistic needs for handling them. Research had to be focused and expanded, with the aid of new kinds of scientific teamwork. Information and ideas had to be assembled. The field had to be mapped and its appropriate divisions identified. Black spots and sources of weakness, confusion, or friction had to be recognized, and appropriate treatments devised. After their defects had been duly diagnosed existing bodies had to be revitalized, reoriented, reorganized, and where necessary expanded or complemented in order to fill gaps.

The whole movement had to be taught to work in terms of concrete, relevant aims, and of a new impetus and coherence, achieved not by amalgamations but through diverse autonomous entities working as one. Official organizations, politicians, industry, and the press had to be educated to revise earlier stereotypes about nature-lovers and to recognize and welcome the new model. The worldwide structure for cooperation and leadership had to be created virtually out of nothing, and to be brought into effective relation with a wide variety of national agencies and groups in many countries. Strategies and tactics had to be developed, such as the priority accorded to cooperation with the inner ring of most closely affected interests, as against premature mass publicity or long-term educational programs at the earlier stages.

It should not, of course, be assumed that today's immense and peculiar problems of redirecting mankind on a course toward scientifically based social evolution could be solved simply by using a carbon copy of yesterday's solutions which have been followed with some success in the case of conservation and care of the environment. As these solutions, however, are based upon research and thorough appraisal of requirements their application should automatically disclose the kind and scale of the problems in this new field, and indicate the means of tackling them. It is the approach, the techniques, and the resolute activism of the conservation movement which could bring success here.

Among fundamental problems which have been common to both fields are a previous failure to appreciate and to identify the challenge; a clinging to wooly outdated attitudes instead of developing a modern guiding philosophy; reluctance to face the need for fuller cooperation within a wider frame of reference; lack of suitable nuclei and capable leadership groups; difficulties and disagreements over how and where to start in on the job; and vagueness about the nature and identification of the adverse forces.

A successful movement must know that it is *for* something and *against* something else. From that knowledge flows a readiness to unite, to adopt aims and programs, to accept priorities and sacrifices, and to keep the score of advances, setbacks, and stalemates. Something begins to take shape and to gather impetus out of the morass of bewildered and frustrated humanity. Neglected knowledge and disregarded ideas suddenly assume significance as the movement becomes conscious of its wants, its needs, and its potential. We have made all this happen in the conservation movement during the past twenty years, as I have described in *The Environmental Revolution*. It could also happen in aid of human evolution and human fulfillment.

One precondition of a successful initiative here is the emergence in influential and informed circles of a full awareness of the need. A second is to find some existing nucleus or midwife organism, able and willing to serve as a point of focus and a catalyst in bringing together enough people of the necessary caliber to launch an effective new movement.

It does not seem too difficult to fulfill these requirements. Through failing for so long to face the need we at least have the advantage that it has had time to become blindingly obvious to many who might earlier have questioned or denied it. The second precondition could be at least partly met by collaboration from the conservation movement. Its members are very much alive to the embarrassments and handicaps to their own objectives resulting from failure to tackle with equal vigor and leadership the parallel needs of human evolution.

This awareness has been strongly in evidence at recent conferences, such as the Second International Congress of the World Wildlife Fund in London in November 1970 where, as Chairman of the Resolutions Committee, I was faced with delicate problems in keeping the recommendations within the framework appropriate for that organization. It would clearly be in the interests of the conservation movement to encourage and facilitate the effective launching of some suitable twin movement which could work in alliance with it for such objectives as have been outlined in the previous chapters, freeing it once more to concentrate upon the range of problems touching Man's harmonious relations with the natural environment.

It must not, however, be overlooked that one feature which has contributed decisively to the success of the conservation movement is at least partly lacking in respect of human fulfillment. The threats and disasters to the environment emerge successively with unmistakable urgency and substance to confront particular human groups at particular places with the imminence of painful and conspicuously visible losses which can be averted only by prompt and concerted action. Each such threat thus generates a powerful motivation, and creates a further battle-proved contingent for the armies of conservation, bringing in many supporters who could not have been contacted and recruited by any other means. The copious and dramatic news coverage powerfully assists this build-up. The necessary challenge and recognizable adversary is automatically provided by the circumstances of each environmental threat. Recently most of the more sophisticated organizations, public and private, have taken much trouble to avoid finding themselves suddenly cast in this embarrassing role, and have tried with some success to claim to be at least potential allies of conservation, and as such to earn a welcome.

In principle the corresponding threat for mankind, apart from the continuing peril of nuclear war, may be identified with the population explosion and the growing danger that unwise use of natural resources may render the world uninhabitable on account of unmanageable shortages and of lethal levels of pollution. It is true that in certain grossly overpopulated cities, regions, and islands, or in smog-ridden conglomerations such as Los Angeles and Tokyo, these evils are brought home unmistakably to the people, who have the power by changing their ways to effect some remedy. On the whole, however, the threat of doomsday, like that of nuclear war, is global and therefore remote to most citizens of most countries. Nevertheless, recent efforts to arouse world public opinion have given promising results. In the next two chapters the population explosion and the complex of natural resources crises which go under the doomsday label will be discussed in their relation to strategy for the future, and to their role in shaping a line-up of constructive response to the emergencies which they represent.

Consideration of recent troubles over national economic productivity and inflation, and many others of a social, economic, and political nature, shows that it is not so simple in such areas to develop clear-cut test cases capable of decisive handling. Nor is it possible to deploy two sides with a plain and readily identified conflict of principles and interests. Although this difference is largely inherent in the situation, it is aggravated by failure to define the new requirements and thus sharpen the issues on the lines indicated in Chapter Three.

Until very recently many examples occurred even in the environmental field where an important case was allowed to be passed over by default because too few people possessed the necessary critical powers and authority to throw down an effective challenge in time. Once the homework has been done to enable a lineup to be created in favor of new and relevant principles, incidents will spontaneously develop where these principles need to be asserted. The formulation and explanation of the issues will, however, be more difficult and less self-evident than in most instances of pollution, destruction of habitat, or threats to fauna and flora. Moreover the maxim blazoned in New York on the 1970 Earth Day that "we have met the enemy and they is us" must apply even more on questions relating to harmony between Man and Man than on those between Man and nature.

Many individuals and groups will feel themselves torn both ways, and will find difficulty in identifying the vital dividing lines and in taking up the appropriate positions. Insofar as the conflict is not between people, but between principles and outlooks which belong to the past and to the future, it is understandable and inevitable that such uncertainties and ambiguities should exist. In any event the object of the exercise is not to bring about destruction and bitterness but to promote, through an immense psychodrama, the appropriate role-playing activities in order to enable the necessary sweeping reorientation and regrouping of people and institutions to be healthily and effectively fulfilled. The objective is to capture the hearts and minds of men. It is accordingly essential to study sympathetically the problems involved in every type of adjustment required and to hold open every acceptable line of retreat and of adaptation which individuals or institutions may wish to take in the interests of self-preservation and self-respect.

Such considerations further emphasize the importance of quality of leadership. But leadership of what? Only after two decades can we identify with any precision the main components of the international conservation movement, and the main interests confronting it. That movement, or important parts of it, must figure prominently, at least in the early stages of a movement for human fulfillment and evolution. Its aims are not only parallel but are interdependent. Its successful operating experience, its organization and techniques, and not least its confidence and prestige would be indispensable for a quick and adequate launching of a new twin movement. This is true not only on the plane of action but on that of the underlying scientific principles and knowledge, especially in relation to ecology and ethology.

A second major component should clearly be the international movement for family planning and population policy. In relation to the need for it that movement has hitherto achieved only a disappointing and inadequate growth rate since 1950, when its status and resources were already at least equivalent to those of the conservation movement. It is plain that accelerated expansion here is of the highest priority, both for its direct contribution to easing pressures and for its indirect influence in promoting new evolutionary attitudes toward human fulfillment. Fortunately there are now indications that such an acceleration is beginning. Equally essential is much more effective scientific underpinning that can only be achieved by expanding research on every aspect of the human potential and its limiting factors.

A third component of immense potential importance is offered by the humanist movement, both organized and unorganized. Even in its existing modest and somewhat ineffectual form this movement plays an increasing part in shaping public opinion and in fostering ideals of human fulfillment. It needs encouragement and recognition to build itself up as a spokesman and champion for values which are entitled to clear public expression over the mass media, as a counterpoise to the excessive and unjustified prominence still permitted to religious propaganda. The utterances of institutions representative of ecclesiastical minorities, unable to retain full credibility and loyalty even among their own ostensible adherents, still enjoy a disproportionate prominence in terms of news and comment.

Between them these three movements—conservation, family planning, and humanism—command the necessary minimum basis of knowledge, experience, contacts, and national and international organization to act, if they will, as effective sponsors to a new movement for human fulfillment and evolution. Reinforcements might be drawn as well from a number of other bodies and interests with such concerns as the reform and expansion of higher education, cultural relations, environmental health, future studies and long-range planning, urbanism, status of women, child welfare, international youth service, and the counteraction of materialist attitudes and of obsession with growth of G.N.P.

Such a list at once demonstrates both the potential for such a movement and the perils in launching it. Enthusiasm is not enough. Substantial and experienced sponsorship is essential. The movement must and should have a strong appeal to the army of the good and just, but that army is second to none in its obsession with fighting the next war in the spirit and by the methods of the last. It would be only too easy for such a movement to fall into the hands of the half-baked or ineffective and to go off at half-cock, misunderstanding the essential needs of its participants and contenting itself with a futile Cinderella status under unserious and second-best leadership. Alternatively, it might well be exposed to take-over bids from thrusting ax-grinders or self-advertisers or from operators looking for a suitable power base which could be ideologically or politically twisted to ends for which they can find no substantial support on an open and straightforward platform.

The task is of most profound and urgent import to the future of mankind. Unless the need to launch it soundly can command enough committed devotion from persons and groups whose *bona fides* and high competence have already been proven elsewhere it would be far better to accept the reproach of doing nothing at all about it. There are already far too many semibankrupt, bewildered and bewildering, amateurish, voluntary disorganizations in the field.

Looking once more at the conservation movement—it was only when that movement began to secure the dedicated time and skilled effort not only of leading scientists and professionals but of men of achievement in public and business life that it ceased to be a nostalgic backwater and became a great dynamic force in the world. It is idle to expect that the enormous tasks of adaptation and renewal of our almost bankrupt civilization can be successfully handled by mankind's third or fourth team, while the best performers are almost wholly diverted to activities whose relative importance in the long run is trivial. It has long been accepted that calls involving national security or political stability must be accorded priority by even the busiest men; the world has to learn that securing the orderly peaceful survival of mankind is of no less overriding status. Men of affairs, however, will not be drawn in by amateurish piecemeal and half-baked approaches to the problem, which waste their time and frustrate them from making a contribution at their customary level of operation. This is one of many reasons why it is so urgent to devise a new comprehensive and businesslike series of linked organizations, capable of coping with the Big Change on a scale and at a standard com-

WAYS AND MEANS: DIRECTION AND GUIDANCE 127

mensurate with the need. Meanwhile, it is as if mankind had elected to discourage and hinder broad evolutionary adaptation to the utmost extent, by enrolling as many as possible of its competent men of action in a distracting and obsessive game of attempting to work the unworkable, and to make progress within a framework of retrogression.

On the subject of money it might well be advisable to follow the fairly successful example of the conservation movement in creating at the international level twin organizations, of which one might concentrate upon publicity, relations with membership bodies, and fund-raising through a series of national appeals. Such a World Fund for Human Fulfillment would aim to complement the countless charities on behalf of the deserving poor and unfortunate, with a long-range constructive program of sponsoring and supporting growing points of new strength and advancement in human standards through all appropriate channels. It would act as a pace-setter and a prod to larger scale action through governments and other institutions of all kinds. By the offer of matching funds it might powerfully reinforce and influence the programs of private foundations and also of United Nations agencies, especially in novel and controversial areas. For this, however, it would need to be sponsored and directed by men and women of the highest standing and probity, and to be advised by specialists and experts assembled and deployed through a sister international organization concerned with scientific, technical, and professional aspects, and with cultural, ethical, and philosophic implications. This might take the form of an International Union for Evolution of Mankind, a title which would readily telescope in accord with current fashion into the acronym INTUNEMAN.

Its role would be to bring together on a world plane functional and national organs to study and monitor progress and performance concerning human evolution, and the understanding and fulfillment of human potential among people everywhere. It would promote, by all suitable means and through all suitable channels, the dissemination and application of such knowledge. It would act as official adviser on all such matters to the World Fund for Human Fulfillment, and so far as possible include among its institutional members all the main recognized institutions and organized groups active within this field in the various interested countries, disciplines, and professions. It would need to develop close high-level consultative relationships with the United Nations Organization, with ECOSOC and the U.N. Fund for Population Activities, and with such specialized agencies as UNESCO and the World Health Organization, as well as with the International Council of Scientific Unions, and with regional groupings such as the Organization of American States and the Council of Europe.

It would need to have a fairly small and effective executive board, a much larger, widely representative supervisory council, and a series of first-rate specialized commissions for such aspects as population regulation, educational advancement, future studies and planning, urbanism, quality of living, development of the noosphere, and evolutionary ethics. Judging by the experience of the conservation movement it could prove instrumental in promoting and coordinating a great variety of useful activity, even over so wide a range of subject matter, if the members of each commission were well chosen from among those most respected and vigorous within their fields, and if they were served by an efficient and dedicated international secretariat, independent of governments and of international bureaucracies.

One of the essential tasks of such a body would be to keep the field under continuous review, and to initiate studies, seminars, conferences, publications, and so forth having to do with as many as practicable of the most timely and promising growing points as possible. Particular attention should be given to subjects capable of factual and objective analysis, leading to wide agreement and to a recognition of common interests and aims.

As an International Union, with a mission mainly but by no means narrowly or exclusively scientific, INTUNEMAN would seek to interest and enroll an ever-widening circle of organized support for such studies in different fields and countries. The recognition and early encouragement of new growth would be one of the most important among its roles. It would stimulate, encourage, and nurse up new specialized or localized bodies engaged in fundamental and applied studies, and also in practical application and development, wherever opportunities exist to contribute to human fulfillment and to the understanding and promotion of evolution toward a higher state.

It is important neither to underrate nor to overrate the contribution such a new structure might achieve. It could not prove a substitute for individual concern, thinking, and study, nor for a social dynamic to give impetus, weight, and direction to the movement toward human fulfillment. However, given such preconditions, it could do an immense amount to fructify the sum of effort and to build up the status and practical effectiveness of the movement in all its branches. A well-run international body of such wide scope can do much to induce narrower sectional interests in various countries to be more cooperative with one another.

One of the essentials for strategic success, such as the conservation movement has attained, is to replace confused and confusing programs of little bits and pieces with convincing and acceptable, broad long-term objectives within which all the detailed tasks and projects can be seen to fit. Such objectives must be given a three-tier structure, ranging from comprehensive fundamental research and survey through applied studies, experiment, and trial development, to effective broad action programs and techniques. Insofar as this would involve creating a worldwide organization for developing and utilizing social science it might do the same kind of job in that field as the IUCN did for ecology. Such international recognition, awareness, and support is urgently needed by the social sciences.

One promising line for an approach to the theme of translating human evolution into a conscious and guided worldwide effort toward human fulfillment will now be outlined to illustrate the possibilities. At the fundamental level the objective would be to involve all nations eventually in a cooperative effort to explore and chart the noosphere and to develop techniques for readier access to it for all, using as an analogy the recent space programs and the International Geophysical Year.

Such a world noosphere program might be comprised of six main parts, distinguished by the different disciplines and groups needing to be involved. These might be tentatively listed as:

(1) Genetic and long-term studies

(2) Health, numbers, and physical capability of current populations

(3) Intelligence, and intellectual and psychological capabilities

(4) Social, including national, family, and group aspects

(5) Cultural aspects, including science, arts, and leisure

(6) Ethical, moral, philosophic, spiritual, and religious aspects

It is inherent in this proposal to concentrate such fundamental studies strictly at the noosphere level, and not to permit any part of them to become involved in politics or in problems of application. Their sole concern would be to appraise the state of Man's knowledge about Man, to encourage more rapid and systematic additions to it, and to create more and firmer links between interested institutions and individuals. For convenience, and as a safeguard against abuse, each of the six parts should be independently organized under bodies created for this purpose from the ranks of leading specialists, somewhat on the model of special commissions of the International Council of Scientific Unions. It might be funded through United Nations channels, by voluntary governmental contributions, under a separately organized International Noosphere Program, which would be restricted to administrative and financing functions, on the model of the U.N. Fund for Population Activities.

Such an approach would draw upon and build up the various small and fragmented existing institutes of advanced studies in the fields of science, medicine, eugenics, ethics and religion, sociology, and the arts. These would thus begin to take up their true role as recognized pathfinders of human evolution and would be seen to form a coherent series of organized expeditions into the noosphere, working in cooperation over the various sectors of a broad front. They would give visible and effective expression to the concept of human unity, expressed by W. H. Auden in the lines:

> And pray that loyalty will come
> to serve mankind's imperium.

Many scientists dislike and repudiate the claims upon their loyalty made by the state and by other incongruous social institutions. By dedicating themselves to such a visible higher quest they would assert their true freedom.

At the second level, that of the nomosphere, a corresponding but differently shaped and organized series of programs and institutions would be involved in monitoring programs and trends, in surveying problems of application, and in proposing actual policies, priorities, and projects to the responsible authorities and generally to public opinion. The work of these applied groups should be determined, and would be criticized and judged, according to the thinking and knowledge emerging from the advanced studies at the noosphere level. This division of labor, and the implied growth of an active and sophisticated public opinion watching and judging the performance and the results from both levels, is essential to the whole approach. Without it the well-known vices of unchecked, secretive, pontifical, and inherently irresponsible planning would repeat themselves on a vast scale. A monolithic structure is to be avoided like the plague.

Fortunately there are already in existence plenty of bodies more or less well equipped to fill many of the roles on this second line. At the international level the more technical fields are partially covered, for example by the World Weather Watch of the World Meteorological Organization, with its global observing system, its global data-processing system, and its global telecommunications network, including satellite services—an admirable and efficient prototype demonstrating plainly what can be done. Other structures that could perform this function exist under the World Health and the Food and Agriculture Organizations, and in connection with international civil aviation, and also (until lately in an ineffective form) with shipping. It is at this level that the special unofficial commissions proposed above for reporting on population and other matters under an International Union for Evolution of Mankind would fit in with their official opposite numbers associated with the United Nations Organization.

At the national level also there is a good nucleus of independent thinking and research bodies such as the Brookings Institute, Resources for the Future, The National Planning Association and the various institutes for the future in the United States, and PEP, Chatham House (Royal Institute of International Affairs) and the National Institute of Social and Economic Research in Britain. The significance and value of such bodies however is still most inadequately recognized, even in supposedly informed circles. They have all suffered from neglect and lack of support during the recent decades of uninspired and disastrous adhockery. Within the ambit of the new type of world approach outlined above such institutions would be capable of making much more important contributions to the process of social and economic adaptation.

Other kinds of body are necessary as well for hammering out and seeing through effective programs of action on the basis provided from the two previous levels. Natural science and technology have achieved fantastic progress with the aid of controlled experiments. Mankind has so far signally failed to solve the substantial but by no means insuperable problems of utilizing the same well-tried principles directly in the service of human and social evolution. One of the most enduringly damaging legacies of the late Adolf Hitler has stemmed from his indulgence of well-publicized and barbarous abuses of the scientific method in relation to human genetics, thus producing in many minds an emotional linkage of eugenics with totalitarianism. This is objectively no better founded than would be a ban on constructing motorways in order to restrain incipient dictatorship.

There is in the West a long and honorable tradition of active experimenting in new social devices, methods, and structures. Among many well-known examples, we may recall the seventeenth-century Invisible College, which led to the birth of the Royal Society and the organization of modern science; in politics the experimental innovations in the constitutions of the United States and of revolutionary France; in education the numerous experiments in teaching from the time of Pestalozzi to A. S. Neill and Dartington Hall; in community settlements the initiatives of Robert Owen, the garden cities and New Towns, the kibbutzim of Israel and current communal experiments in the American west and elsewhere; and in the arts such initiatives as the Bauhaus, the Royal Court Theatre of Chelsea, and the Diaghilev Ballet. What such initiatives have in common is that they are influenced neither by commercial nor technological nor party political pressures, and that they can succeed only by matching sound original ideas and practical means of implementing them with full acceptance and commitment by at least a minimum body of like-minded or converted supporters.

Unfortunately they also have in common other features which go far to explain the relative rarity of successful social as against technological innovation. In the absence of public appreciation and acceptance of the role in human evolution of the noosphere and the nomosphere, they have to face the drag and inertia arising from public disbelief in the normality and desirability of social evolutionary change. This has meant that the vast majority have either viewed such experiments with total disinterest, or have actively disliked, discouraged, or even obstructed or prevented them from being carried through. Even among the more enlightened minority, who would be ready to have a go, many have been overawed or blackmailed into withholding their participation or overt support, thus further subtracting from the potential resources available for social innovation, and adding to the stresses and problems to be faced by the usually inexperienced and inexpert promoters. Moreover, the institutional structure is heavily biassed against experiments. Regulatory and licensing authorities view them with disfavor when they have to seek even routine authorization, while grant-giving bodies tend to be supervised by safe personalities who are ready to give support only on terms which rule out most bold and potentially significant social experiments or inquiries as too untried or dangerous. Fiscal regulations are often also adverse.

While exactly the same attitude long prevailed in the technological sphere, the two world wars enabled technologists not only to break down but virtually to reverse this situation, so that fears and guilt were more likely to beset respectable bodies which *declined* to back untried new inventions than those which took even unwarrantable financial risks with the taxpayers' money in doing so. What is clearly necessary now is a fresh corrective which will insure a longer and cooler look at the desirability of rushing into new technology when it does not clearly serve a valuable social function and will at the same time give a fairer wind to those prepared to face the tribulations of engaging in timely and promising practical experiment in the social realm.

One possible approach would be to increase public funding for such bodies as a Social Science Research Council on condition that it supports a large-scale program of studies of varied types of potential advance and diversification in various fields of community development. Such a program might be complemented not only by private grant-giving bodies, such as foundations, but possibly by an autonomous, publicly financed Social Science Development Council, which would be able to take some part in enabling promising projects to be tried out sufficiently for their significance and value to be properly assessed. It might be a condition of such grants that every opportunity of measuring and recording results for the use of social scientists should be taken to a satisfactory standard of accuracy. It would help in achieving such advances if more social scientists would understand that their profession has yet to justify its existence fully in the eyes not only of the public but of natural scientists. If social science is to win the respect of informed opinion it will have to develop a self-respect of its own, to restrain recruits from flocking to it for inconsistent motives and proving unable to exercise enough self-control to avoid compromising their own and their colleagues' professional integrity by public excursions into the politics of their subject, and even by engaging in crude violence on the streets or on the campus. The contribution which the world expects from social science is much too important to risk its frustration through such unworthy deviations.

The belatedly grasped opportunities of adventure playgrounds and nursery schools, the Duke of Edinburgh's awards, such new integrated groups of school and community facilities as at Countesthorpe near Leicester, the long-lost Peckham Pioneer Health Centre, and many other examples illustrate the kind of need and opportunity which exists. It is somewhat ironic that the British taxpayer has for many years paid for an endless succession of human guinea pigs to spend a couple of weeks enjoying the amenities of the Medical Research Council's center for studying the common cold, without any perceptible progress being achieved in its prevention or cure. Had a comparable program been launched for practical testing of techniques of handling social problems, putting public money into it would have been unthinkable. Yet big industry is more and more coming to support comparable workshop methods for the training of managers, and for the solution of management situations.

There is here an unresolved problem of according recognition and status, and of giving effective reinforcement during their most creative years, to the true pace-setters and pathfinders, who largely determine whether and whither civilization advances. Election to a prestigious academy was an early device of this nature, but academies on the whole have tended to look askance at the bolder innovators, preferring the safe second-rater. Belonging to them has often brought more fetters than aid to creative work. A foundation such as the Nobel Prize does not compromise the freedom of the recipient, and does provide him with a useful sum of money, but its award is more difficult to justify and brings less professional status in the case of the Peace and Literature prizes than in the field of natural science. National systems of honors, whatever may be said in their favor, are virtually inapplicable to the types of individual creative effort here under discussion, at least until it has been going on so long that recognition is superfluous.

There does, however, appear to be a need and a promising opportunity for a new kind of *early* recognition to be given to those who are manifestly capable of exceptional creative productivity in all fields relevant to cultural development in a wide sense. All the arts, from painting, architecture, music, and theater to landscape design, films and television, printing, and fashion; all the sciences, both fundamental and applied; all the professions, from law and medicine to engineering and management; all teaching, exploration, sailing, and sport might be embraced. Up to a set limit of, say, one hundred, elections could be made at the rate of some twenty a year to the status of Pathfinder, on the basis of nominations and supporting evidence decided upon by the current Pathfinders. The award, open to men and women aged twenty-five and over, would carry a tax-free expense allowance of, say, up to £5000 ($12,000) a year, available for expenditure on travel, on secretarial assistance, on a quiet place to work (comparable to the successful Russian writer's country *dacha*), on equipment, books, or other tools, and on other items helpful to creative work, excepting mistresses and the various kinds of drugs. Once elected the Pathfinder would enjoy a five-year term, after which he would have to stand for reelection on his record during it, facing all competition from new challengers. Those failing to secure reelection could try again at any time and meanwhile would retain the equivalent of an honorary fellowship without emoluments.

While such a scheme has obvious limitations it seems to offer the following advantages. It would be open to and tailored to the needs of the younger creative people from twenty-five upwards. Annual vacancies would occur automatically at a steady rate and would not depend on dead men's shoes. Success would bring a really useful windfall of extra resources flexibly available for any purpose even indirectly related to the performance of creative work. Having offended the Establishment would not necessarily prejudice success. The danger of missing reelection would offer a deterrent against going to seed after having arrived. The existence of such a rewarding distinction would form a target for ambition from school years onwards and would help to counterbalance the rewards offered by more ratracing careers. Finally the provision of such modest resources out of national taxation for the encouragement of all kinds of creative performance would give fresh incentive and self-respect to all engaged in creative activities at every level and in every field.

For the most part the initiative for studies and for pathfinding projects in personal and group relations must be private and voluntary, with the benevolent encouragement but not the participation or control of the state. The state, however, has a right and a duty to set firm ground rules for kinds of experiments which subject society at large to undue risks or nuisance. Certain kinds of drug-taking, which lead to permanent addiction, or to the creation of lawless commercial interests, or to gross interference with the use and peaceful enjoyment of public places, should be pursued if at all in conditions effectively insulating them from becoming intermingled with a vulnerable and unconsenting society. On the other hand social tabus and prejudices about sex, dress and conduct should not be admitted as an excuse for self-righteous majority opinion to prosecute or frustrate minorities in living their own lives as they choose, so long as they do not themselves directly harm or endanger others. We are entering a period in which opportunities, resources and techniques render possible a vastly expanded range of experiments in ways of living. This period immediately follows one in which unorthodoxy and experiment have been unjustly and ruthlessly repressed either by law or social pressures or both. How to encourage legitimate and rewarding initiative without exposing society and its vulnerable elements to abuses as unjustified as society has been accustomed to inflict upon unlikeminded minorities is a subject meriting more thought and discussion.

Here is the point of transition from the realm of social discovery and pioneering to that of testing and developing its results in terms of everyday life. Conservationists, like ballet companies, film directors, football teams and plant breeders have found that the most powerful aid to the rapid attainment of high standards and of adequate growth is the build-up of an enthusiastic yet critical and well-informed supporters' movement to serve as a stimulus and also as a bridge between the small creative group and the large inert mass of inarticulate population.

In most advanced countries the evils of a largely passive us-and-them relationship between governed and governments are becoming ever more plainly recognized. The citizen whose role is merely to cast a vote every few years personifies an unworthy and unworkable travesty of democracy, encouraged and exploited in the interests of overcentralization by the power-hungry secret manipulators of mid–twentieth-century legislatures and bureaucracies. Any democracy worth the name must tap the immense resources spread throughout the population, the resources of concern and humanity, of talent and expertise, of initiative and helpfulness, and help them to find a focus through broad and diverse channels into organisms which can parley on level terms with their political administrative and managerial servants, sustaining what they find good and criticizing or rejecting what is unacceptable or half-baked. Conservationists have grasped this need, and have acted on it so skillfully and vigorously that where the environment is at stake even the largest public agencies and business interests now find it politic to tread warily in shaping their policies and practices so as to satisfy a mature and informed public opinion.

The need for equivalent homework and for a matching public dialogue exists in many fields. This need will grow with more progress in curbing and partially dismantling that outdated and mischievous institution the national sovereign state. In place of a series of tightly organized monopolistic power centers claiming, often falsely, to speak and act for a homogeneous national population, we are beginning to see a decentralization of authority and initiative to regional and local levels, accompanied by an overt or unacknowledged sharing of sovereignty with a growing group of supranational or international organizations, official and unofficial.

So far as it goes this trend is encouraging. But it will only work if public opinion can see beyond the illusion that any official, or for that matter unofficial body, can cope unaided with the earlier thinking and sifting stages essential to sound decision-making. This blind-spot in social awareness has been the cause of untold misery and loss even in allegedly advanced countries, whose entire capability for adaptation to the needs of the future is only marginally superior to that of the late dinosaurs. If, or rather IF, it proves possible to remedy the acute deficiency at the level of fundamental thinking, research, and social experiment it will still be essential to develop means and channels for receiving, discussing, and coming to conclusions upon the results, independently of political parties and of other major vested interests and above all of the central bureaucracies. These will only serve the citizen faithfully and efficiently so long as the citizen knows enough, and is pertinacious enough, to demand and tolerate nothing less.

I have already outlined some proposals for fulfilling this requirement in *The System* (pp. 356–359, U.S. edition). Referring to the success in Britain during World War II of the Bureau of current Affairs and of the Hansard Society, I suggested that something roughly equivalent should be reconstituted to provide an authoritative and impartial source of information and explanation about Parliamentary activities in suitable form for use by all interested citizens wishing to keep up to date with public affairs, either generally or on any particular subject. The Parliamentary material should be supplemented with much else from United Nations and other appropriate international sources, and from local government and other responsible public bodies. (It would also be important to add news and reports from bodies engaged in studies or experimental projects over the whole field of social adaptation.)

Such a citizens' information bureau would arrange for lecturers, films, visiting discussion teams, and many other forms of communication. Informally organized citizens' groups, wherever constituted in accordance with simple requirements, should be entitled to its free information and liaison services, which would provide a full range of agenda material for frequent meetings on matters selected as being of common interest. Existing bodies such as political parties, Rotary Clubs, Women's Institutes and Townswomen's Guilds, trade union or cooperative branches, civic societies or trusts, and charitable and religious organizations would be encouraged to belong. Frequent visits of inspection would be made to local institutions and centers, and more specialized interchanges would be promoted. At first it would probably be necessary for a liaison representative from the central information body to advise on a model constitution.

As it would be essential for such citizen clubs to function as visible, lively, friendly, and fully representative neighborhood gatherings, belonging to a national family of similar clubs, they could not directly undertake functions of an executive or specialized character. For such purposes however it would be possible, as the local civic societies have shown in British towns and the naturalists' trusts in the counties, to establish more compact and practical twin bodies acting as general trustees and promotional agencies for related tasks, including the raising and administration of a community fund with charitable status, negotiations for grants from other quarters, and the fostering of temporary or permanent offshoots for particular tasks. Such a division of labor would resemble that already proposed, on the model of the conservation movement, at the world level.

All such ideas are apt to look visionary unless or until they are put into practice. Anyone who had dared twenty years ago to suggest the need and the practicability for creating a world conservation movement for the environment such as now exists would have been greeted with ridicule. In the end it is a question of leadership and response, and that in turn is a question of people. If the kind of effort for responsible human evolution which has been indicated above is accepted as needful in the present full emergency over the survival of man, it would seem to be a contradiction of all that we know of human evolution to question the possibility of enlisting enough response to meet the challenge.

6

THE POPULATION EXPLOSION

A distinguished economist, now deceased, pointed out that in the long run we are all dead, which is true enough if *we* refers only to those now living. But we the members of mankind also include many who are not yet alive. It is essential that we the living learn without delay to treat these unborn fellows of ours with much less loutish selfishness than this generation has so far shown toward their vital interests.

No words more vividly express a prevailing lamentable attitude than "I want it now." Nothing could more starkly expose the extent of the transformation required to achieve responsible participation in the task of pressing forward human evolution. Adjustments, adaptations, compromises, and concessions are going to be required on a vast scale, and nowhere more than in relation to future human population.

Any honest consideration of the meaning of a "wanted child" quickly reveals that what was wanted beforehand may have differed from what was wanted during pregnancy and again at birth, during infancy, and many times later. Human wants are often ephemeral and trivial, but the human biomass on the earth is lasting and extremely heavy in its burdens. Some means must be found of establishing a *modus vivendi* between the two.

A fleeting and imponderable impulse leads to a ponderable and enduring tax on resources. The acuteness of the current population problem, bad enough in terms of sheer expanding numbers, is immensely aggravated through its occurrence at the precise moment in time when every individual has been persuaded and enabled to demand more and more of everything. The more greedily such demands are persisted in, the more urgent and drastic becomes the required limitation of numbers, if harmony between man and environment is not to be irrevocably destroyed. The 1970s are seeing both levels of total population and levels of per capita consumption never previously equalled, and very doubtfully sustainable for long ahead.

In contrast to the situation twenty years ago, when I was first led to study global population trends in detail, the elementary facts and figures are now widely available, fairly generally understood, and no longer seriously contested or evaded. A general knowledge is accordingly assumed in what follows, which will deal first with the quantitative and then with the qualitative aspects, and finally with the discussion of issues of policy.

In 1970, estimated world population passed the 3600-million level and was then currently increasing annually by 2 percent, adding some 75 millions each year, of whom nearly two thirds were in Asia. During the previous five years both the average birth rate and the average death rate had fallen to about 2 per 1000 population, while children under fifteen years continued to form some 37 percent of humanity. The highest birthrates were in Africa (Dahomey 54, and Sudan, Niger, and Rwanda, all around 52 per 1000) and the lowest, just over 14 per 1000, in Europe (Sweden, Luxembourg, and East Germany). Apart from the freak case of Kuwait, which doubled its population within nine years, the fastest-growing population was that of Costa Rica, oddly enough one of the most sophisticated Latin American countries.

Of 33 countries which registered 50 percent or more excess above the already excessive world average rate of population growth (2 percent per year), 12 were in Latin America, 11 in Asia, and 10 in Africa. The countries coming out at half or lower of the world average included only one in Africa (Gabon 0.9), 1 technically in Asia (Cyprus 0.9), the U.S.A., and 19 European territories, including all the 6 largest. Following the spread of death control, death rates of 20 or more per 1000 persisted only in Bolivia and Haiti, in Indonesia, Cambodia and Nepal and in no less than 27 African countries, headed by Upper Volta with 28. The earth's lowest natural growth rates were in East Germany, followed by Austria, Hungary, Belgium, and Finland, and then by the United Kingdom with one quarter of the global average. The oldest nations (with under 24 percent of their people below fifteen) were Sweden, East Germany, Luxembourg, West Germany, Hungary, Switzerland, and the United Kingdom. The youngest, with 48 percent or more below fifteen, were Honduras, Costa Rica, Ecuador, Nicaragua, and Togo.

According to United Nations projections, a world level of 5 billion is to be expected by 1985–1986, and at the medium estimate some 6 billion by A.D. 2000. (At constant fertility the total then would surpass 7.5 billion, or double the present figure.) If the medium projection is arithmetically extrapolated to 2050 it rises to 11 billion, only leveling off fifty years or so later at around 13.5 billion. The high variant would go on rising until around 2150, to a then level of 30 billion. The optimistic "low" variant would flatten out by 2050 at around 8.5 billion.

It has taken the more developed countries, whose population

THE POPULATION EXPLOSION 145

is by no means yet stabilized, over a century to halve their average birth rates, from about 39 to about 19 per 1000. The less developed countries still have birth rates averaging about 40 per 1000. In order to stabilize population growth even by 2100 they will need to achieve in the next sixty years what took the more advanced countries over a century, by coming down to half.

The scale of the problem is stupendous. At the more modest estimate Asia alone will contain by the year 2000 a billion more people than the entire world population as recently as the end of World War II. Both East and West Africa face 50 percent increases over the next fifteen years. India will by then far exceed today's greatest national population, in China.

Experience shows that population forecasts of this span are subject to wide margins of error in the present state of the art, and in the current exceptional demographic situation. Given, however, that all but the youngest adults of A.D. 2000 are already born, even the greatest conceivable deviations will do little to mitigate the already forseeable problems. There is no reason to suppose that the kind, degree, and pace of the remedial measures indicated would be in any major way affected at this stage.

According to the U.N. medium forecast the immediate trend anticipated is:

Year	Population
1970	3,632,827,000
1975	4,021,863,000
1980	4,456,949,000
1985	4,933,975,000
1990	5,900,000,000
2000	6,130,000,000

The low variant would cut this to 5.4 billion at A.D. 2000—a reduced increment only from about 66 to about 50 percent. For comparison the current thirty-year period 1961–1991 is estimated to increase total population in England and Wales by less than 20 percent. Yet judging by the experience of the initial decade (which has now elapsed) even provision for less than 3.5 million extra persons in ten years in such a wealthy and organized urban country has stretched resources quite seriously. By contrast in the coming fifteen years a country now with less than one third the population, such as Algeria, is expected to cope with an extra ten million, and Nigeria with nearly 30 million.

If a highly expert working party were set up on a worldwide basis to investigate the practical problems involved in coping with this deluge of bewildered young people, it would face a formidable agenda. Among other things it would need to consider:

> Whether, and if so how and where, supply shortages would be likely to arise on a scale calling for emergency or extraordinary governmental or international measures to meet them?
>
> What kinds of steps can be taken to insure that supplies which are economically capable of being improved or expanded in anticipation of growing needs do not lag behind, for example, owing to shortage of development capital?
>
> In cases where insufficient or no expansion appears possible, what steps can be taken to ration, or to provide substitutes for, inadequate supplies, in order to insure that unduly harsh consequences are averted?
>
> What kind of timetable is foreseen for the development of stringencies and possible breakdowns on likely assumptions concerning the course of population growth?
>
> What kind of educational and informative campaigns should be initiated in order to insure that consumers, suppliers, and other interests are forewarned of expected difficulties, and how can such campaigns be most effectively linked with those for family planning?
>
> At what levels of population growth, and of increasing density, must it be expected that sudden and severe strains may arise, threatening health, law and order, distribution of goods, and other vital services?
>
> In which parts of the world are strains likely to become greatest earliest, and conversely which countries or regions can be counted upon to be able to solve their own problems

as they go along, or to be able to extend specific kinds of aid to others?

What kinds of disaster aid should be organized, in addition to provision being made for natural catastrophes, in order to mitigate suffering and damage through this great manmade tribulation?

For how many decades are special international measures likely to be necessary, and how quickly can any essential emergency measures be replaced by effective local action?

Such a working party, if not in the usual way left until too late, could do much to educate and inform national governments and public opinion, and to enable practical advance preparations to be made. It could also, perhaps more than anything else, lead the complacent, the ignorant, and the wrong-headed who still exert so much drag on the urgently needed mass awakening, to get it into their heads that there really is a price to pay for the rake's progress of twentieth century procreation, and that it will be a heavy and a bitter one.

Any such measures can only be helpful to those who have to conduct the agonizing and belated struggle to halt the reckless overproduction of people. That struggle badly needs a well-founded strategy, some of the implications for which fall to be discussed next.

Given that the population explosion obviously cannot go on forever, the fundamental strategic question is to determine when, at what level, and how it is to be halted, and whether or not that level will be reached so late and so high that a major subsequent reduction will be urgently essential.

First, as to the timing: The later the halt the higher the population level at which it will occur. On an admittedly optimistic view it is just possible that certain fortunate and well-prepared countries may be able to reach Zero Population Growth during the 1980s. East Germany, Belgium, Finland, Sweden, and just possibly the United Kingdom might be among these. They do not, however, weigh at all heavily in pulling down the world average, although any such examples will be of great psychological significance.

Among the world's seven largest populations (China, India, USSR, U.S.A., Pakistan,* Indonesia, and Japan) there are three which are fairly well advanced toward checking population growth—the U.S.A. and USSR, which are expanding by only half the world average, and Japan which is fractionally higher. Of the rest only China, so far as the figures can be relied on, comes out just below the world average, while Pakistan is the worst, being sixty-five percent above it. As these seven countries make up well over half of world population any substantial reductions which they can make will be of overriding importance. If, for example, they could collectively halve their present increases by the turn of the century they would have done something effective toward setting a manageable task for the years after 2000.

Fortunately the 33 worst exceeders of the world average, mentioned above, are largely small states, apart from Pakistan. The other 10 in Asia total less than Pakistan between the lot, while the 12 in Latin America aggregate even less, at around 123 millions. The 10 in Africa account for only 74 millions. The combined present populations of the very high breeders are therefore only around 470 millions, or roughly 13 percent of the world. It may well be that they will need a full century to get down to ZPG as a group, and it is doubtful whether it would be either necessary or rewarding to try to push them much faster. Several may be expected themselves to take quite energetic measures, while others will be hypersensitive to any suspicion of interference. Incidentally, Brazil, which has been perhaps most articulate on this issue, actually shows up somewhat better than the South American average and is not among the twelve.

Alert opportunism often pays best in such matters, and there is much to be said for leaving the most backward to sort them-

* Pakistan is taken as a unit as of 1970 before the secession of Bangla Desh.

THE POPULATION EXPLOSION 149

selves out, and concentrating on encouraging and assisting the more promising starters. Islands such as Puerto Rico, Barbados, Malta, Cyprus, and Singapore are compact enough and often keen enough to set good examples. Japan is of exceptional significance in this context. Even particularly favorable regions and cities such as Berlin, Brussels, Stockholm, New York, London, and Aberdeen could with advantage be encouraged to become demonstration areas in the movement toward Zero Population Growth.

While the complexities and difficulties should not be overlooked neither should they be exaggerated. The United Nations Population Commission report of 1969 concludes that "Birth rates under premodern conditions would not often have been lower than, say 35 per 1,000, and rates in the range between 40 and 50 per 1,000 were probably typical." Around two centuries back, when population began to increase substantially, death rates seem to have averaged around 34–40 per 1,000. Statistically the current explosion is due mainly to the rapid fall of death rates to a world level of around 14 per 1,000, while average birth rates have stayed up at around 35, thus opening a 2 percent annual excess of births. But it was only as lately as 1900 that the average birth rate, even in more developed regions of the world, first fell as low as 34; a century earlier it had been nearly 40.

The present world falls in terms of birth rates into three broad groups. The countries of North America, and of Europe (except Romania and Albania) together with Australia, USSR, and Japan, have fairly low birth rates in the 14–21 per 1,000 range. Argentina, New Zealand, Cuba, Uruguay, Barbados, Puerto Rico, Taiwan, Singapore, Israel, and Cyprus are also below 30. All these countries combined, however, only account for less than one third of world population. Even so they include some, such as Israel and Singapore, whose rate of population growth exceeds the world average.

A further significant group consists of countries whose birth rate has already been reduced below the level of 35, which roughly represents the lowest normally attainable without some measure of birth control. These promising beginners do not include a single African country unless we can count Mauritius, and only a single Latin American country, Chile, to add to Argentina, Uruguay, and Cuba already mentioned, plus the Caribbean islands of Martinique, Guadeloupe, Trinidad, and Tobago. In Asia however they do include the most important of all, China, with Ceylon and perhaps by now Malaysia.

Not only is this group of incipient growth reducers disappointingly small; it shows no indication of being quickly expanded, since with the sole exception of Brazil no other important country has yet got below 40. Pakistan at 50 and Indonesia at 47 are the biggest among the virtual nonstarters, but India at 42 (a level over 20 percent above China) is of paramount importance, since it represents over one seventh of the human race, and is still lagging with an excess of 0.6 percent above the world average in population growth.

Even marked reductions in birth rates are of no avail if they are matched by further reductions in death rates, as is often the case. In Africa, at least 27 territories still have death rates of 20 or higher, while Asia has only 2 still at this level, with an average of 15 for the entire continent, and Latin America matches North America with an overall death rate lower than that of the United Kingdom. It follows that almost any reduction of birth rates in Latin America and much of Asia should represent an equivalent drop in population growth; in Africa and the rest of Asia it might well not.

This brief analysis calls attention once more to the important point that the contemporary world is full of a great variety of population problems. Only in one sense can there accurately be said to be a world population problem. However diverse the situations may be they nearly all add up to a resulting annual increase far higher than the modest 0.4 percent prevailing at the start of last century, which itself involves a doubling within 175 years. Is this bunching of demographic levels in the unprecedented high range of 0.4 to nearly 4 percent a mere accident, or does it reflect powerful trends, in addition to death control, making for a big spurt in human numbers?

The question is almost impossible to answer definitively, but most recent consideration strongly suggests that an affirmative answer is the most likely to be right. The more we look into demography the more we are struck by the spread and persistence of settled norms which come to be accepted by many as unchanging and unchangeable, and in contrast by the occasional abrupt and widespread shift from one norm to another, such as has occurred within living memory over much of Europe.

A further peculiarity about recent decades, despite World War II, has been the relative freedom from natural or manmade catastrophes great enough to show up markedly in demographic setbacks. It would be very rash to assume that this immunity will continue even to the end of this century. Recent events in what is now Bangla Desh, for example, demonstrate that population reduction by catastrophic means is a continuing and may well be a growing contingency.

To summarize the argument of this chapter so far, we have to think of ourselves as being caught in the acute early stages of an explosive worldwide population growth unprecedented in its pace, its scale, and its indiscriminate and hazardous impacts upon natural resources. Only a couple of decades back we lacked the theoretical knowledge, the techniques, and the information sources to understand more than very vaguely what was going on, and what prospects and problems it was opening for the future. Gradually, and still inadequately, the more elementary gaps in our knowledge are being filled, and a picture is taking shape which is of horrifying complexity, difficulty, and danger for us all. It demands cool, intensive, and cooperative international effort on the grand scale.

Clearly a large part of that effort must be applied to the rapid reduction of birth rates by every acceptable and effective means. At the same time large-scale preparations are needed to mitigate the inevitably painful and damaging situations which cannot now be prevented from emerging during the coming decades. In face of this threat to the very survival of mankind there are no resources to spare for playing about with nuclear armaments or with spaceships. Yet the message of the impending population impact has so far attracted more lip service than serious action at top political levels, and by the time it gets through, many disasters which could be averted by immediate large-scale preparation will have become inevitable.

Some possible lines for such precautions have been indicated. Although both Latin America and Africa seem certain to more than double their populations by A.D. 2000, and thus to plunge themselves into avoidable problems which may take a century or more to contain, it is in Asia that the menace is largely concentrated, and especially in the southeast and middle south. The Soviet Union and East Asia have already lowered their population growth rates below world average levels, and, although the prospect before China of accommodating another 200 million by 1985 is daunting by any standard, China has more experience, and perhaps more capability, of coping with such immense demographic stresses than any other nation.

Much more anxiety must be felt about the extra 350 million to be packed into the Indian subcontinent and the 150 million into Southeast Asia, where economic, social, political, and administrative breaking-points could easily be reached, in some areas sooner rather than later. A good deal of experience now exists concerning the diagnosis and treatment of symptoms of undue stress in these regions, and it should not be unduly difficult in technical terms for adequate contingency plans to be prepared in cooperation with governments concerned. Unfortunately, as recent experience has shown, the extent to which actual cooperation will be effectively forthcoming remains in some doubt. Demographic and political stresses readily become fused in an unmanageable hotchpotch.

Pursuing our strategic analysis we need to adopt some planning assumption in answer to two key questions:

> When, and at what level, can we expect global population growth to cease?
>
> How far is it necessary and practicable to assume that a reduction will follow to below peak levels?

Although the United Nations projections are statistical exercises rather than forecasts, and although their reliability rapidly decreases as the dates become more distant, they do enable us to determine with a very high degree of confidence that global population growth must continue well into the twenty-first century. It is perhaps around the region of A.D. 2030 that the first serious possibilities of equilibrium can be sought, although it would probably be more realistic to set this back several decades further.

"Equilibrium," however, is a debatable term in this connection. It is abundantly clear that if and when the world as a whole statistically reaches Zero Population Growth this will not be based upon uniform conditions, but will represent the net product of three quite distinct demographic sectors: one with declining population, one with still expanding numbers, and a third which is more or less stationary.

Subject to catastrophic developments, it would seem most likely that the countries already mentioned as possibly attaining Zero Population Growth within the 1980s would also be those which might form the core of a declining population bloc from about 2000 onwards. Such a bloc might include virtually all of Western and Northern Europe (except perhaps Iceland, where the winter nights are very long), and such South European countries as Italy, Greece, and Portugal, together with most of eastern Europe, and not impossibly the USSR and U.S.A. Eventually the adherence of China and Japan should not be ruled out, bringing the total to around 40 percent of the world—a base large enough to make even a modest overall reduction a significant offset to continuing growth at a reduced rate elsewhere.

Politically and psychologically it appears of high importance that the goal of worldwide Zero Population Growth should be set soon, officially, and with the utmost determination to achieve it earlier rather than later next century. For certain purposes, notably the drain on nonrenewable natural resources, and the build-up of cumulative weight of public opinion, it would be the global progress that would count for most. But in many other respects it might well be that serious and even catastrophic regional and local difficulties might continue to occur despite a reassuring world average trend. Global targets would need national targets to match them all along the line.

This line of thought suggests that a world program should lay particular stress upon two concurrent aims:

(1) To create by A.D. 2000, and thereafter gradually to expand, a pacesetting bloc of advanced countries, ready and able to pass beyond ZPG and to move into gradual reduction of existing population levels through the twenty-first century, thus demonstrating the advantages of net reduction and helping to offset continuing expansion elsewhere.

(2) To develop progressive plans aimed at insuring that by 2030 no more than a small minority of territories, and an insignificant fraction of world population, would still have failed to achieve reductions of crude birth rates to 20 per 1000 or less.

A longer-range target, say for around 2060, would be to reduce crude birth rates in the vast majority of countries to around 13 per 1000, which is the estimated level for Zero Population Growth, assuming full utilization of presently available medical knowledge throughout the world. (Insofar as further medical discoveries affecting survival were made and generally adopted, this figure would of course require corresponding revision, but it provides a yardstick meanwhile. It is slightly lower than existing birth rates in Sweden and Luxembourg.)

It is not possible to forecast with confidence whether the implied world population peak level of the order of eight or nine billion would be accepted as permanently tolerable if and when it is actually reached in the middle of next century. As a planning assumption, however, it seems wisest to assume that the conclusion then will be to move toward a gradual reduction aiming to get back to not more than current levels by somewhere about 2300. By adopting such an assumption we will insure that alienations of land and exploitation of natural resources which may be unavoidable will be regarded and handled as potentially temporary transfers, to be later made good, rather than as permanent and irrevocable, and as therefore justifying irreversible destruction. Purely as a personal view I would be happier to contemplate getting down eventually to something closer to 1 or 1.5 billion, but such a level could not usefully be considered in anything like existing circumstances, even as a long-term goal.

The discussion so far has attempted to place statistical values on the aims which are indicated for a practical effort to salvage our civilization and our natural environment, in face of the insanely philoprogenitive excesses of the twentieth century.

In 1928, when I carried out the first national bird census of a wild species in England and Wales for the heron, *Ardea cinerea*, the total of breeding pairs proved to be just below 4000. At that date the human population was 39 million, or about 5000 times as great. So effective, however, is the mechanism by which herons regulate their numbers that forty years later their population was virtually unchanged. So inefficiently, by contrast, were human numbers regulated that in the same short period they rose by a further 10 million. Of all higher creatures *Homo sapiens* is the most recklessly undisciplined in reproductive habits.

The precise means used by the herons to achieve such an admirable balance are not yet clear. It is, however, known that in some way social restraint limits the numbers qualifying to enter the adult breeding population, which has never expanded in any year by more than 20 percent above the statistical normal. In favorable years a growing number continue as nonbreeders, whereas a severe winter involving heavy mortality is compensated by a sudden drop in this nonbreeding buffer stock, bringing the population back to normal within about three years. (After 1962–1963 recovery took about seven years, probably owing to the effects of toxic chemicals.) In other words the controlling variable is not family size but the proportion of parents in the total population. By contrast, when conditions are exceptionally favorable, modern Man embarks upon earlier marriages and a smaller ratio of unmarried persons in the community. Perhaps the herons have something to teach us. Should it be *Ardea sapiens?*

It is now time to turn from population control to people, and to consider the immensely difficult issue of reconciling such aims with their feelings, their habits, and their capacity to think and act in the interests of their children's children. At the outset it is essential to be clear about who the people are who are directly responsible for reproduction. In considering the natural regulation of bird populations it is necessary to take into account three main elements composing them: the juveniles and immatures which are still unready for breeding, the reproductively active adults, and the other adults who for various reasons do not take part in nesting. The reproductive pattern as a whole depends on the relative proportions of these three elements, no less than on the number of eggs laid and of broods reared.

It is helpful to follow a similar approach in assessing human reproduction, in which it is possible to distinguish ten different stages or categories, listed below:

Human breeding or nonbreeding groups

(1) Infants and juveniles, physiologically still incapable of reproduction

(2) Adolescents, capable but still socially inhibited from reproducing

(3) Persons restrained from reproduction by old age, ill health, impotence, etc.

(4) Adult virgins and others, by choice permanently or temporarily reproductively inactive

(5) Vasectomised, or otherwise artificially removed from reproductive activity

(6) Sexually active only while fully safeguarded by contraceptive methods

(7) Sexually active without being fully protected by contraception

(8) Seeking reproduction outside marriage

(9) Married and seeking reproduction

(10) Married or unmarried and resorting to abortion rather than contraception

(In addition to these permanent categories there are many who at times fall out of their normal categories on account of illness, travel, divorce, etc.)

Between one quarter and one half of all persons living fall in the first two categories. In England and Wales the proportion would be appreciably above one quarter, to which should be added some 30 percent above reproductive age, leaving well under half the population in all categories after the first three.

The total married population is almost exactly half the whole, but this overlaps substantially with 3. It seems unlikely that at any given time more than one quarter of it, or an eighth of the total population, fall in the vital category 9 which accounts for the great majority of births.

In statistical terms it is clear that there are two complementary or alternative routes open toward achieving a decline in population, or a check upon population growth. The one usually emphasized is to persuade or press married persons into having smaller families. It is, however, no less effective, and may up to a point be less difficult to encourage a number of people to abandon reproduction entirely by switching from 7, 8, and 9 to 4, 5, or 6.

A larger nonbreeding element in the population would bring several advantages. *Ipso facto* those who could thus be persuaded are likely to include a high proportion of the less interested and less responsible parents, whose offspring are more vulnerable to emotional instability and to juvenile delinquency. Also it is more costly in money and land, and more difficult, to provide family houses which are only fully occupied during a relatively small part of their life; permanent nonbreeders raise no such fluctuating problems. No doubt too, unwise social pressures on those who do not really want or have the capacity to rear families cause widespread unhappiness and maladjustment, affecting society in diverse ways. There is much to be said for setting the bias the other way and expecting would-be parents to demonstrate their keenness and sense of parental responsibility.

For parents to continue to have families as large as they please is not merely essential to social justice and to the general acceptability of population policies, but is a necessary means of conserving values and experiences peculiar to the large family. It is far more legitimate, and socially beneficial, to exert even considerable pressure to restrain reckless and merely infatuated couples from precipitately bringing into the world children whom they shortly afterwards begin to neglect or disown, than to impose any restrictions on those for whom the family is what counts. Even homosexual couples, although still so often persecuted and ostracized, set a far better example in not irresponsibly saddling society with enduring consequences of a fleeting folly.

A reversal of social pressures toward procreation and a strong new emphasis upon readiness to assume and carry through the full responsibility as being the only legitimate moral title to having children are two of the primary conditions of a socially sound new pattern, in harmony with a sane attitude toward human population recruitment. If, as we legitimately can and must, we decline to accept mandatory state intervention in this great emergency, we cannot justify stopping short at a negative and unhelpful line. We have an honorable obligation to propose and back some less objectionable alternative which can be expected to achieve a similar result. The more we can enable and encourage those who do not wish to reproduce to succeed in not doing so, the lighter will be the burdens on society, and the more freely those who really do wish to reproduce, and really will fulfill to the end the corresponding responsibilities, can go about their creative and socially vital role.

It is to such ends, rather than to harassing young girls who have carelessly become pregnant, or persecuting harmless sexual deviants, that modern society should turn its energies. Not only would a solution of the population problem be furthered, but society would be relieved for the future of an immense burden of unhappiness, emotional conflict and disturbance, marital disharmony, and delinquency and crime, which are the byproducts of the diametrically opposite pressures hitherto exerted in society's name, and far too often in the name of Christianity.

While there are no data available to quantify the reduction in candidates for parenthood which might be achieved, there is little doubt that it would be significant. The development of more effective means of minimizing the number of unwanted children conceived prior to or within marriage is a familiar further potentiality, and although the extent to which this would reduce total births is controversial it would clearly be a substantial help, and again bring other benefits on the side.

An additional area in which easing of population pressures could go hand in hand with relief of other strains is presented by the problem of births to very young parents. While some of these are genuinely and responsibly sought, a great many are the result of rash impulses which increasingly interfere with higher education, break up young marriages, and put improper obligations on the welfare state. More, and more fully manned family planning clinics and other advisory services could do much to save the inexperienced from falling into traps of this kind on such a large scale.

The thought here is to closely coordinate steps toward a solution of pressures of population growth with steps to concentrate reproduction among those people who genuinely believe in it as a lasting priority in their own lives and can therefore rear offspring of higher quality benefiting from much more love and care.

Clarification and progress have been handicapped by the muddled assumption that only state interference by means of legislation, tax adjustments, and even some form of compulsion can "solve" the population problem. The sum of existing experience would indicate that if anything the opposite is true. Population may be a public affair, but it results from private activities which are rightly highly unamenable to any specific external regulation. To ignore this would not only be ineffectual for its immediate purpose but would be counterproductive in creating barriers and resistances tending to block spontaneous trends toward adaptation of private conduct to fit in with the realities of population. Handling of population policy is indeed a critical test of the soundness or otherwise of public appraisal of the true role of a modern State.

Where the state can and should help is in adapting existing laws and institutions so as to assist rather than to hinder the individual in acting responsibly on all that affects population. There should also be a deliberate and massive state-assisted move to break down and to replace out-dated and prejudicial public attitudes and expectations concerning population. Not only have narrow-minded interest groups long used their lobbying powers to secure and bolster up legislation for unwarranted public interferences with private sexual conduct; not content with this they have sought to intimidate and blackmail persons acting within the law from exercising rights of which the bigoted minority disapproved.

For example, for many years it was generally believed in the United Kingdom, on advice from the highest official quarters, that so-called male sterilization by vasectomy was unlawful, except in circumstances so special as to be a negligible quantity. Only during the sixties it occurred to the Simon Population Trust to take new legal advice on this matter, which was such that the Trust were enabled to initiate a nation-wide experiment involving thousands of volunteers. Not a single attempt to bring a prosecution resulted, although the law had not been changed by one iota since it had been falsely misrepresented to preclude any such activities.

Copious claims to highmindedness and Christian principle are evidently quite compatible with indulgence in lying and blackmail on the part of still influential reactionaries. It is useful to bear in mind that those who seek to invoke state interference in the personal lives and morals have personal lives and morals themselves which in the circumstances can fairly and properly be scrutinized in public. They should not count upon a continuing relative immunity in this respect. When the worm turns the world may benefit from a worm's-eye view of its persecutors.

The climate and prevailing trend of a culture is closely bound up with the composition and attitudes of its most articulate and actively influential groups. In this respect the twentieth century in countries of western culture has had a peculiar and frustrating record. The Industrial Revolution and the odd Victorian mix of religiosity, materialism, and imperialism in its various guises had built up a powerful and deeply entrenched ruling system which, as the century opened, was coming under penetrating attack from a few articulate and determined critical movements, including Marxist and Fabian socialism, an individualist brand of liberalism, and from the mainly literary apostles of greater personal freedom as against restrictions imposed by law and custom on rights of women and young people, on sexual conduct, and on many other matters such as licensing laws for alcoholic drinks, Sunday observance, censorship, and divorce.

The development and timing of the conflict between these opposing opinion groups, one in power and the other in opposition, have shaped the course of cultural transition during the first three quarters of the century. Gradually the opposition has succeeded in whittling away this or that part of the formerly solid front, in driving in wedges and eventually in breaking through at various points and outflanking or partially demoralizing the previous cultural regime. But the process has proved so interminably extended, that those responsible for these dearly bought victories have tended to run out of steam and to relapse into a posture unsuited to the ensuing tasks. Instead of being ready to take the strategic initiative in shaping and leading the new phase of culture, they are stuck in the roles of critical opponents of a series of father figures who have largely faded away.

This great deficiency is nowhere more conspicuous than in relation to population. The population explosion has not merely been an historical accident; it results from the preaching, the education, the supposed social and economic interests, and the inherited prejudices and superstitions of the recently dominant elements in western culture. It will respond to nothing less than an equally comprehensive, dynamic, articulate new set of idea-systems, of policies, of programs, and of organized interest groups and institutions expressing fresh values, among which the firm and thorough limitation of human numbers occupies a central position. The lazy and muddled belief that somehow the needful adaptation will be achieved by a multitude of low-grade groping interchanges between unserious and ill-equipped individuals and groups simply will not do. The task challenges our utmost capabilities; it must be tackled with professional concentration and skill, and with sustained and well-directed effort on many levels and in many fields. To make, as many now do, the assumption that the necessary containment of the population explosion can be achieved simply by a narrow set of family planning measures and some wishy-washy propaganda is to waste time that cannot ever afterwards be made up. Kinds and levels of reproduction are inseparable functions of kinds and qualities of culture. To seek to modify them inescapably means seeking to modify fundamentally the culture which produced them. The sooner this elementary point is thoroughly grasped the more hope there will be for our children.

In trying to supplement the essential but inadequate family planning approach it is perhaps most promising to focus upon those areas of the broader culture which most closely bear upon population. Obviously one of the most important is the status of women. Economic and technical change, and the new capability of adequately reproducing the species without involving most of the mature women for most of their time, require a complete rethinking on this subject. The status of women is, whether one likes it or not, very largely dependent upon what men expect, demand, enable, and permit. It is highly discreditable that so many women today should have good cause to feel such frustration and lack of confidence in this matter being adequately attended to that they feel impelled to resort to crude and desperate demonstrations. The men who so largely mold cultural patterns could and should have made a better job of it.

It is a paradox of the ratrace of the affluent society, and of the anachronistic power game which obsesses politicians, administrators, and top managers that while the men overwhelmingly monopolize the positions of greatest personal stress and effort it is the women and young people dependent upon them who suffer most from hollowness and frustration.

If we reflect upon the intense thought and dedicated effort recently lavished upon problems of racial relations in Britain, and compare this with the equivalent attention which has been allocated by leading men to the no less significant problems and stresses besetting their own womenfolk, the contrast speaks for itself. In terms of quality, although perhaps not in quantity, much the same applies to the generation gap and the relations between parents and their young. And these are only two among many urgent issues for the neglect of which a heavy price has daily to be paid. Somebody or some body ought to keep such gaps and priorities under review and be able to insure, as the conservationists have done, that chronic neglect of them ceases to be politically possible.

Here it is possible only to sketch the required agenda and to suggest in outline some possible approaches. As for mankind in general, the key to a new deal for women lies in the one word, fulfillment. The role of women in bearing and rearing children has to be deeply and constructively harmonized with their role as people. The first can and must come to play a less dominant part, while the second unfolds and broadens. Excellent as are many of the women's organizations and the women's journals it is neither realistic nor fair to leave so much of the struggle to resolve this intractable problem so largely to their unsupported efforts. To bring about satisfactory conditions of living for women is also a problem for men, whose record in attending to it is not good. Indeed, the chronic difficulty which our culture exhibits in making tolerable provision for the feminine half of mankind is a further symptom of something badly wrong with it.

During the latter centuries of the Middle Ages the domineering and uncouth barons, knights, and squires were taken in hand by a group of gifted and gently influential women and converted, at least partly, into the cultivated and well-mannered types for whom the age of chivalry is still remembered with respect. No comparable civilizing influence has yet been exerted upon the busy promoters of the modern ratrace and the modern international power game. In this respect Woman's Lib also looks more like an additional symptom of the problem than a genuine step toward its resolution.

Thorough analysis would probably show that a high proportion of the basic handicaps under which women now suffer represent factors no less inimical to human interests as a whole, to which men have persisted in turning a blind eye. One clear example is the absurdly excessive proportion of human productivity which continues to be earmarked for warlike preparations and for the extravagant toys of high technology. Consequently resources are not available for countless facilities in education, family planning, urban design and renewal, public transport, and so forth, where women are often the main sufferers.

Disappointment is often expressed at the limited results in those fields which have resulted from votes for women and their participation in legislatures and local government. While there may be something in this criticism it is manifestly unfair, where the alternative options, costs, and benefits have never been properly worked out and presented, and where the necessary resources are being permanently hogged by the well-entrenched bosses of the military-industrial complex. The belated and unsatisfying "great debate" over the United Kingdom joining the Common Market, like the previous debate on a third London airport, has plainly demonstrated the total incapacity of the academic and political worlds to present to the electorate a plain, honest, comprehensive, and accurate statement of big alternatives and their implications for the future. This is readily explicable in view of the obsession of both politicians and academics with myths about the past and hasty improvisations to tide over the present. Until a more future-oriented culture begins to emerge, such shoddy performances are all that we can expect.

It is unfortunate that it should still at this late hour be necessary to insist upon such overriding background problems at the expense of urgently needed concentration upon the specific and concrete needs for bringing about a diminishing quantity and a rising quality of human population. Some of the underlying problems of social and family structure are, however, discussed in a following chapter. It is in those areas that any satisfactory population policy must set its roots.

7

THE PROSPECT OF DOOMSDAY

Closely linked with the threat to man's future posed by the population explosion are a series of other formidable threats arising from pollution of the environment and from the overuse of land and other natural resources. After long neglect certain of these threats have lately stirred up intense public concern through the knowledge and skills, the devotion and the tenacity of a small number of conservationists in North America and in Europe. It must be borne in mind, however, that when a novel and highly complex subject, still relatively unexplored, bursts so suddenly upon public attention the presentation is inevitably unbalanced and incomplete. Even by the mid-seventies we must expect to see things in a different perspective. This will result partly from the mass of new research and study which has been triggered off, partly from the developing response of other parties and the more mature dialogue between all the interests concerned and partly because those who have been most energetic and articulate so far in expounding the problems have been more keenly interested in some aspects than in others of equal importance.

It is not among the purposes of this book to add to the already voluminous and often excellent detailed literature, especially relating to environmental pollution. Nor does it seem profitable to attempt to assess which particular facets have been thoroughly researched and evaluated, and which are still largely matters of inspired or perhaps uninspired guesswork. The pitch and volume of the various voices, the varying caution or dogmatism of the prophets, forecasters, and analysts, and their diverse interests and scope should all be appreciated as presenting public opinion with a range of material for choice and judgment. Once it is conceded that the problems themselves are real, great, and urgent, and that they intimately concern all of us, there is much to be said for the kind and degree of difference of opinion, of treatment of information, and of tone which has characterized in its early stages the great debate on care of the environment.

This debate is still in full swing, and is visibly screening out the more viable ideas and programs from the ephemeral, the exaggerated, or the merely mistaken. In so doing it is contributing not only toward a solution, if there is any, but is providing valuable training and experience in a new type of exercise for world public opinion. If any degree of harmony between Man and nature is to result it cannot be an imposed harmony. It must be the outcome of just such widespread and open discussion as is now taking place. Having well and truly launched the debate we now need to insure that it does not fail to cover the whole agenda confronting us and that it enables all those who have questions to put to satisfy themselves about the answers.

Underlying and aggravating all other problems is the ever-present population explosion. This has been treated separately in the previous chapter for three reasons. Unlike the others it is in a literal sense a human problem, arising from human desires and presenting itself entirely in human shape, with multifarious human consequences, some of which will be pursued further in later chapters. Owing to the dominant position now assumed by Man in the biosphere his runaway increase in numbers has repercussions upon it more varied, more severe, and more dangerous than any of the other problems which are little more than particular identifiable facets of the same thing. And finally, as we have seen, although there is not one world population problem but many distinct territorial problems adding up to one global mess, it remains true that virtually every territory in the world is at this moment facing a population problem of some kind, and either struggling or failing to struggle with it.

Human numbers, however, have been expanding for many millennia. Although the rate of growth and the absolute numbers involved are now much higher than ever before, that in itself would not explain or justify the present widespread and well-founded fears of an imminent approach of doomsday. Their justification rests upon the limited resources now and prospectively available in relation to the claims upon them, and to human competence to conserve and manage them. The problems on this supply side of the balance sheet can conveniently be arranged into a series of categories, beginning with those which are more or less fixed and intractable and going on to others which, although currently severe, are capable of extensive modification within fairly short timespans.

On this basis the obvious starting point is the limited amount of unused reserves of non-renewable resources such as minerals and fossil fuels, in terms of number of years' visible supply. If we are serious in expecting our technological civilization to continue flourishing even at its present level we should be able to point to the whereabouts of at least one hundred years' future supplies for all the main natural materials on which it vitally depends. In fact we are in most cases well below such safety margins, and in some important instances are gambling on large and early replenishments or on huge technological advances to avert forced changes of an inconvenient and in some circumstances catastrophic nature. It is true that, like those of Malthus, the warnings of early forecasters to this effect appeared for a time to be discredited by unforeseen developments which postponed for a number of decades the anticipated consequences. In the case of nonrenewable resources these developments have included the bringing in of supplies from remote torrid or Arctic sources, or even from beneath the sea, which were previously unsuspected or inaccessible. We are already well advanced in the transition from high-grade, readily accessible supplies capable of safe and fully economic exploitation to lower-grade, more remote, and precarious reserves acceptable only through combined aid from brilliant higher technology and from inflationary national economies able to conceal or absorb the rise in real costs.

While it is true that more sophisticated techniques of exploration may be able for some time yet to go on finding, large extra reserves of lower quality or accessibility, and that advanced technology may make it possible to exploit them, the writing is on the wall. Equally the rosier dreams of replacement of natural by "manmade" synthetics are fading. It is now realized that many of these substances are themselves dependent on massive use of natural resources, if not in the form of raw materials then in the shape of vast inputs of energy involving also vast discharges of pollutants back into the biosphere.

Dr. Norman Borlaug, the winner of a Nobel Prize for his contribution to the Green Revolution by breeding higher-yielding strains of cereals, stated flatly that all he had been able to do was to buy mankind a little more time to put its house in order. Industrial scientists and technologists have tended to be carried away too uncritically by the mid-century euphoria to realize that precisely the same applies to their own limited advances. Far from assuring mankind of an indefinite future, their inventions and their unfounded optimism have merely led millions of ignorant decision-makers to persist in courses which now confront mankind with the harsh alternatives of very drastic readjustments or of catastrophic emergencies, or quite probably a mixture of the two. The sad fact is that there really are limits on the resources available to Man, and that the only illimitable element is human gullibility.

What is true of extractable nonrenewable resources is equally true of the land itself. Contrary to the still persisting claims of optimists lacking the necessary knowledge, the earth's surviving virgin lands have kept their virginity for very good reasons. Modern ecology, backed by the techniques of the life and earth sciences, is at last beginning to probe in some depth into the potential productivity of these lands. The result in almost every case is not to uncover bonanzas for human settlement and profit but to show the wisdom of our prescientific ancestors, who tried everything once, in choosing to wrest a living from the land elsewhere. Having adopted for ourselves standards of ease and comfort in transport which for a time made many areas inaccessible to civilization, we look for great opportunities once such areas are opened up to us. We readily forget that aboriginal peoples with no such inhibitions have long since explored most of the lands until recently classed as "unexplored" by westerners. The thoroughness of their exploration is attested by the very small number of plant species valuable as food or raw materials, which missed being exploited by our illiterate neolithic ancestors.

There are of course a few substantial exceptions. As in the case of other natural resources, it is possible to bring into use with modern techniques areas of fertile land which were previously ruled out by inhibiting factors which we have only just learned how to master, such as disease, lack of water, contamination of water, and difficulties of physical access. In terms of the levels and growth of population a century ago such additions would have amounted to a valuable source of relief and improvement of human conditions, but for a generation so reckless as to expand its biomass by 75 million a year it is only a drop in the bucket. The sustenance of an extra 3.75 million tons, annually at compound interest, of human flesh and bone takes more than that. People unfamiliar with the total surface of this planet tend often to lose sight of the fact that its cover consists for the most part either of ocean, snow, and ice, naked and often precipitous rock, or barren waterless desert. After ten thousand years of hard trying man is still not within sight of making a living or of establishing permanent residence in these places. Humanity's multiplying billions are therefore competing not for a share of the whole earth but for a share of that residual fifth of the earth which alone is humanly usable, at least in theory. So far the situation is that some 85 percent of the planet has defeated all human dreams of putting it to continuous use of any kind. The realistic prospect of significantly reducing that percentage within the coming decades is negligible. Indeed, owing to abusive land management practices, to be mentioned later, it seems more likely to expand than to diminish.*

Unfortunately what little thought and discussion have been given to the limiting factors on human population growth has been concentrated mainly on the cruder arithmetic of meeting demands of food and raw materials. Problems of living space have received little attention, although with rising standards there is a formidable expansion in the area required per person for services such as transport, education, and recreation, as well as for work space, dwelling space, and other purposes. The reconciliation of these demands in terms of available sites is one of the greatest growth occupations of our time, although few realize it. Physical planners, housing administrators, developers and real estate dealers, agriculturalists and foresters, mining groups, local authorities, landscape designers, land use specialists, and others are engaged in a perpetual struggle to fit a quart of largely unmixable activities into a pint pot. The stage they have reached bears a close resemblance to that which technology has reached in utilizing less accessible lower-grade deposits, or which agricul-

---

* The breakdown of land and water areas is more full dealt with in Chapter Three of *The Environmental Revolution.*

turalists have reached in exploiting even the more hazardous opportunities for increased yields. Once more, those who really know what time it is are aware that limits exist and that we are quickly being forced up against them. What happens next?

The question at once arises: How well are we conserving and how effectively are we managing these precious limited land resources? Almost incredibly the answer is that we are currently engaged in destroying and irreparably damaging them on a scale never previously imagined, as if there were infinite reserves to replace them, instead of virtually no reserves whatever. The processes at work are so widespread, so varied, and so complex that conservationists are only just attaining a reasonably comprehensive synoptic view of them, and being able to chart their geographic incidence, their functional origins and relations, and how near they have come to bringing about final and irreversible loss of resources (Fig. 4).

They are most conveniently reviewed under four categories. First comes the once-and-for-all, overt, and usually massive direct destructive impact, characterized by clear felling of forests without replanting, strip-mining, or open-cast working without replacement of soil and vegetation, blasting of coral reefs, and other activities resulting in swift and lasting dereliction. Second come the various types of abusive management, such as overgrazing, overburning, overcropping, and persistence in practices causing serious erosion or loss of moisture. Although the seriousness of damage in this category is immensely increased by such development as opening up new highways, or new access to water, the actual damage is done largely by people whose ignorance is plain and is linked with illiteracy and lack of education. In most other cases the damage is the work of highly educated ignoramuses and barbarians, often with university degrees.

A third category of destruction, in which this latter group often specialize, is the reckless substitution for well-tried and healthy ecosystems of half-baked substitute patterns promoted and expensively maintained by copious use of chemical additives and

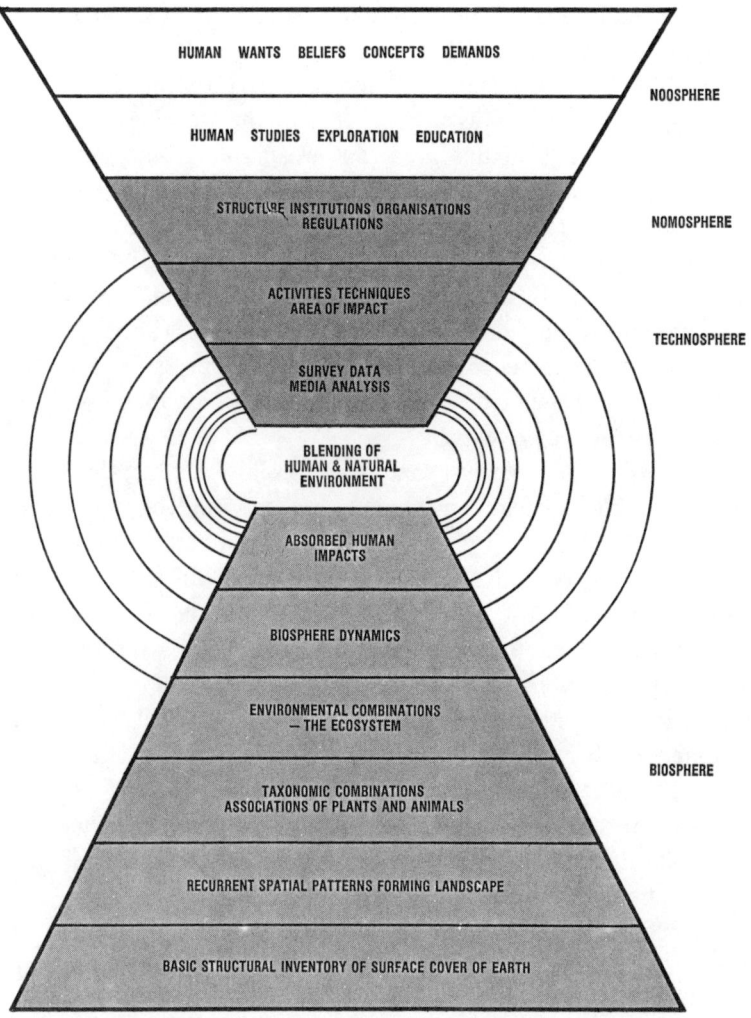

FIG. 4
RELATIONSHIP BETWEEN HUMAN PROCESSES AND STRUCTURAL LEVELS OF THE BIOSPHERE

of mechanical interference. While there is in principle nothing wrong with the replacement of a natural by an artificial ecosystem, it can cause lasting injury to natural resources if embarked upon in ignorance and in haste, as it so often is.

Finally, there is the now only too familiar problem of pollution of land, air, and water as a byproduct of the workings of man's technosphere. It is in this area that we currently encounter the greatest and also the least predictable threats to the survival of mankind. While most gross pollution is still localized in the region of high industrial activity between latitudes 30 and 50 North, fresh centers and fresh types are proliferating in many countries, and dangerous pollution is building up through airborne and waterborne substances all over the planet. Outer space has also been intensively polluted, with consequences which may not show themselves for many years.

Modern man's reckless and irresponsible conduct has thus created problems of unimaginable complexity and of the utmost peril for himself and all his fellow creatures on earth. In terms of absolute numbers he has bred up to levels of infestation of his environment amounting to nothing less than a plague of excess humanity, with all that that implies in terms of overdrafts on resources and of involving catastrophic methods of forcibly reducing his population unless rational correction can still be effected in time, which is highly questionable. He has greatly aggravated the problem by synchronizing the most rapid growth of population ever recorded with the attainment of total numbers moving into critical imbalance with resources and with vastly enlarged consumption per head.

It might have been supposed that, being confronted by record rates of population growth at record absolute levels of numbers and with record average consumption per head, a rational species would at least be taking special care to conserve its natural resource base. But no, the vital natural resources on which man is dependent for survival are not merely being consumed but are simultaneously being destroyed, badly damaged, or just wasted,

THE PROSPECT OF DOOMSDAY 175

faster than ever before. In such circumstances it is remarkable that prophets of doom have been so slow to emerge and that there are not a lot more of them. They have an easier case to argue than those like myself who stubbornly cling to the contention that all is not yet necessarily lost, not to mention the sheer boneheads who see nothing to worry about.

The onus is on those who take less despairing views not to try and rebut the proposition that man is currently headed for self-destruction, which must by now be obvious to all thinking people, but to indicate practical and realistic means by which a new course compatible with survival can be set in time. Until such means have been devised there is no choice and no clear alternative for the many millions of current adherents of the human suicide movement, and therefore no chance of promoting the necessary mass defections from it and enlisting their support for a rival movement toward human survival and fulfillment.

Taking the broad categories indicated earlier in this chapter it is not difficult in terms of higher administration to frame a series of measures and instruments adapted to tackling the adverse trends and, given adequate support, to bringing about a reversal. This involves complementing and correcting the bias of the various exploitative agencies at international and national levels by establishing organs of long-term planning and trusteeship having powers of supervision and review in the continuing general interest.* (It also involves drastic changes of common attitudes and values which are discussed elsewhere in this book.)

In the case of nonrenewable natural resources this would take the form of an international office to assemble, assess, disseminate, and consult with governments and interested parties about the present and anticipated rates of consumption and the proven and potential reserves of all the significant metals and other minerals, including fossil fuels, and free renewable resources, including

---

* The first of these, an Environmental Fund, Secretariat and Governing Council has been authorized by the United Nations General Assembly as this book goes to press.

atmospheric and marine. The future demand data already well provided by the United Nations Population Division in such publications as its *Demographic Yearbook* would thus be matched by equally authoritative and objective data relating to essential supplies. On this basis either the Economic and Social Council or a more specialized world representative body, aided by technical working groups, would be able to inform world public opinion and national governments of the prospects and issues, and to develop policies for reconciling so far as possible the interests of present and future producers and consumers.

It would be clearly advisable for each of the main countries concerned to create its own national counterpart center of study and review of the implications of natural resource exploitation. For example, certain countries, such as Australia in the case of coal, are already experiencing anxiety as to whether large and apparently advantageous immediate export contracts will not within the foreseeable future leave important local industries short of essential supplies on the spot. In extreme cases, such as Nauru, exhaustion of the only significant natural resource may involve finding an entirely new economic base, or even mass abandonment of a devastated island. Quite apart from the conservation problems involved there are evidently urgent economic and social reasons for setting up a comprehensive service of information and study concerning the reserves, production, and consumption of nonrenewable resources in the light of long-term trusteeship needs. An early exercise on these lines in which I took part was published by PEP—*World Population and Resources* (1955).

While working of minerals tends increasingly to be in the hands of financially strong undertakings capable of participating in such long-term controlled developments, the opposite is true of the land itself over large areas of the world. Although the sponsorship and concern of the United Nations for the scale and standards of provision of National Parks is much appreciated by conservationists, posterity may find something paradoxical in this when it is contrasted with the utter lack of international concern over the massive and widespread devastation of immense areas of desperately needed soil, water yields, and vegetation cover by fire, by pointless overgrazing, by erosion, and by deforestation.

The Food and Agriculture Organization, with all its expertise, contacts, and resources, has achieved surprisingly little in checking this rake's progress, and it has become apparent that a new approach is needed. Such an approach might take the form of a World Land Bank, provided with sufficient funds to enter into large long-term contracts with developing countries willing to set aside for sufficient periods substantial areas of threatened land, such as forests and poor grasslands, with adequate provision for safeguarding them from encroachment and abuse inimical to maintenance of fertility and plant cover, and for carrying out wherever necessary ecologically sound programs of rehabilitation, reforestation, and so forth.

A worldwide program on such lines would have several great advantages. It would provide a financial inducement to governments to check and to begin reversing the worldwide destruction of land and natural resources. It would provide much local employment in remote areas without the need for more than simple training and equipment and would therefore help to relieve the economic pressures making for shortsighted practices in such poorly endowed areas. It would turn the attention of governments to problems of environmental care which they have hitherto been prone to neglect, or to treat as of low priority. It would also yield a growing number of demonstration areas showing the value of land conservation. For the past forty years a program on somewhat similar lines has been operated successfully through organized Soil Conservation Districts in the United States. There is nothing unduly novel or speculative about it. Once governments can be brought to survey the state of their own land resources, and to utilize international aid where they need it, the widespread dissipation of resources which has been a blot on the past three decades may gradually be brought under control.

Actions which suddenly destroy or irreparably damage land

are in a distinct class, and are more often the work of large- or medium-sized exploiters intent only upon cashing in and getting out. It should be accepted as a principle of civilization that every government, as trustee for the national land, should insure that no such act of any kind or on any scale can ever be carried out without advance study of its significance, consultation over its effects, and authorization only upon strict conditions for remedial treatment. Such a system has been operated with great success in the United Kingdom during the past quarter of a century in respect to open-cast or strip-mining of iron ore and coal. After deposits have been surveyed and evaluated, a detailed application for permission to mine is submitted to the minister and published, containing full particulars not only of the proposed operation but of plans for complete and immediate subsequent rehabilitation at the charge of the mineral extractors. Whenever necessary to meet objections a detailed public inquiry is held before a ministerial decision is reached. So much expertise has been developed that it is normal for the soil to be significantly more productive afterwards than before.

If the environment is to be successfully conserved, and if trusteeship for the land is to become a reality, all must understand that nowhere upon earth will owners or occupiers of land, or developers, be permitted to act as judges in their own cause whether or not to embark upon operations of any kind which may destroy or damage the land for future generations. Certainly there will be occasions when at least a risk of damage must be accepted for other valid reasons, but the validity of these reasons should always be tested first, and all who may be affected should be given a fair hearing before any irrevocable step is taken.

This becomes all the more essential now that big machines can go in and within a few hours or even minutes can put an end to historic structures, or significant ecosystems, or to amenities prized by the community. If all that is now known about the proper conduct of such operations and the subsequent restoration were generally adopted, a vast amount of senseless and selfish destruction could be averted, while still fulfilling the requirements in aid of which it is perpetrated. It may well prove necessary to limit purchase or use of certain environmentally destructive machines to operators who can show that they fully understand and will faithfully observe the essential environmental restraints demanded in their use.

As the world still has so much to learn on these matters it would be desirable for all authorities entrusted with decision-making on such applications to publish annual reports listing with sufficient details the authorizations which they have given and refused, and the reasons. Such reports should be analyzed and reviewed on an international basis, in order to secure worldwide interchange of experience and knowledge.

Problems of abusive management always reflect a complex of anthropological, sociological, cultural, traditional, and economic problems which must be studied in some depth if the administrative agency concerned is to function with success. Such studies will point the way to the right educational approach, and to possible needs for fiscal or other measures such as financial subsidies or deterrents, supplies of free fuel to relieve extreme pressures on relict woody vegetation, or incentives to change methods of cropping or levels of stocking with domestic animals. There is a big task here for conservationists and others to persuade and demonstrate to politicians, administrators, and agricultural advisers the lines on which conservation principles can be made effective in face of the stubborn and delicate human factors involved. Not only deep understanding and much tact but firmness and a sense of the urgency of remedial action are called for.

Turning now to the substitution of one ecosystem for another, we are on new and little explored ground. It is true that the fundamental problem has existed since before the neolithic revolution. Indeed subsistence cultivation, the purposeful elimination of predators upon livestock and game, and selective extraction of trees from forests are practices of this nature which go far back into prehistory. In such examples, however, the natural ecosystem was modified only locally or temporarily or to a relatively minor extent, not affecting its continued functioning as a whole. During historic times irrigation, elaborate terracing, forest clearance for agriculture and tree planting, and other developments gradually created a series of secondary landscapes which in the older settled districts gradually superseded the primary natural areas. These have now led on to more complete substitutions, sometimes on a large scale, of artifacts such as cities, industrial and transport facilities, mines, and reservoirs. By virtue of their command over certain technological tools and methods engineers, chemists, economists, and other ecologically illiterate groups have moved in with ill-considered projects for more or less total transformation of existing ecosystems in many parts of the world, creating severe hazards and injuries in an attempt to correct supposed defects in a preexisting ecosystem, or to obtain theoretically attractive improvements in production.

Insofar as the interests and disciplines behind such misguided activities are fairly compact, and in most cases at least partly educated, there is a physical capability for communicating with these groups and helping them to understand the ecological principles relevant to their activities. Steps to this end have alread been initiated, and it is to be hoped that the light of ecology will soon penetrate even into the darker corners. It was with such thoughts that I gave to my book *The Environmental Revolution* the subtitle: *A Guide for the New Masters of the World*. We must educate our masters, and we must hope that they will not be slow to learn. Administratively there would be formidable difficulties in an alternative approach, such as devising some kind of licensing system for interventions calculated to modify an ecosystem.

An interesting approach which has recently been adopted in the United States under the Environmental Protection Act is the requirement for an Environmental Impact Statement to be included in every project application which can have significant effects upon environment. Early experience showed how far many promoters of such projects were from appreciating the factors involved, and how to incorporate safeguards against them, but there are some indications that the message is getting through. If a similar requirement were embodied in planning authorization procedure in Great Britain it would help to tidy up and consolidate a series of looser measures to the same effect which have long been applicable.

This brings us to the last and in many respects the most urgent, dangerous, and complex category of all—the deliberate, regular, or occasional, and the unrecognized or indirect pollution of land, air, and water. Once again we must begin by recalling that human pollution is an age-old activity. Indeed, an important part of our knowledge of certain vanished cultures is derived from their middens and similar sources. Aside from the multiplication of numbers, and the widespread partial or complete replacement of natural by artificial ecosystems, modern civilization has vastly expanded the scale, range and potential destructiveness of the technosphere, and the mass, variety, and volume of substances which it extrudes into the biosphere, purposely or unwittingly.

The first reaction of conservationists has usually been to await perceptible lethal symptoms appearing within the biosphere. This has been the signal to embark on what has sometimes proved a wild goose chase to isolate some agent which could be responsible for the symptoms, and to trace back where it comes from, how it travels to its destinations in the biosphere, and what can be done to treat its effects, to block its dissemination, or to cut it off at source, which may even be in some distant other land. This was a case of doing things the hard way. Ecological knowledge of normal states, and of the nature and extent of natural deviations from them, is still often rudimentary. Apart from all the difficulties of interpreting and accounting for such deviations they may be totally missed. An odd example of this occurred in the exceptionally well-worked field of north temperate zone ornithology after World War II. An observer in a position to watch a pair of peregrines (*Falco peregrinus*) at close range at an unusual nest site high on the Sun Life Building in Montreal made the surprising discovery that their eggs can be destroyed by the parents themselves pecking at them. Thus alerted, ornithologists elsewhere found similar instances, but for years there was no clue to the cause.

In 1959 representations were made to the Home Office in Britain on behalf of racing pigeon interests for the removal of the special protection enjoyed by peregrines. The Nature Conservancy advised that there was insufficient up-to-date ornithological evidence on the status of the peregrine. At the Home Secretary's request a survey of numbers and distribution was arranged through the British Trust for Ornithology. This led to a further surprise. Instead of being on the increase, as the racing pigeon interests had assumed, peregrine breeding population proved to have declined spectacularly since about 1955, especially in southern England and Wales. The decline had been gradual and was marked first by the failure of peregrines to hatch their eggs, followed by failure in succeeding years to lay, and then finally by desertion of the eyrie. During 1962 in Britain, peregrines were found absent from 191 out of 432 territories visited where they had bred annually, and only 92 pairs (or 21 percent) could be found rearing young.

Next the Nature Conservancy obtained analyses of peregrine eggs, which proved to be badly contaminated by chlorinated hydrocarbons. Through the work of the Conservancy's Toxic Chemicals and Wildlife Section, set up in January 1960, a scientific basis was established for a far-reaching scheme of regulating the use of toxic chemicals on the land in Great Britain. Although only voluntary, this achieved sufficient success to halt, and in places to reverse, the decline which had cut the country's breeding population of peregrines from about 700 pairs before and after World War II to little over 70 percent of this by 1962. Had it not been for a fresh impact of a different type of pollution on peregrines breeding on the coast, the 300 young birds reared annually by

THE PROSPECT OF DOOMSDAY 183

1971 would already have almost made good the population loss of this excellent indicator of ecological welfare. During the same period, the comparable sized American peregrine population east of the Mississippi had fallen to zero and stayed at zero.

The peculiar interest of this case is its light upon the timing and duration of the impact on the biosphere of a new and deadly chemical, irresponsibly disseminated by man, and of the time lag in detecting its occurrence, in proving the connection, and in remedying the worst of the traceable effects in the field. It happens that reasonably reliable population counts of the peregrine both in Great Britain and in the U.S.A. were made around 1940. It was a lucky fluke that a pair happened to be nesting so conveniently for close observation on the Sun Life Building, that they happened to be early victims of such chemicals as DDT, and that their symptomatic and arresting behavioral response happened to be promptly observed and recorded by a competent ornithologist—something which would have been immensely more difficult at a normal eyrie.

It was again chance that some four years after the impact of toxic chemicals had hit the British peregrines an ill-informed but strongly opinionated Welsh pigeon fancier should have made himself sufficiently tiresome to the Home Office to lead them to the rare expedient of inviting a national investigation of the facts, and that this should have happened to come at the very moment when the story of what was occurring first became traceable. It was a further lucky coincidence that, almost simultaneously and quite independently, the Nature Conservancy had brought into existence a special toxic chemicals and wildlife section without whose expertise the proof that the peregrine's decline was due to particular toxic chemicals might not have been obtained. In all it took some four or five years after the first marketing of the chemicals concerned before they began to hit the British peregrine population seriously, and another eight to ten years before the facts were fully ascertained in the field and the link between the decline and the use of toxic chemicals became strongly suspected. Only a further approximately eight years were needed to establish the link, to diagnose the source of the trouble, to prescribe appropriate remedial action, to secure voluntary agreement among the interests concerned, to disseminate the necessary information on a nation-wide scale, and to secure such changes of practice in the trade and on the land as were needed to check and in some regions to reverse the effects on the peregrine population.

Even given a good deal of luck it is quite remarkable to have carried through so complex a process of research, survey, diagnosis, and successful remedy within so short a period, without even having to secure any fresh legal powers. It is on the basis of this and a few other somewhat similar successes that I tend to be fairly optimistic over the possibility of checking and reversing the potential for doomsday which modern pollution undoubtedly contains. It must, however, be stressed that the methods used in this instance through the initiative of the Nature Conservancy were infinitely more scientific, more expeditious, and more comprehensive than those which would normally be adopted in the British and probably most other civil services. On the other hand, now that background knowledge is much ampler and more widely understood, and now that agricultural and medical scientists have ceased publicly contesting the established ecological facts, the time required for action should obviously be reduced.

One clear lesson is the need for maintaining a regular and comprehensive network of monitoring, on a global scale, a substantial number of indicator elements and species, to give early warning of changes which may point to ecological dangers or deterioration. After discussion of this problem at the Varna General Assembly of the International Biological Programme in April 1968 plans were examined, under the auspices of the International Council of Scientific Unions, for launching such a system. Many difficulties were however encountered in defining and agreeing upon a manageable range of parameters which could be satisfactorily interpreted and effectively and economically covered on an international scale. As usual also there were difficulties concerning the required level of expenditure and the ways and means of raising the money.

It is essential that such comparatively secondary obstacles should not be allowed to stand in the way of equipping the world with its urgently needed early warning system against the further ecological hazards which are undoubtedly imminent. It might well be that some of the readings and inferences produced by such a monitoring network could from time to time prove embarrassing to governments in various parts of the world, who would be faced with a temptation to try to dispense with their publication, at least in an undoctored form. For this and other cogent reasons it seems essential that the network should be under continuous international scientific inspection and supervision, and that its findings should be in the form of scientific publications. On the other hand not only the cost but difficulties of maintaining the necessary trained personnel and specialized equipment at the right places would point to the need for delegating the regular monitoring in the field so far as possible to scientific institutions already suitably located and engaged in other programs.

A possible partial solution is provided by the gradual spread of what are coming to be called "biome stations" under the International Biological Programme and in other connections. I have been much impressed by the current work and future potential of several of those which I have visited. The latest was in Alaska in July 1971, and I do not think I can do better here than to quote from my report on that occasion:

> Modern science has been slow to appreciate and to adapt itself to the immense needs and opportunities for comprehensive multi-disciplinary studies of the environment—of its working mechanism, its potential, its vulnerable points and of the nature and limits of its adaptation to human technology and human use. This shortcoming has begun to be made good only since the launching in 1964 of the International Biological Programme, under the auspices of the International

Council of Scientific Unions and with the active support of the world's leading academies of science. Although principally a biological initiatve the IBP has drawn in many geographers and other earth scientists, as well as some physical and social scientists, in the most important international series of projects yet developed concerning the study of environment.

Such study cannot be made wholly or mainly in the laboratory: it has to go out in the field. It cannot, however, be carried through without a wealth of instrumentation and a series of sophisticated techniques, hitherto largely the monopoly of laboratory research. It therefore needs experimental areas accessible and convenient for large-scale, continuous, well-equipped investigation. This inevitably modifies and injures the study area, which therefore requires duplication, and also must be matched with control areas of undisturbed natural character. It is essential to guarantee the freedom of such working sites from intrusion of other uses which would write off the scientific investment. It is also essential that such costly interdisciplinary teamwork shall proceed in the closest communication with other related scientific projects in various countries, in order to eliminate avoidable duplication of effort, and to ensure prompt adoption of new techniques and rapid assimilation of relevant results.

With that object the International Biological Programme organised much of its work in terms of Biome Projects. Of these one of the most important and quickly developing is the Tundra Biome, in which scientists in Alaska play a leading part, especially near Fairbanks on the University of Alaska campus, at the Arctic Research Laboratory in Barrow, fronting the Arctic Ocean, and on the North Slope at Prudhoe Bay, using the installations and resources of the oilfield. At the summer peak of field work in July 1971 no fewer than 75 scientists were working on this program in Barrow alone. It accordingly forms one of the largest, best coordinated and best equipped projects ever undertaken in field biology. The impressive review of work in progress and of interim findings already produced confirm the effectiveness and fruitfulness of this approach in contrast to sporadic individual efforts of the recent past. The ready enthusiasm for integrated and programmed teamwork displayed by the largely very young group of assorted scientists taking part represents a revolutionary departure from earlier isolationism among ecologists. The challenge presented by the impending oilfield development has lent a new urgency of purpose and a new applied significance to research which, although of fundamental scientific importance, might otherwise have dragged on over many years.

What is taking shape here in Alaska will form one of the prototypes and growth points for the fast expanding science of ecology and for the scientific understanding and care of the world-wide environment. Moreover, since so many of the scientists enjoying this new experience are still on the threshold of their careers, it is bound powerfully to influence the development of a type of scientific and technical intrastructure which Alaska so badly needs, and which may well enable its development to be transformed on late 20th century lines. It is of the utmost importance that the wider significance of the tundra biome project should be fully and generally understood. Continued support should accordingly be given to the comprehensive long-term build-up of environmental science at the University of Alaska and the Arctic Research Laboratory.

The function of fostering, and promoting communications with, such international biological stations has been taken up by the International Union for the Conservation of Nature. It is to be hoped that before long the tundra, the boreal forest, the temperate and tropical forests, the savanna, the desert, and other leading terrestrial freshwater and marine biomes will all possess their network of properly equipped base stations for field studies by earth and life scientists of all countries. Among their functions should be the maintenance of regular precise monitoring of suitable environmental parameters, and of ample fully safeguarded natural areas close at hand, on which opportunities for permanent or repeated research projects can be assured.

While such stations must be envisaged as falling within the scope of existing ecological and conservation programs they illustrate the kind of parallel possibilities which might equally be developed on the human ecological side under the auspices of an International Union for the Evolution of Mankind.

Writing after so much attention has been focused on this aspect by the United Nations Stockholm Conference, there seems little point in pursuing further here the discussion of ways and means whereby the various types of pollution which have given rise to what are often termed the doomsday series of forecasts and warnings might be checked and contained. Many excellent proposals have been outlined, and there is an impressive worldwide activity in many different states. One valuable feature of these discussions has been their success in bringing out of obscurity and into effective contact with their governments many good scientists and conservationists in various countries who had hitherto been without any channel for making available their information and advice. Without adopting too optimistic a view of the outcome of Stockholm, it is already clear that, for all the disappointments of its aftermath, it has produced a singularly comprehensive and well worked-out set of studies of these problems and their possible treatment. Future organizations will also have the benefit of Maurice Strong's well-sifted recommendations which will be increasingly felt in the course of the current struggles for effective world action.

The threats presented by pollution in its many forms may be the most dramatically menacing, and the most immediate of the environmental dangers facing mankind, but it is arguable that they are also the most readily manageable and in many cases the most ephemeral and unlikely to persist in anything like their present form.

The classical and legendary peasoup fogs of inner London, which brought so much misery, ill-health, dirt, danger, and inconvenience, lasted through enough decades to be thought of as inseparable from the city. Yet they were brought to an end so thoroughly that fewer and fewer now recall their peculiar acrid embrace, which after two or three days made the eyes smart and breathing unpleasant as the dank, dense, brown air surged through sore nostrils and choking lungs. In those days one hardly reckoned it a real fog so long as it remained possible to set out across the street without finding oneself back on the same side. Traffic movement became impossible, and even starlings flighting to their roosts got hopelessly lost on the way.

Less spectacularly, the burden of filth in the Thames has been so reduced that once more different species of fish are actually able to live in it. Although still unusual during the first phase of counterattack against pollution such remarkable victories clearly indicate that it can be halted and reversed. The very depth and breadth of public concern, and the toughness of the countermeasures which the public now demand and tolerate, are fair evidence that the political as well as the technical possibilities exist for bringing it under control. Meanwhile, by all means let the prophets of doom continue their good work in full cry. Without it they might well prove right.

8

THE QUALITY OF LIVING

In earlier times chronic failures to attain a higher quality of living could plausibly be attributed either to Divine Will or to the incurable evils of the rule of rival princes, or simply to human limitations and destiny. One of the greatest of modern challenges has been to demonstrate beyond rebuttal that shortcomings in the quality of this generation's living are the fault of this generation, and of no one or nothing else. The rigid barriers against any desired new pattern of living have been breached, at least for large groups in the advanced countries, but people have not known and have made little effort so far to understand how to take advantage of these breaches and to pass through to new ways of human fulfillment. The vast new resources at the disposal of mankind, won with so much effort and ingenuity, and so much risk to the environment, are being squandered on wars and washing machines.

What do we mean by quality of living? How do we map out the range of possible options, and the criteria for choosing between them? How do we educate and train ourselves to produce, and above all to be able to appreciate and to thrive upon, better things in our way of life? What are the physical limitations governing improvement in quality, now and in the future? Can "human nature" be changed, and if so how? What is the strategy for a shift toward higher quality of living, and how can this strategy be applied to create the necessary social dynamics? Such questions are daunting, but unless we can make at least some steps toward answering them it is idle to expect improvement, and we may well find things getting steadily worse.

Holding firmly to ecological and ethological principles we must seek quality in terms of encouraging diversity and interplay rather than uniformity and dominance, of long-term sustained yield rather than of sudden spurts and tangential deviations, of effective cycling and recycling of energy rather than of consumption leading to waste and pollution. Above all we must continually and vigilantly work for full evolution of human potential, rather than against it or in disregard of it as now. It follows that the dominance of the technosphere must be curbed, and that human activity in the noosphere must be vastly expanded, as a stimulus and guide to creating, through the nomosphere, a new environment congenial to fulfillment.

It follows that politics as recently understood (together with its lackey, economics) must be removed from its central role in human affairs. It is demonstrably counterproductive to seek to filter all new thinking and response to challenges through organisms so stupid and rigid, and so amenable to sectional manipulation, as the party political machines which have done so much harm in the United States and Great Britain during the past century, and the kind of amateur administrative mechanisms which go with them. Once we understand that our role on earth is not to be tools of priestly or secular mythology and power politics, but to understand and to tend the health of a most complex and delicate living organism called mankind, we need to rethink our central nervous system accordingly. Our sick society in its sick environment calls rather for the ministrations of something more resembling a comprehensive medical service, drawing upon a wide range of scientific knowledge and expertise to treat the great pathological conditions of our time, and to set mankind on the road to mental and physical recovery.

The tensions, stresses, and distortions, which create so much unhappiness among so many, are predominantly traceable to a small number of chronic evils of our civilization. One of the most obvious is war-making between sovereign states, together with its preparations and its aftermath. It seems safe to say that never in history have so small a minority of mankind believed in, desired, or seen any justification for war "as an instrument of policy" or as an instrument of anything else that can serve as a disguise for human folly and aggression. Yet by sheer command of the levers of power in an inherited system the military-industrial war complex is still able at this moment to divert to its support a colossal share of the world's product. Forty years of disarmament conferences have left mankind saddled with greater arms burdens than ever before.

The credibility of this war-making capacity is, however, steadily being undermined, partly by the extravagant destructiveness of modern weapons, but paradoxically also by the ineffectiveness of these weapons to cow the spirit of resistance so long as life goes on. Never has Clausewitz's dictum that the defensive is the stronger form of warfare rung truer. Never have the mightiest armed forces had so much to fear from ostensibly weak opponents, and consequently from the withdrawal in disgust of domestic backing.

The present uneasy truce with militarism cannot long continue. It seems almost certain that by the 1980s the battle to dismantle and disband conventional armies, navies, and air forces will be fairly launched. A decisive step to eradicate major war-making capacity on the part of sovereign states cannot much longer be deferred. Indeed one of the most substantial remaining obstacles to this development is the poor progress made in preparing for its economic and employment consequences to be cushioned by suitably massive programs for peaceful construction. Unless and until industry and organized labor can see such alternative outlets there will be a built-in drag on this essential part of the Big Change.

Fear is an important component of modern stress. Fear of wars and their consequences is one of the greatest contributors to this. Another is fear of unemployment, stimulated by the observed instability of modern western economies, and the alarming loss of income, status and self-respect which unemployment can bring so suddenly upon its victims. It has long been obvious that there is a disparity between the productive capabilities of modern mass manufacture, even before automation, and the capacity of financial and distributing mechanisms for taking up the entire output on an economic and steady basis. Fluctuating distribution and consumption imposes a stop-go rhythm on industrial and primary producers, leading to uncertainty and to economic slumps. Thanks to the dominance temporarily accorded to the technosphere, and the failure of economists to calculate its true long-term costs, the happiness and welfare of many millions have been staked upon the continuing gamble of finding profitable means of disposal for immense amounts of short-lived and quickly obsolete products which are whimsically termed "consumer durables."

In the United States the preoccupation with unloading these products has led to the prostitution of television as an instrument for brain-washing potential purchasers into accepting the kind of social attitudes and the kind of Madison Avenue hogwash which seems best calculated (at no matter what social sacrifice) to make the consumer receptive to even the most unnecessary commodities.

This highly artificial process has contributed much to the inflationary and psychological pressures which disfigure contemporary western society. Indeed a large part of the relief of human misery that came when the dominance of religiously inspired moral despotism over personal conduct was broken has been rapidly offset by the commercially inspired amoral despotism of mass production and mass selling.

The other major source of stress which needs mention here is pressure of human numbers, already discussed in Chapter Six.

All these complexes, including war, inflation and mass consumption, unemployment and population, have to be regarded as reservoirs of stress and seats of disease in the body politic. A society less addicted to superficial political antics, and more in earnest about understanding the causes and the cures of its own sickness, would approach such problems with something of the attitude and method appropriate to the elimination of malaria or of tuberculosis. Just as we have atlases of the occurrence of various diseases it would be possible to devise atlases of stress, using appropriate physical and psychological indicators to locate the sources of anxiety in work and living environment. We are coming to recognize the connection between the health of people and the wealth of rivers, forests, oceans. Similarly we have to appreciate that an essential first step toward improving the quality of life is to minimize the incidence of stresses and tensions, of fears and imposed distortions of personality which make people unfit to maintain and appreciate a higher quality of living.

In our pursuit of harmony we must never forget that it remains a minority ideal. It would hardly be an exaggeration to say that, however unwittingly, the mass of mankind is dedicated rather to the pursuit of disharmony, and to activities which make harmony difficult and improbable.

On the fundamental plane perhaps the gravest and most stubborn complexes are those which direct collective human effort toward unrestricted tool-making for "the conquest of nature"; those which perpetually and unremittingly prepare and organize human societies for internecine warfare; and those which promote and enforce the subjugation of women to men. All three of these evils are centered in the male sex, and not one of them will be neutralized without massive and persistent enlightened feminine influence, which is far from being the same as Women's Lib.

The attainment of harmony implies a mature and settled outlook and a satisfying role in society. For this each person needs a private identity which knits together and fulfills his or her psychological needs and personal aims in life, and which is recognized by others as a firm basis for relationships with them, and for social status. This need for an assured identity is even more difficult to satisfy for women than for men—a fact to be borne in mind in considering the feminine aspect of the problem. Given identity there is a continuing requirement to be able to integrate general or particular inherited elements, such as aggression or some particular weakness or talent, with many learned and acquired additions, and to reconcile the whole with harmony toward other human beings within a total environment. Every factor involved in quality of life must be considered in such a context.

Evolution takes place in response to challenge. It has been the tragic lot of this and recent generations to be compelled at immense sacrifice to respond to challenges such as the two world wars which were unnecessary, futile, and diversionary from much more urgent human tasks.

Even when major wars are not actually being fought, their legacies of political and economic distortions and their crippling influence on the advance of human fulfillment remain dominant factors. Much of the violence and dishonesty which plagues our modern societies has been disseminated, with official approval, in their own armed forces. Any effective move in the direction of a higher quality of living must not leave on its flanks garrisons dedicated to hostile concepts which await the next opportunity to resume their retrograde activities. Like slavery, such activities cannot be stopped so long as interests and networks are permitted to remain in existence which have no other function but to perpetuate them. National politicians, who have so long been subservient to these interests and gullible to their misrepresentations—as Vietnam has once more dramatically demonstrated—must be left with no further escape routes for dodging the main issue.

At the same time much study and planning is needed to devise and launch new challenges of far-reaching magnitude, which, unlike wars and space travel, will shift the focus of challenge from man's tool-making to man's intellectual and moral capabilities. Citizens of leading western nations have recently been far too careless in permitting huge resources to be taken from them in taxes and to be misapplied to speculative high technology at the expense of requirements far more valuable to mankind. Politicians and administrators should be left in no doubt that these days are over, and that social cost-effectiveness will be narrowly scrutinized in future. What could we not achieve with the thousands of billions of dollars invested during the past two decades in the vain pursuit of prestige?

The quality of a culture rests basically upon the duration and richness of its inheritance from past generations, but is limited at any given time by the quality and composition of the inputs contributed during the formative years of each new generation by parents, by schools and universities, and by other articulate groups and individuals. Not only the substance but the methods of teaching and of disseminating information play a decisive part. In recent years the quality and amount of knowledge have immensely expanded, but there has been an equally significant growth in the variety and scale of transmitting media. As a result new channels of communication have vastly expanded human awareness and sensibility, enabling new and more diverse choices to be made in the range and composition of elements in the quality of living. This new awakening has results in direct opposition to the attitudes and patterns imposed by the mass production and mass distribution regime which immediately preceded it. The fighting out of the issue between the two will be a major theme of the seventies and eighties.

It is now apparent to all that during the middle decades of this century the United States and other advanced countries have seen a highly successful attempt by a powerful group of financial, marketing, and advertising interests to combine the technical resources of modern mass production and of modern applied psychology in order to generate an immense and highly profitable consumptionist economic pattern. This has been geared to the systematic creation of new wants for material processed products, and the competitive satisfaction of these wants at vast expense in energy, waste of resources, pollution and the stimulation of inflation and social discontent.

Many millions have been led by the biggest confidence trick in history to suppose that this huge operation was carried through to meet their demand. They are slow to realize that more often their demand was skillfully engineered in order to reap the profit of meeting it. The game was perfectly apparent to acute observers fifty years ago, when it was only beginning. Few at that time, however, were pessimistic enough to forecast how massively it would develop and what immense evils, cultural, environmental, and social, it would bring in its wake.

Among these one of the gravest is the confusion which it has caused between the admirable concept of a high standard of living and the particular distorted pattern of technology, industry, and marketing which has been developed to meet these sectional designs. We now face the dreary and difficult task of retracing our footsteps and rediscovering what options exist for alternative high standards of living which are at least relatively free from the gross vices of this one. In tackling this task we are bound to reflect upon the ease with which allegedly educated nations have been conned in this way, and to lay blame upon education—especially the education of women, the main targets of this campaign. At long last there are signs that the expanded body of graduate citizens is slowly becoming more resistant to such specious seductions and more ready to ask searching questions and to decline to accept the inacceptable. It is only because of this new spirit, most plainly exemplified in the conservation movement, that the presentation of such an approach as this book outlines may not be a waste of time.

Any cultural base which may now have emerged for a more sophisticated and discriminating style of living is however still highly localized and horribly precarious. An ecological survey of cultural activity would show only pockets or narrow zones of lush growth islanded in the midst of broad tracts of monotony and retardation, which in turn would be flanked by sheer cultural deserts. In considering quality of living therefore, whether we like it or not, we are stuck with an elitist mission. It is only where such islands and zones of relatively rich cultural activity exist that a basis can be found for beginning.

Thanks to human imitative tendencies, any progress toward a higher quality of life can in favorable conditions spread quite fast, helping both to create a demand for and to supply something better. Indeed it seems probable that, unless such a rapid spread can be brought about, the original initiatives will be too precarious to last. At the outset, however, such indicators as clusters of graduate citizens, research and higher teaching centers, museums, theaters, art galleries, concert halls and music festivals, bookshops, restaurants, and craft displays must serve to indicate the most promising growth points. Higher quality of life cannot be imposed or magically communicated; it must emerge on the basis of an already developed capability for it, and an urge to satisfy the accompanying demand.

Given such a basis, changes become possible in a wide range of material elements in consumption. Many, although by no means all, of the daily needs of a well-educated modern man can be provided with relatively little expenditure of money and materials. It would be possible to list all the goods and services which are consumed by different income and occupational groups, bringing out which groups make heavier than average use of which goods and services, and which goods and services involve the least drain on scarce resources and least incidental pollution. It seem probable that even today the most highly educated groups and persons engaged in creative mental work would already emerge as the least burdensome on resources and the environment.

Negatively, therefore, we need to identify the range of products and services which impose the greatest strain upon resources and cause most pollution. Having done that we need to study which are their heaviest users and to what extent it appears that economics in use could be achieved immediately through greater efficiency and substitution and in the longer run through re-education and if necessary through taxation and differential pricing. A restriction on certain lines of advertising may well also prove necessary. Positively there is a need to discover more about the satisfactions in terms of items of consumption, which correlate with higher education and with creative activities, and to consider what more might be done to explain and disseminate these values, especially in areas where the cultural level appears adequate but its full implications in changed consumption remain to be seen.

Conversation, music-making, singing and dancing, viewing films or transparencies, reading books (but not newspapers), painting, writing, sailing, swimming, walking, and many other civilized activities represent a very low hourly use of resources. Anglers, sailors, shepherds, bird-watchers, and lovers of landscape find enduring satisfactions which involve minimal consumption of materials. Enhanced sensibility and trained mental aptitudes reduce the need for grosser types of demand. People today have been deliberately persuaded to cut down on such satisfactions, profitable to themselves and the environment but not to the profit-makers. In view of human suggestibility, and of the barriers and deterrents which have been created, it is no longer possible to ascertain with reliability what people really want in conditions of free choice.

Some years ago I was dining in a hotel in Chicago. The bar

was not separated from the restaurant, and behind the bar was a large television set showing a boxing match in full swing. The accompanying noise was such that it caused me some distress, and as none of the few people at the bar seemed to be attending to it I beckoned the woman supervisor and mildly inquired whether they might not still be able to follow the match if the volume were turned down somewhat. She gave me a curious look and said, "I'm glad you've complained. Until a customer complains I can do nothing." She went and turned it down to a tolerable level, and I noticed several of the other diners signaling their appreciation.

Shortly afterwards she came back to me and asked "Is that better?" By now my scientific curiosity was aroused so I looked at her quizzically and remarked in my British accent, "Well, it's not so bad as it was, is it?" She at once responded "You're quite right, I'll turn it off," which she then did. A delicious silence ensued. Those in the bar showed no sign of noticing; they had been shutting out the sound anyway, at whatever cost. Nearly all the Americans in the restaurant however conveyed their intense relief and pleasure at an intervention which it would have seemed un-American for any of them to make. I was left with the impression that my own suffering was fully matched, if not exceeded, by theirs. As this noise background had been foisted on them by commercial interests as part of the American way of life, they dared not protest against it, in those days before reaction against pollution became respectable.

I tell this little tale as illustrating the danger of assuming that people like what they get, when they are barred from getting what they like. Superficial opinion polls and market research can be highly misleading after so long a period of systematic brainwashing. It would require prolonged experimental studies in depth to distinguish preferences between currently offered choices, conditioned by commercial advertising and publicity, and eventual choices following release from such background propaganda and presentation of a full range of alternatives.

Unfortunately the protagonists of consumptionist economics are well aware of the restriction of profitable opportunities which goes with the emancipation of consumers to adjust to a higher quality of living. It is no accident that American television not only has to carry the world's heaviest load of commercial drivel in overt sales messages, but is also the most firmly and permanently restrained from developing types of program which might even indirectly lead viewers to indulge in thinking for themselves and to question the background philosophy involved.

In Britain, where the BBC has given a balanced and genuine service to viewers over a wide and diverse range of serious subjects the conflict has been fought out on less unequal terms. There has consequently been less need for the issue to preempt attention in other fields, such as the campuses of universities and demonstrations in the streets. In Britain, the 1952 commercial campaign to dominate the television channels along American lines was stoutly contested and was only partially successful, the channels being divided between the two rival schools of commercial subservience and public service. For some years the outcome was in doubt, but gradually the boring banality of most ITV programs and the arrival of increasing reinforcements for more discriminating standards from expanding higher education have tipped the balance. It now seems very improbable that the British will be wholly subjected to the fate which has befallen Americans.

Owing partly to this moderation, Britain has been slower and less forthright in developing consumer protection agencies than the United States, where Consumer Protection, Inc., was launched on a successful career more than forty years ago. Quite recently Ralph Nader developed, with immense dedication and skill, a critical approach in depth which is having an impressive impact not only on specific industries but upon the background philosophy of business. Closely comparable in scope and method with the conservation movement and converging on its broad conclusions, the Nader phenomenon is one of the most significant of our time. It has no political connections or overtones, and its impact is made not by mass support but by the highly specialized and professional work of a small and deeply committed elite. Yet its political implications are tremendous, and it has quickly clocked up a remarkable series of productions and of achievments in action. It affords convincing testimony that the kind of approach whose wider application is advocated in this book really works. It also further documents the contrast between that approach and the obsolete and ineffective methods still favored by many politicians and reformers.

Recent studies, such as those carried out on M.I.T. computers by Professors Jay Forrester and Dennis Meadows for the Club of Rome, have (whatever their shortcomings) confirmed the close interrelation between components of living standards, pressure on natural resources, amounts of pollution, and growth economics. It is through such interplays that the conservation movement becomes increasingly involved in global economics and social policies. In order to minimize pollution it is essential to conserve resources, to moderate the rush for economic growth, to check the multiplication of mankind, and to change over to a way of life involving much more quality and rather less quantity, especially in terms of energy use and waste.

When Queen Philippa of Hainault so opportunely invented fashion six centuries ago she brought a much needed stimulus to the depressed economies of both her native and her adopted lands, and she caused the court of Edward III of England to throw away much clothing which had seen plenty of wear and probably begun to stink. Her successors today have geared up the pace and extent of changes in fashion to an absurd degree, involving a waste which is aggravated by the demand for rare skins and fabrics and for materials involving disproportionate expenditure of energy. A higher form of culture would be consistent with a less frenetic output of couture.

There are plausible grounds for believing that future standards of living will involve a smaller tonnage of resources consumed per person. As Professor Barry Commoner has pointed out, current

United States consumption per head of food and clothing materials is not greatly above that of thirty years ago, but owing to shifts to manmade fibers and unnaturally produced foodstuffs these end-products now require immensely more raw materials and fuel to produce them and engender far more pollution. A partial return to more natural fibers, and to foods in due season, would much reduce the strains on the environment in affluent countries and among their suppliers. A reversal of sheer waste, which has greatly increased in affluent throw-away societies would also help, both in conserving resources and in reducing refuse.

Some practices, such as needless use of motor transport for short distances, overeating and smoking, superfluous packaging, overheating of dwellings and public rooms and indiscriminate distribution of unread advertising matter could be cut down with advantage to health and well-being and could substantially ease the strain on resources. Many of these practices, insisted upon by the promoters of consumption, not only fail to bring happiness but are boring, troublesome, and merely a drag. As this simple truth becomes evident, more and more people are inclining toward a simpler and less extravagant pattern of living. It is because of this growing trend that we can look forward with some confidence to the rejection of consumption.

For the past several decades it has been fashionable to picture the pleasant problems soon to arise when automation and technology enable the work of the world to be completed in far fewer working hours, leaving the larger part of human time and energy for leisure. The technological progress and the corresponding economic growth have come about, but where has all the leisure gone? It has been strangled at birth by those who direct mankind's economic affairs. Such margin as remains for leisure is diverted from those busy men who most need it for refreshment and perspective to a body of unfortunates who are expelled from the working population, sometimes permanently, by some chance circumstances which render them unemployed. Most of the potential general increase of leisure is mopped up by the artificial creation of new alleged wants, to pay for which overtime must be worked in many cases.

All men are equal in being endowed with 8760 hours in every year of their lives. Of these very roughly 2760 can be regarded as preempted for sleep (until some satisfying substitute for it can be developed), leaving a gross 6000 (or less in the case of long sleepers) for everything else. Deducting a further 1000 to 2000 according to circumstances for meals, washing, dressing, and all other daily or periodical items of routine personal maintenance there remains an effective balance of some 4000 to 5000 annual hours to be split between "work" and "leisure." Assuming as a norm a working year of 220 days, each of 7 hours on average, the residue for all kinds of leisure should be approximately 2500 to 3500 hours. If however, as seems not unreasonable, human affairs were so organized as to concentrate the working year into say 160 days of around 5 hours each, net leisure would increase to a range between, say, 3200 and 4200 hours. Travel, including journeys to work, could account for between 200 and 1000 of these, leaving between 1500 and 4000 hours of what may be termed freely disposable leisure.

Different people will be subject to diverse and quantitatively varying charges on this fund of time, some of which will be regular and precise while others will be more flexible. For example, caring for children and dependents, extended shopping, and personal domestic ploys will usually claim higher priority while television, radio and cinema, playing or listening to music, sports, pastimes, and recreation, politics and voluntary social activities, and direct or telephoned conversation will be fitted in as conditions permit.

Against such a background it becomes possible to review the annual expenditure of man-hours in the light of the main evolutionary objectives. Among the strategic considerations here might be:

    (1) to minimize the number of man-hours compulsorily absorbed by the state

(2) to safeguard everyone, and especially those in higher managerial, administrative, and professional posts, against being placed in the position of having to put in more than, say, 1500 hours a year at a main job

(3) to identify and thoroughly evaluate types of use of time which carry with them a high demand upon resources, and to study the possibilities of reversing advertising and publicity pressures so as to exert influence against rather than for such activities

(4) to identify, encourage, and where necessary subsidize activities which usefully or enjoyably absorb large amounts of time with relatively low demands on material resources

It might even become advisable to adopt some kind of luxury tax on disproportionate expenditure of resources through such demands as those for large private vehicles, sports and "fun" cars, newspapers of above a certain size, packaging above a minimum level, nonreturnable containers, mail advertising, and so forth. The proceeds might usefully be spent in subsidizing less wasteful and polluting activities, consistent with educational and cultural advances.

The aim in this chapter has been simply to sketch in terms of quality of living a few of the practical possibilities of remolding policy and practice so as to reduce the stress of modern living and its excessive pressures upon resources. Such remolding should begin to favor the development of inner resources and talents, and a more civilized concentration of both work and leisure in directions according with evolutionary needs.

9

PEOPLE IN SOCIETY

People need and create society, but society is apt to devalue people. People are always problems, and many people make big problems. Big problems mean that people are diminished, for in their shadow no person amounts to much, nor can a person be treated as more than a conventional unit. In such circumstances even good and imaginative administrators are compelled to give less and less attention to human personalities, and to think more and more in terms of an impersonal mass.

When I am in the Syrian desert a dark speck appears on the horizon, moving as if to pass me by at a distance. Soon the speck changes course toward me and proves to be a camel rider who wants to talk. He is a man; I am a man: we have something to exchange, however briefly, as unique beings, and that makes the deviation worthwhile. The encounter is positive.

When I am in New York, on the sidewalk at a rush hour, a formidable torrent of human shapes bears down on me, jostling me on either side, moving suddenly across in front so close that I must break step, or treading literally upon my heels. I assume them to be people like myself, but they adroitly conceal the fact, thrusting by with set expressions like automatons, and totally ignoring the existence of myself and their fellows, although we enjoy no more individual distance than starlings on a ledge. I am gradually overcome by a profound malaise and loss of confidence. I feel my very identity beginning to be eroded. Dehumanization is setting in. The encounter is negative.

The more densely people congregate the less attention they can give to one another. In some great cities it is already necessary to fall to the ground in distress in order to attract any human response. Before long, no doubt, even that will pass, and the crowd will just march on insectlike over any prostrate bodies which happen to fall in their path.

Personally I lament this trend, and I do not accept that it is either inevitable or justified. To me it seems axiomatic that the common aim of all people should be to enable people in each generation to become better rounded and fulfilled, and to enjoy more freedom and opportunity than before. To bring about a situation in which educated young men and women have to choose between becoming rat-racers or drop-outs does not give me pride or satisfaction.

Since I was born I have watched the pound sterling lose six sevenths of its value. It is my impression that being born a human being has been devalued by roughly as much during the same period. The more people per square kilometer the less liberty per person, and the less individuality. World population by A.D. 2000 will probably be four times what it was in 1900, but *people* in a true sense could be fewer.

Human numbers and their trends being what they are, the task of rehumanizing society is intensely difficult. Problems and policies must inevitably, for several generations at least, continue to be handled on a mass basis. That is, however, no justification for failing to make a vigorous start at the opposite end, by developing more and more suitable activities on an intimate and human scale, and by so organizing the larger activities that they can be decentralized and delegated in different patterns suited to different preferences and needs.

In Chapter Six on the population explosion people were considered in ten different groups in relation to their role in reproduction. Of these five were sexually inactive, and of the others only two could be regarded as both sexually and reproductively active.

The population explosion results from the fact that there are currently too many people in these two actively reproductive groups, that they join them too early and stay in too long, and that they observe norms for family size which far exceed the requirements of Zero Population Growth. If fewer people came to desire inclusion in these groups, and if they were willing to join at a higher average age, to drop out earlier, and to be content with fewer children in the average family, the population explosion could be brought under control. It will be observed that this formulation does not postulate any particular spread of birth control, nor does it imply any but voluntary measures. It does however imply substantial alterations in patterns of living and in social attitudes, and this is an aspect which the present chapter is intended to explore.

Quantitative aspects have been discussed in Chapter Six and the quality of living in Chapter Eight. The remaining requirement concerns the changing of the social structure to favor the necessary quantitative readjustments, and at the same time to favor a wider choice and a richer content in the ways of life which individuals are free to lead within a more civilized society.

Hitherto, despite successive gains in the struggle to win tolerance for minority opinions and habits, the main weight of the system has been felt by those who for one reason or another wished to lead their own lives on lines other than those prescribed from above. To change one's spouse, or even one's job or domicile too frequently, was to become an object of adverse criticism, or even ostracism. Conformity was the thing, even if it only meant paying lip service to inacceptable beliefs and standards.

The great counterattack, which has won enough ground for the growth of a permissive society, has so far only peripherally modified the legal and institutional framework handed down from the dogmatic past. In a growing number of countries there has been repeal of a growing number of the grosser and more detailed interferences with the freedom of the individual over matters of individual belief and conduct. Yet neither the reformers, nor the custodians of the *ancien régime* under which we still live, have given much thought to the implications of a restructured society, in harmony with what modern people actually think and feel, and their preferred ways of life. Here is another immense area in which overdue homework cannot longer be postponed. This chapter can attempt no more than to sketchily indicate how a serious approach to it might be developed.

Since people consist of men, women, and children it seems best to start by considering the framework and the social standards governing the relationships between them. Of course this consideration must take account of economic and social conditions generally, and above all of population aspects. But it is on people, and on the opportunities and responsibilities which go with the status of a human person, that our eyes should focus.

People today have to live in a world society which is in a literal sense degrading them. Obsessive manipulators of power, narrowly dogmatic theocrats wielding what they quaintly term spiritual authority, professional political extremists, exponents of economic materialism and of perpetual growth targets in G.N.P. and population, chiefs of the military-industrial complex, and plenty of others do not want to know who people are or how they feel, but simply to get the best seat on their backs.

An ecological approach to social evolution leads in a quite different direction. It views as a whole the social and the natural environment, which offers rewards and satisfactions, but also presents dangers and checks to the individual and the group. Society is in error when it modifies or replaces rewards and deterrents which work along with evolution by others which for religious, political, or social reasons induce people to deviate from the course most consistent with evolutionary progress. Evolution demands that selection pressures on the community should work toward the creation and maintenance of a wide range of opportunities for human fulfillment, and that selection pressures on the individual should tend to favor one or another of the most promising choices among such opportunities.

Ecological processes promote diversity, and thus maintain stability. Human institutional processes seek to foster conformity and uniformity, and thus tend toward instability, as does monoculture of crops. To rethink the entire range of social institutions in such terms is a giant task, but it seems to be inescapable, as an agenda for the future.

Evolution works through selection, and selection works through sexual choice and reproduction, and thereafter through the nurture and survival of the young. It follows that sex relations, marriage, and child-rearing are the decisive areas for any adaptation of human society along evolutionary lines. People, being human, sensed this long ago, but they have not until lately made very much progress in face of the stubbornly retrogressive attitudes of church and state and of the underlying System.

The essential problem can be quite simply stated. Adult and adolescent people expect and require more and more complete freedom in their interpersonal relations. The survival and evolution of society calls for fewer and better-tended children, conceived and reared by the sustained cooperation of responsible and competent parents. The two needs are irreconcilable in terms of the institution of marriage as it now stands. That institution is founded on the creation of a life-long tie between a man and a woman for the central purpose of procreation within a permanent family. There is much stress on parental authority and little regard to the quality of parental performance. Backed by the strongest religious, legal, and social sanctions, marriage seeks to compel all, whatever their nature and wishes, to at least pretend to adjust to a narrow and obsolete concept, which is in head-on collision with the needs of population policy, and which perpetuates an immense sum of misery for many husbands, wives, and above all children.

The logical conclusion of recent changes in attitude would be plainly to recognize that there is a popular demand and a social need for two distinct forms of marriage. The first, which may be termed *social marriage,* provides simple legal recognition of the decision of a man and a woman to live together and to form a recognized pair, while preserving the right to have the union dissolved by consent at any time. Thus far society and the state have no legitimate ground for interference or denial of the joint wishes of the two partners, provided that they both agree and that they refrain from prejudicing the rights of others.

The second type, which may be termed *family marriage,* goes beyond the relation between two adults and aims at producing and rearing children. In the modern effort to meet demands for the first type, the responsibilities inherent in this second type, and, above all, the interests and happiness of children, have been largely sacrificed. If human evolution is to have any weight in our affairs it is here that fresh thinking and thorough reconstruction is urgently needed. It is one thing to accord respectable married status, with wedding rings and marital homes, to openly self-centered men and women who want to be free to call the whole thing off at the drop of a hat (if they possess one), and to change partners *ad libitum* or *ad nauseam.* Their right to do this must be staunchly defended. But it is quite another thing to place the future quantity and quality of the human species at the mercy of such whims.

It is paradoxical, in a period when science, especially biological science, is enlightening us about the paramount importance of parental care, and about the methods by which apes and other animals sometimes excell our own human performance as parents, that it should be fashionably regarded as progressive to reject and ignore not only this new knowledge, but much which was successfully followed through in past generations. Whether it really adds to the fun of short-lived unions to embark on them as if they were to last forever is arguable. Whether this approach should be pushed to the point of bringing children into the world and then tearing their lives apart is not. Society does not permit high-spirited people, who have never learned to drive, to take fast cars on the highway and to shrug off the casualties with impunity when they crash. Society should, and soon must, take a more serious responsibility on similar lines for the welfare and happiness of children, and for insisting that those who choose to beget them shall live up to their chosen role, and shall see them fairly and safely launched into adult life.

The implications are plain. Children should to the utmost possible extent be brought into the world within marriages which are soberly meant to last and are reasonably calculated to be capable of providing the necessary continuing love and care for them. Provision should therefore be made for a second stage of marriage, not normally to be embarked upon less than a full year after the first, bringing with it a series of legal obligations, as well as privileges, related to parenthood. Prospective parents should be under obligation to complete at least one of a series of alternative courses of instruction and practical experience in the art of rearing children, linked with a universal network of nursery schools. In running these, both prospective and actual parents should actively participate.

Prospective parents should also solemnly renounce rights to seek divorce until they have seen their children through at least the more vulnerable period of their childhood, if not until they have reached adulthood. A national trustee for children, with sufficient local deputies qualified by training and personality, should have a definite status, accepted by those embarking on parenthood, to be consulted and to advise in cases of difficulty or distress affecting the interests of children. The trustee should have wide discretionary powers for insuring the provision of special community services of various kinds for children, and he should have adequate financial resources to give emergency aid. He or she should not be merely an adviser, but a source of help when it is needed.

In return for society's new recognition of the right to form and dissolve sexual relationships without hindrance or penalty, people of reproductive age should be expected to recognize that the act of reproduction carries responsibilities of a different order, and of a far longer duration, than the sex act, and that it is the right and duty of society to insure that these responsibilities are treated with the seriousness that they deserve. Improving methods of birth control enable, and the rejection of self-righteous arbiters of conduct now permit, a distinction to be made between sex relations and parenthood. What is needed next is a restructuring of marriage and of other relevant social provisions, to take account of and to support this novel and potentially highly progressive situation.

This restructuring requires a modern scientific basis, provided by ethology, ecology, and the social sciences. A growing amount of valuable research and experiment has been done on the early development, learning capacities, and psychological requirements of human infants, following clues largely derived from behavioral studies of animals, and taking account of the important common elements involved. To some extent, although so far on a disappointingly small scale, such studies are supported, and their results applied, by pioneer experimental groups and institutions in the educational and social field. What is still totally missing, however, is a network of points of focus to make this new knowledge available to, and to see that it meets the needs of, those most intimately concerned—the parents themselves.

Our culture is coming to recognize that higher education is

not merely for learning classics or science, but is a gateway to all kinds of activities where human intelligence and concerted intellectual advance are involved. Should not parenthood itself be regarded as important enough to qualify for comparable treatment? Should there not be a College of Parenthood, supported by those who desire personal access to the latest findings, and who wish to cooperate with research workers, social workers, educationists, and others in trying them out and assessing their practical value and implications?

Such a college, with ancillary groups up and down the country, could sponsor demonstrations, provide films and other visual aids, maintain records, give awards, and arrange visits and tours by specialists and groups from other countries to compare experience and methods. It should generally act as a center of excellence and an effective stimulus to public recognition of the art and science of parenthood, of the rewards of doing it well and the penalties (both for the individual and the community) of doing it badly. There would be strong arguments for publicly endowing such a college, which could hardly fail to save the money of taxpayers in terms of future productivity and public service, and of reducing crime, delinquency, and unemployability.

It seems advisable to think in terms of a threefold constituency, composed first of active parents in relation only to their own children, second of parents interesting themselves in helping generally with the upbringing of other children (for example, through participating personally in the running of nursery schools and adventure playgrounds), and third of prospective parents and others, of school age upwards, who would interest themselves in preparatory studies and ancillary activities extending, for example, to baby-sitting.

Such a College of Parenthood, if effectively staffed and supported, could go far to fill the strange and discreditable hiatus in our modern society, which finds it worthwhile to provide elaborate public mechanisms for discovering and bringing to the notice of farmers the causes of obscure deficiency diseases in crops and livestock, but somehow regards it as quite unnecessary to sustain and disseminate scientific research directly related to the quality and capabilities of future citizens. But for the antiscientific bias so long handed down in our educational system such an anomaly could not have persisted into these days.

It is in that same area that we must seek the cause of the curious and nearly universal resistance to learning, except as a stage to be gone through with as good grace as possible by young people who cannot afford to miss it. It seems so obvious now that Man is essentially a learning animal and that his happiness from the cradle to the grave is largely bound up with taking opportunities to acquire fresh knowledge. There is something badly wrong with an educational system which treats education as something that finishes at some set age, and which does not regard the study of the learning process as one of its essential functions. Given the great modern expansion of higher education, it seems very probable that our current state of ignorance and of intellectual incapacity will appear as hard to credit by the end of the century as dwellings without sanitation are now.

Against a background of fuller information, and more general willingness and ability to learn, the task of learning to be a competent parent will assume a new complexion. It will appeal to bright and vigorous young adults, often mindful of unfortunate deficiencies in their own upbringing, and accustomed to want to find out what science has to offer in other fields of interest to them. Such a group can act as a catalyst and a growing point for new standards of parental performance, sadder and wiser in the knowledge that their own parents were in error in supposing it to be sufficient merely to rebel against and to try to reverse what they in their turn had suffered as children. Rebellion is not enough, although it is a useful spur to learning how to do better, if the opportunity for that is provided.

In the struggle to secure more freedom for married adults the interests of children have often come off worst. There is a case for compensating children for their deprivation of much of the former security assured by an old-fashioned marriage. One way of doing this would be to invite every new parent, married or unmarried, to make and put on public record a solemn pledge recognizing the prior claim of each child for consideration and support during all the years before reaching an age of independence, and the duty of securing the child's health, education, and welfare. In case of apparent default on this undertaking, and of failure to satisfy the national trustee for children, the parent could be called on for an explanation before a children's court or equivalent body. This would have the power to require and to supervise remedial measures in the case of parents unwilling or unable to fulfill their responsibilities.

Parents seeking divorce during the currency of such a pledge would know in advance that a searching inquest into their record as parents, and an exhaustive consideration of the interests of the children, would take priority. Where necessary very long delays could be imposed as a deterrent against attempts to rush into the break-up of a marriage without the fullest regard for the future of its children. Awards of alimony often seem to favor the interests of a small class of adult females fortunate enough to place well-to-do husbands in the position of getting rid of them early in life. More frequent and larger maintenance awards to trustees for children of broken marriages would help to spread public awareness of the need to look before leaping into thoughtless parenthood.

The making of such a pledge might well, in the case of parents having their children baptised as infants, become an accompaniment of the christening ceremony, just as civil marriage registration accompanies a church wedding. In other cases it could be synchronized with or linked to registration of a birth. There seems no good reason why an unmarried mother ready to take sole responsibility for the upbringing of a child should not be eligible to make such a pledge on equal terms. There could be no legal compulsion to enter into the parenthood pledge, but parents declining or omitting to do so would have to reckon on being required to give correspondingly stronger evidence of their fulfillment of all obligations in case of any question arising. It would be legitimate to give some preference, other things being equal, to parents who had taken and kept the pledge. Above all, every opportunity should be taken to build up the status of the parenthood pledge, and of its signatories as symbolizing the newly heightened interest of the community in advancing the interests and prospects of future citizens, and the newly enlarged responsibilities of those choosing to undertake the high role of a parent.

As has been previously indicated, such a series of concrete steps to encourage and underpin improvements in the upbringing of children would be likely to give powerful assistance to the urgently needed world population policy. On such a basis it may still be possible to permit and even encourage large families among those who have that vocation, and to secure big reductions in the birth rate by inducing people to think very seriously in advance about whether they really wish to incur parental responsibilities which they will no longer be able to repudiate later with impunity, or to treat as a bottom priority in their pattern of life.

The shallow distinction between "wanted" and "unwanted" children does not go nearly far enough. Far too many children in both groups are born and bred on the assumption that they can be left to take their chance with a minimum of parental love, care, and time devoted to them. A pledged child, whether wanted or not before conception, would be in a very different situation. The aim of human fulfillment should begin to be realized both before and from the moment of birth.

While it is not possible to assess the immediate and long-term quantitative effects of such a qualitative change there is reason to believe that they would be very substantial. In the United States inquiries among married women have indicated that between 1960 and 1965 as many as twenty percent of all children born were unwanted, and in the case of fourth and fifth children the proportion was between forty and fifty percent. If this is the case in a country which is among the most advanced in birth control, there is clearly an immense amount to be done merely in minimizing the unwanted element among all births. Even among wanted births, however, a more rigorous advance consideration of the responsibilities involved, once it becomes plain that fulfillment of these responsibilities is to be insisted upon, would lead to a further reduction, through the dropping out of intending parents whose motives are trivial and careless, or are due to mere fashion based on circumstances which no longer apply.

The essential point here is to avoid the mistake of simply making propaganda for fewer births, but instead to demonstrate, through all possible media and in many different ways, that the world will expect future citizens to have been given a far better start in life, and that better *must* mean fewer. In this way it will be possible to tackle the population explosion at a less superficial and more effective level, with a minimum of state intervention, and with that intervention concentrated in areas where it is generally accepted as legitimate, in connection with child welfare, health, and education. In this way the qualitative needs of human evolution and the quantitative requirement to cope with the population explosion may be made mutually reinforcing. Apart from obviously inacceptable measures of coercion there can be no shorter cut. Such an approach, however, requires a world campaign on a truly massive scale, sustained through entire decades.

Among the evident advantages of developing this strong stress on quality as a key to the containment of excessive quantity is the favorable opening which it offers for a realignment of attitudes on the part of adherents of traditional values—not least the Roman Catholic church. If society rallies behind the concept of responsible parenthood, and of enhanced care and respect for each person as an individual from the outset of life, the arithmetical necessity for simultaneously reducing human densities and numbers in order to assist in realizing this ideal can gradually become acceptable as a reasonable price to pay. Population control becomes an instrument to further accepted higher values, rather than a tool of secular policy. Given thorough study and dissemination of the doctrinal implications in terms of present-day conditions, such an approach might greatly facilitate the attainment of an agreed revision of practice, which could have inestimable benefits, especially in such regions as Latin America. It should not be difficult to render untenable persistent resistance to the unquestionable proposition that where human numbers are concerned more means worse.

If greater priority is to be given by society to the responsibilities, rather than merely the rights, of parents it becomes necessary to consider some of the implications for men, women, and children. Taking the men first, it is obvious that, especially at the higher job levels, a substantial proportion of the best young executives and specialists in their thirties and forties are presently placed in the position of being unable to do justice to their parental role and at the same time to satisfy their employers and their own self-respect among their colleagues at work. In the growing number of cases where the work involves frequent and distant travel the dilemma becomes even more acute, throwing severe strains not only on the family but on the marriage.

When study is made of what this is all in aid of, the answer is often disillusioning. Obsessive competition for markets, resources, and power, efforts to speed up progress by shortcuts which often prove to have been illusory, and concentration of talent on trivial and unworthy goals too often underlie such real and irreversible human sacrifices for marriage and the family. The acquiescence of wives and children is bought by furnishing the means of keeping up with the Joneses.

That this vast distortion of living patterns, and this forfeiture of the most intimate human values, has been carried out in the name of a higher standard of life is one more of the crazy contradictions which the illogicality and gullibility of twentieth-century Man has brought to pass. Positively it has been facilitated by the concentration in the modern business corporation of authority, managerial techniques, and the capacity to bring in ambitious men. The comprehensiveness and exclusiveness of this economic structure is thrown into sharp relief by the plight of those who are fired or drop out from high posts in it.

There is also, however, a significant negative side. When World War II threatened, those of us who were needed for planning and preparation were quietly called in by the authorities and set to work on duties which took precedence over our continuing peacetime jobs. The changing military situation decreed that these should no longer have first claim on our time and energy.

Why should it need a war to cause society to take an interest in defining such priorities? Without going so far as to propose an Act of Parliament to compel overenthusiastic employers to desist from encroaching on the leisure of their young executives at the expense of their wives and families, it does at least seem time to focus a good deal of study on this aspect of modern life. To set and publicize minimum standards of time and energy which husbands and fathers should be in a position to devote to their families, and which should not be whittled down by demands from their employment, seems a possible line of redress. There is no reason to doubt that good employers would respond.

The present situation could hardly be more at variance with the needs of human evolution. Instead of an equitable distribution of the growing potential for leisure, there is an enforced excess of leisure for those who fail to make the grade or to stand the pace in modern employment conditions, and a growing stress and deprivation of leisure for those who perform best and are consequently often barred from bringing up their children properly or from taking due care of their wives. This whole distortion is neither reasonable nor necessary; it is a by-product of social negligence and lack of imagination. As such it has been accorded next to no attention; the existence of the problem would scarcely be known were it not for the well-justified moaning chorus of women sufferers from its effects, which are, however, by no means confined to them.

The immense recent changes in the human condition have confronted women with profound problems of adaptation which have so far been discreditably neglected. Insofar as reproductive and parental functions, spread over from twenty to thirty or more years, have hitherto dominated the pattern of feminine life, death control has brought much more drastic changes to women than to men. Far fewer babies need be born to maintain family and national complements of new recruits. The human race could carry on nicely if half or more of adult women never had a single child, or alternatively if the vast majority produced a single child only. But a single child constitutes a tie and a responsibility not much less than that of a normal family.

Insofar as the matter lends itself to rational solution it would seem more sensible for a large number of women to devote their lives, as they are now free to do, to activities other than reproduction. But how many women wish or would be content to follow that course? In any event those who do not so decide are now faced with a span of twenty or more years of active life after their parental responsibilities are over.

From any angle, therefore, women are faced with new problems of adapting themselves to prolonged years of activity in replacement of or in substitution for bearing and rearing children. A growing number choose or are compelled by economics to try to combine both.

The stress and conflict involved in such a double life should be at least partly capable of sympathetic resolution. For this a threefold approach is indicated. First, the education and training of girls should be searchingly reappraised and redesigned, by such methods as have been brilliantly followed through in the Biological Sciences Curriculum Study at the University of Colorado. (See page 96.) In this way the sum of what is available for teaching, the complete requirements of those to be taught, and the full range of available methods of teaching it would be reviewed, through a program of successive trials and experiments yielding the necessary feedback of results to assist successive revisions and improvements, and to enable teachers to be trained or retrained in the methods to meet the problems of the taught.

Such a comprehensive program of educational renewal should be absolutely freed of any obligation to insure that the teaching of girls conforms to the teaching of boys, unless the trials show that course to be best. No doubt there would always be a diversity of demand sufficient to insure a full range of choice.

The second part of the approach should be in terms of women's employment and the minimization of obstacles to switching between home and office or factory tasks. Modern recognition of the importance of environment at work, of human relations, and of other aspects previously neglected is leading toward a situation in which the units of scale and the interpersonal relations in workplaces need not contrast so starkly and inhumanly as often hitherto with homemaking patterns. Far from being ignored or discouraged these tendencies can be given full play in an effort to reduce stress both for men and women and to provide a background favorable to flexible cooperation.

The third part of the approach would center upon the resolution of conflicts and problems concerned with the home and family. It has been left largely to women's periodicals to bring these conflicts and problems into focus and to enlist scientific, medical, design, and managerial help for working out remedies and lines of treatment. Considering the changes in the quality and coverage of these periodicals over recent years they appear in the main to have done a valuable and effective job so far as possible within the limitations surrounding them. But much more is needed.

Perhaps the most promising line of structural adaptation might be to enable the family to develop within a closer, more flexible and less rigidly institutionalized social context. Such an approach was tested on a small scale forty years ago by the Peckham Pioneer Health Center which, like so many such initiatives in our sluggish society in Britain, proved to be far ahead of its time. Under this approach the community would provide, either directly or by grant-aided voluntary effort, a series of services sharing a wellequipped and spacious common home for the benefit of families containing children under, say, twelve years of age. Medical and health services, physical education, audiovisual facilities, and many types of informal education, games and pastimes, hobbies, information and advisory services, nursery care, and all other activities relevant to the upbringing of children (other than formal education) would be included.

Such centers should be designed, indoors and outdoors, to demonstrate and further the highest standards which the local community can reach in the interests of its future citizens. Flanked by the school on one side and the home on the other, it would round off the wide world of opportunity for children at all stages from the nursery to adolescence and would offer a continual stimulus and relief from the narrowness which either the home or the school or both can impose.

Although construction and maintenance in the widest sense should be a responsibility of the local authority, it would seem desirable for most of the actual running of activities to be entrusted to appropriate voluntary groups, or picked teams of parents and older children, involving a high degree of social responsibility and direct self-government, and a minimum of externally imposed rules and programs.

Many advantages would, as Peckham long since proved, flow from such a comprehensive community–family approach. Pivoting upon the mothers, it would assure them of a status and a continual diversity of interest, which would more than compensate for what they have lost since the small dispersed family replaced the older, more comprehensive, and sometimes matriarchal model. Whatever talents and enthusiasms they could muster would find a valued outlet, since most of the activity would depend on voluntary teamwork, with only an essential nucleus of trained full-time and part-time professionals. Women with previous experience in medical, education, and social work, or in offices, shops, workshops, and gardens, would be able to maintain their skills without neglecting their families. Strains on family budgets would be relieved by such a wide range of free diversions. Pets could be kept and gardens tended. Incipient talents among children could not only be detected but fostered and encouraged, if necessary by calling upon external specialists. Psychological disturbances and handicaps could be unobtrusively watched over and treated without removing the children concerned from the background of the healthy child community. Parents could be regularly informed and, where desirable given training, in the arts of parenthood.

Administratively it would become possible to replace the dreary proliferation of ad hoc "social services" scattered in separate premises by a close-knit family of family services. Wherever possible such family centers should be sited alongside more conventional community or civic centers, theaters, town halls, larger swimming pools, and schools or colleges, thus contributing to a more vigorous and balanced cultural life, spanning all age groups and all social needs. Out of the lively experience and training of the family center would grow interests and habits of community living which could continue throughout life in successive contexts, including local government and other forms of active citizenship.

Expensive as the provision of a network of such family centers would inevitably be, they would have a clear investment value in saving many other forms of public expense. Not the least would be in reducing misfits and delinquency, and in providing more alert and responsive pupils for the extremely costly education system, which is currently compelled by lack of such a preparatory support structure to cope with so many extraneous problems and to suffer so much unnecessary drag. As parents would themselves be relieved of much of the spending which the raising of children currently involves there seems no reason why they should not be able and willing to contribute something to the running costs, even though capital items would be charged entirely to the community.

School holidays, weekends, and periods of domestic illness or dislocation would prove much less of a strain with a family center operating on a year-round basis to cushion their impact. The lot of mothers working part-time, and of all those without home helps would be sensibly eased. But above all the family centers would make available, on tap to everyone, modern knowledge, facilities, and amenities which are frustratingly inaccessible even to those who have the education, persistence, and money to seek them out today. Thus the potential richness and diversity which our civilization holds in its hidden interstices would be unlocked and opened out, so that the younger generation in particular could enjoy it and benefit by it at the right age, rather than being left, as now, to discover it in bits and pieces when it is too late to avert deprivation.

As an organ of human evolution such a family center model would fill one of the most serious and indeed disgraceful gaps in our supposedly advanced culture, which leaves so many wives, mothers, and children so badly deprived of the essentials for their health, happiness, and fulfillment. It would fit in at the right stage of the life cycle and at the right central position in the local community. It would not necessarily take precisely the same form everywhere. Some communities might prefer to have it centered, as Peckham was, around a humane and broad-minded group of doctors of medicine practicing within its bounds. Others might prefer a more collegiate or a more recreational pattern.

There is scope for much variety and above all for experiment and study both of and in such centers. One obvious immediate need is to restart where Peckham left off, and to gain further experience of the ways of creating and running such centers over a period of years as a basis for their general adoption. It seems reasonable to suppose that such family centers would go far toward redressing the most serious deprivations and frustrations which presently bear so harshly and inequitably upon mothers and children.

When men in carefree mood stake £10 of the future income of every man, woman and child in Britain on such a binge of high technology as the *Concorde* it is the resources needed for such essential services which are being foolishly dissipated. It is not true that the nation cannot afford these essentials, but it is true that the nation cannot afford the type of leadership which has frittered away on largely abortive prestige projects the resources needed to sustain them.

Such truths, however, are not popular, and those who voice them must expect to be looked at askance. The massive redeployment of resources will come because it must, but it will come too late to avert vast evils to mankind, as well as to Man's environment. Moreover, the more time lost in producing a comprehensive, convincing, and practical program of the true priority objectives for future public investment, the longer will be the delay before necessary changes are made. The current dissipation of resources is the counterpart of the current failure to think out and spell out the nature and the scale of human deprivations, not in terms of charitable palliatives but of effective preventive and constructive measures for the long term.

However valuable the family centers may be they do not touch the needs of teenagers, who have passed beyond the stage when the centers can be expected to cater for them successfully. Insofar as teenagers are increasingly seen to be in rapid transit from a childish to an adult role, some of their needs will best be considered in the context of junior citizens in the next chapter, especially where interest in the workings of society and equipment for participation in it are concerned. There are, however, specific aspects of their needs which differ so much from those both of children and of adults as to call for separate provision. Gregariousness, segregation by age group, and having somewhere to make a lot of noise at all hours are obvious examples. Self-reliance and independence, adventure and mobility, freedom to experiment in personal and group relations, and scope for testing capabilities and for discovering identity are others. Modern adult society has a poor record for noticing, understanding, and adapting itself to those needs, and must be held primarily to blame for the suspicions and even hostilities which have flared up across the generation gap. The mental laziness, the lack of imaginative sympathy for others, the complacent assurance that nothing need change very much, and the accompanying misuse of adult authority to block up the safety valve have cost society dear. Having brought about a degree of alienation, and frequent overt and even violent outbursts which are inexplicable and unmanageable on such wrong premises and in terms of such wrong attitudes, many adults have retired into a half-frightened, half-injured, and passively resigned posture which goes little beyond permitting an uneasy and unproductive truce.

We are overdue for a really serious and searching combined effort to find out what is wrong with the relations between teenagers and adults. Although the problem is international it resembles the population problem in taking different forms in different countries, adding up to somewhat similar results.

Evidently there is always in the background a painful sense that adults have made and are making a disastrous mess of the conduct of affairs, and that adolescents are cast both in the role of spectators who are powerless to intervene and in the role of heirs whose heritage will be the resulting shambles. I am in full agreement with that analysis and in deep sympathy with their undeserved predicament. Insofar as arguments such as those of this book have any force and influence, and insofar as the Big Change itself is smoking out those responsible for the shambles, we can look forward to a gradual reduction in background conflicts and tensions which may permit a more constructive and integrated approach. That was impossible so long as teenagers were merely exhorted to get ready to take their places in a society whose values they despised, whose leadership they distrusted, and in whose managerial competence they had no confidence.

It is evident that however seriously such background features affect the situation, the generation gap and its accompanying conflicts and sufferings take practical shape within each home. While the teenagers are under intense biological and educational strains, or those of adjustment to a regular job, their parents are often badly fatigued by a decade and a half at least of family responsibilities and of accompanying financial worries, and are ill-trained and ill-supported in performing their critically delicate role at this final stage of upbringing. Society, having given next to no thought or help to their problem, merely receives and bemoans the results in terms of a torrent of delinquency, alienated and uncooperative young employees, drugs, promiscuity, and other forms of escapism. Of the minority who care and try to do something, most are committed to such obsolescent and ineffective methods as boys clubs.

One way of relieving the strain would be to make it easier for teenagers to get away for a time from their own parents, with whom relations may be temporarily fouled up, or whose other commitments and circumstances may cut across the grain of their own teenagers' interests. A simple system of direct exchange between homes, either in the same or in other countries, could prove a solution in a number of cases, provided a sufficiently well-informed, skilled, and tactful clearinghouse mechanism could be created to make the right contacts. Opportunities also need to be provided for teenagers in appropriate cases to be accommodated away from home under light supervision in conditions of group self-government. It may be the feeling that teenagers and their parents are stuck with each other in a situation of tense deadlock which aggravates the trouble in many cases. If it were known that there were ways of escape, that knowledge alone might encourage the finding of a modus vivendi without recourse to them.

Ugly and stressful environment is undoubtedly also a common factor in some of the worst teenage conflict situations of urban society. There can be little doubt that far-reaching improvements in physical environment will contribute toward mitigating such situations, even though they can hardly be expected to achieve much unsupported by constructive treatment of other aspects.

All this demands a great deal more adult time and effort devoted to servicing, guiding, and supporting teenagers through what is often the most critical period of their lives. In a nation the size of Britain the equivalent of at least a quarter of a million full-time workers in this family field, outside the educational system proper, would be by no means too many. Against such a background of greater parental responsibility, partnered by greater community assistance for the upbringing of their offspring, it becomes possible to envisage the kind of changes which may be practicable in the role of women. No longer condemned from birth to spend much of their lives conceiving, bearing, and ministering to children, and being unable either to come and go freely or to learn and carry through an outside vocation, women will be able to make for themselves a series of successive decisions to shape their lives: whether to embark on professional training, whether to embark on an active sex life, whether to enter a marital relationship, whether to become a parent, and whether as a parent to concentrate on the home or to participate actively in a group of community services centering on the family, or whether by more passive use of such services to carry on a career of some other kind, subject to meeting the psychological needs of the children. The fundamental new factor is that instead of being socially or economically dictated these choices should become genuine and personal for women. Inseparably linked with this effective personal choice is the need to be fully prepared for making it at each stage, on a basis of education and knowledge, and the need to be ready to stand by the obligations and responsibilities which it implies, especially where the choice involves having children. Neither the freedom of choice nor the need for making it with knowledge and responsibility makes sense separately; they must go together.

It is possible here to indicate only some of the many implications. It will gradually become apparent what proportion of women really want to bear and rear children in conditions of free choice but of enhanced responsibility. As traditional imperatives recede, and as birth control continues to improve in accessibility and in effectiveness, it seems a reasonable hypothesis that at least a somewhat smaller proportion of women will embark upon childbearing, and that more will devote their lives to other patterns, more similar to those of men. As the dangers and inconvenience of the gross excess of human population come home to everyone, commonsense and social responsibility will lead those who do start families to have regard to easing the pressures in which their own and others' children will have to grow up. In this way mankind may be delivered both from the continuance of reckless procreation and from the equally undesirable course of state regulation of family size. The period during which such a civilized option will remain open is, however, quickly running out. Unless the tide of babies can be turned beyond Zero Population Growth during the next few decades, compulsion or catastrophe will become the only remaining choices, if indeed events do not meanwhile take over.

Very few nations are sufficiently sophisticated and socially mature to show the way. Those nations of northwestern and western Europe, of North America, and of Australasia have a most urgent and all-important duty to do so, and to do so quickly. It is idle to hope that the teeming and suspicious billions of Asia, Africa, and Latin America will follow, so long as no one really leads. A few demonstrably successful examples will not only be more valuable than unlimited propaganda; without them nothing else can be of much value in relation to the scale and urgency of the need. While the boneheads of England, as of other lands, continue to argue that the country is not overpopulated the last chance to give a lead is being lost.

10
CHANGE AND THE CITIZEN

By a convenient ambiguity the word *citizen* means both an inhabitant of a populous center and an individual having adult rights in a state. For more than two thousand years the changes have been rung on these twin abstract roles within regimes alternatively democratic and despotic, centralized or decentralized, republican and monarchical. At times the citizen has emerged as a proud and privileged figure with a real voice in the running of a prestigious and flourishing kind of large residential club. At other times he has been no more than a frightened and oppressed cipher, thankful to take refuge in the anonymity of his insignificance. Sometimes he has been bandied about, without consultation or ceremony, from one ruler to another, and even from one state to another. At others his sense of solidarity with those sharing his racial, linguistic, geographic, and often religious background has trapped him into becoming the tool of power-hungry and ambitious nationalist leaders. Self-determination, once hailed as the passport to liberty, has not necessarily bettered his lot.

It is surprising how little of significance has been added to our thought and understanding of fundamental political relationships during the past two thousand years and more, since Ancient Greece demonstrated just how fast and how far a community dedicated to the exploration of the noosphere and the nomosphere could travel. The modern obsession with technology and material success has aggravated the neglect of the nomosphere in recent decades. Advances in scientific knowledge, and in managerial and political techniques, must certainly have afforded a basis for new developments in political philosophy and science of an order different from anything which has so far emerged. The landscape is one of cobwebbed ruins, of intellectual slums, and of politically derelict areas. Politicians, bureaucrats, and their subservient academics and acolytes are broken reeds clinging to a complacent satisfaction with the System which is shared by hardly anyone else.

To start with it seems time to reconsider the whole concept of sovereignty and the pretensions based upon it. In view of modern changes in every aspect of human affairs, and of the diplomatic recognition so briskly accorded to so many new regimes of questionable antecedents, it seems difficult to continue to give much weight to historical derivations of authority, except insofar as they accord with, and sentimentally bolster, a viably enduring regime still able to command acceptance and to provide practical validation of its status. The flatteringly named Great Debate in Britain over adherence to the European Community led to the ventilation *ad nauseam* of concepts of sovereignty which, insofar as they ever were valid, have ceased to be so in today's international relations. Curtailment of sovereignty in that sense is now an everyday happening. Decisive votes in both Houses of Parliament on the principle involved have probably buried that issue under the lumber of history, so far as relations between states are concerned. What is more disturbing, and remains unsettled, is the extent to which outworn fictions about sovereignty can continue to threaten, at least implicitly, the personal rights and liberties of individual citizens, as for example in the notorious misapplication of the Official Secrets Act.

The appropriate kind of state for the late twentieth century is not a sovereign state but a common service state, which derives authority and attracts loyalty (if at all) from the competence, humanity, and consideration with which it performs on behalf of its citizens those tasks which they could not so well carry through otherwise, and which represents them with resolution, goodwill, and efficiency in participating with other nations in the civilized guidance of world affairs. While many will no doubt dismiss such a concept as utopian, recent trends of public opinion give reason for doubt as to whether any kind of state not prepared to move at least some way in this direction can count upon even the very minimum essential loyalty and support from its citizens as well as enough external recognition and respect to be truly viable in future. Even where breakdowns in political leadership result in a dictatorial regime for a temporary period, the justification and maintenance of the regime can no longer rest securely on other than empirical grounds.

In an ecological setting the state represents no more than an organism for performing a particular set of functions inseparable from many other functions and incapable of being hierarchically differentiated from them without assuming a cancerous role in the entire society of which they form part. It is possible for an organism to develop and obey the messages of a decision-making center for certain purposes without that center becoming entitled to, or capable of, going beyond its strictly service function, important as that must be for the welfare and survival of the organism. Moreover, any tendency to make decisions which are beyond the powers or will of the organism to carry through immediately aborts the decisions. While the precise application of ecological principles to government remains to be worked out it is becoming evident that a growing number of citizens are coming to think and act and react to government along these lines. A continuance of outmoded and unjustified assumptions and claims on the part of those who currently administer the machinery of government will encounter growing friction.

It follows that an organism which deliberately chooses to make or through incompetence drifts into making, decisions beyond its inherent powers becomes nonfunctional and must therefore rest its authority on usurpation, pretence, or mystique rather than upon what may legitimately be regarded as natural law.

Anyone having to work partly on ecological problems and partly in public affairs is constantly confronted in the latter field with a peculiarly myopic attitude toward the frame of reference and the processes involved, and toward the time scales governing their responses and interactions. No attempt is made to construct, and constantly to adapt, some credible model of the working relationships and the context of political interventions. Instead of a self-balancing political ecosystem, in which each action elicits its inevitable response, there seems to present itself to the protagonists something more like an imaginary theatrical stage, the political arena, vividly lit and displaying only two hues, black and white.

In that unreal world shortsighted operators cling to, or reject and oppose, combinations of well-worn words to which they attach meanings, suspicions, loyalties, and hatreds only comprehensible within their own ephemeral and subjective local context. In order to verify this one only has to wade through political debates and commentaries of another nation or of a different, even quite recent, period. Is this esoteric indoor game, so recently invented, really the only or the best means of settling political issues? If so, cannot it at least undergo a more civilized and rational evolution, in accordance with the lessons which have been learned in awakening public opinion to the environment, with minimal help from politicians and political parties?

When there has been time to study in depth the relevance of

ecological and ethological approaches to public affairs there is every reason to expect that significant advances will occur in our understanding of these matters. As an example it would be interesting to look into the time factor, and the relation between short-term, medium-term, and long-term aspects. An ecosystem operating today is founded upon and is currently recycling cumulative results of past activity, as well as new inputs. The relationships between these are well defined, and their respective limits are traceable. The past shapes the present by ascertainable processes and to ascertainable degrees, and this remains true whether change is gradual or catastrophically abrupt.

Similarly Man's progressive exposure to the noosphere, the nomosphere, and the technosphere is continually depositing layers of discarded ideas, outmoded styles and attitudes, and worn-out or obsolete information and experience. In order to reveal Roman London we have to excavate many feet of intervening rubble from intermediate periods. In the same way man's social evolution is perpetually, although invisibly, laying down varved layers resulting from extinguished *Zeitgeist*. If we as historians or archaeologists bore into these layers we learn something of past intellectual and aesthetic climates, but much that was most intimately and vitally bound up with what was thought and felt and done in those days escapes our blunted sensibilities.

Less justifiably, and less explicably, we permit the same obtuseness to blind our current handling of affairs. I am old enough to have lived through and personally witnessed the laying down of several of these time strata on which we tread today. I' have been vividly aware of their landscapes and flavors, just as I taste the distinctions between continents and countries in the course of a long journey. In neither case have I found it necessary or sensible to become fettered to one rather than another.

Different places and different periods have different climates and demand different responses. Whether or not we travel in space we all have to travel in time, yet many even among educated persons have apparently never bothered to learn how to adjust to it. Often one must regret, more or less poignantly, seeing things of value pass into discard to be trodden thoughtlessly underfoot. Often also new features emerge which are unpalatable or even threatening. The screening process works badly in both directions, and efforts to improve it give slow and sometimes abortive results. Yet this is what life is like.

The ecologist, ever conscious of the inherent tendencies toward balance, which we check and distort but cannot overcome, finds compensations which are perhaps less readily perceived by others. It may even be that in the long run the current devaluation of the individual and of human individuality may prove to have been a necessary price to pay for the enthronement of mankind above the stupidity and selfishness of particular human groups and generations. If so it may be well worthwhile. While paying lip service to the rights and foibles of the individual, political operators have had little difficulty in exploiting his vanity, gullibility, and greed to move in directions clearly contrary to the general interest. Individualism in business has been the excuse for much shameless despotism and exploitation of numerous individuals.

From this standpoint the most important criterion for judgment on political strategy is not between left and right, between socialism, liberalism, and traditional conservative capitalism, or between Christian and non-Christian beliefs. Rather it is between evolutionary and counterevolutionary regimes, parties, and policies. If we accept evolution as a fact, and therefore want to make the best of it, we must appreciate that certain political approaches, institutions, and programs are better adapted than others to enabling and furthering man's social evolution in accord with the fulfillment of his potential. It is therefore important to be able to apply this criterion in practice and in detail.

We are bound to identify as counterevolutionary all regimes based on fixed dogma which must be adhered to and which cannot respectably be changed. Unalterable institutions and rigid continuing programs and privileges for a party, a class, or a racial element are equally incompatible. From time to time counterevolutionary obsessions and attitudes are vividly revealed by some moment of decision, such as that which showed up the British Tories and the French Fourth Republic over Suez, or the docile and retrograde British Labour majority in their vote against joining the Common Market on October 28, 1971, when most of those with wider experience insisted upon saying "Yes" to it. Such dramatic confrontations dividing a great political party throw a searchlight beam upon the processes by which evolutionary needs and concepts infiltrate and modify the bigotry and bone-headedness to which all political parties are prone.

Legal bans on birth control and divorce, repression of freedom of opinion, and discrimination in access to higher education are other clear instances of counterevolutionary policies. Even though some counterevolutionary manifestations may appear right in the short run, they cannot be right in the long run. Because evolution is a practical process, and because it functions through so many different forces and channels, any counterevolutionary course must be uneconomic, and may also soon prove politically and socially unsustainable.

Owing to these strategic considerations, correct identification and sound following through of evolutionary courses must be regarded as essential. Within that principle, however, it will often be necessary to apply further criteria as between alternative courses, none of which is identifiably counterevolutionary. The principle is an aid to political judgment but not a substitute for it. Insofar as it inclines toward keeping future options open rather than purporting to close them, it in fact involves the exercise of more judgment rather than less. It also demands taking a longer view than has been customary in party politics.

If the nations of Europe are to succeed in harmonizing their relations within the community more study in depth will be required of the undercurrents which have so often caused misunderstandings and conflicts between them in the past. It is conceivable that to some extent cyclical processes may be at work, as they have been shown to be on a quite different plane in relation to animals such as lemmings and snowy owls.

By way of illustration, rather than as a documented proposition, it is interesting to reflect upon the hypothesis of a realized time lag of around a century between major human impacts and their digested and generalized repercussions. Such impacts must be traceable in terms of reactions among substantial groups of people.

On this basis the trauma of the Norman conquest of England in 1066 and the immediate creation of a vigorously interventionist central government in England forms a convenient starting point. The Conquest was completed in 1071–1072, with the suppression of the last risings in England and the abandonment by Malcolm of Scotland of his unsuccessful resistance. A century later the Anglo-Saxons gained a place in the highest levels of government with Thomas Becket, who was murdered in 1170 and canonized in 1173. Courts of justice and the national finances were organized and the first university was created, at Oxford, at this time. Ireland came under English suzerainty, but England came under the Pope. The fusion and modernization implicit in the nature of the Norman victory had suddenly come to pass.

A century later, with the accession of Edward I in 1272, continuous English Parliamentary history begins, England becomes organized as a commercial state on a basis of flourishing boroughs. After a further century another decisive stage was reached at everyday level with the emergence of the English language, in which Parliament was first opened in 1362 and Chaucer began writing about 1369. Following the Black Death, this period also sees the winning of freedom by serfs, the emergence of a wool-based capitalist economy, and the first moves towards Protestantism under Wyclif and the Lollards.

One more century later the defeat and death of Henry VI in 1471 marked the end of medieval England, and also of the power of the feudal barons, while Caxton's printing of the first book in English gave the means for an accelerated spread of the new learning and of Renaissance values. New men, and indeed whole new classes, emerged.

In the sixteenth century the corresponding decade marked the opening of the high Elizabethan age, long recognized as a turning point in English history, with the birth of Shakespeare, the final breach with the Pope, the founding of the Royal Exchange, and Francis Drake's operations in Latin America.

Passing on to the late 1660s we find the formative years of organized science through the new Royal Society and of the Royal Navy under Pepys and others. Newton's law of gravitation (1672), Wren's rebuilding of London after the Fire, and Milton's *Paradise Lost* mark the emergence of new perspectives. The building of a long line of great country houses marks the maturity of a new governing class.

Around the corresponding stage in the eighteenth century the years around 1770 are crucial for the origins of the Industrial Revolution (Arkwright's spinning machine and Josiah Wedgwood's Etruria pottery, 1770; the first cast-iron bridge, at Coalbrookdale, in 1773; James Watt's steam engine, perfected 1773) and of the Agricultural Revolution (Coke of Norfolk at Holkham, 1772), and modern scientific exploration (Captain James Cook's first voyage to Tahiti, New Zealand, and Australia and Bruce's journey to the confluence of the Blue and White Niles). The breach with the American colonists, the *Letters of Junius,* and the vindication of freedom of publication, the decision of Lord Mansfield in Somerset's case that a slave is free on landing in England (1772), the first edition of the *Encylopaedia Britannica* (1771), and the foundation of the Royal Academy illustrate the gains made possible by the breakthrough of a century earlier, and the decisive influence of this turning point. Modern man had arrived.

In the equivalent years of the nineteenth century we have the British North America Act, inaugurating Dominion Status for Canada, and wide extension in Britain of the right to vote in 1867, Galton's foundation of eugenics (1869), Karl Marx's *Das*

Kapital and J. S. Mill's *The Subjection of Women*, W. E. Forster's Education Act and Jowett's election as Master of Balliol, the adoption of competitive examination for entry to the British civil service, and the culmination of the great debate on Darwinism, arising from the publication of his *Descent of Man* (1871). The storms and stresses initiated by the Industrial Revolution had fairly broken out.

Whether the course of the Big Change will be accepted as conferring equivalent landmark status on these latest years is too early to discuss, but it may at least be said that they have not been stagnant or uneventful, and that they echo the themes of discord of a century earlier.

In introducing these reminders of historic events associated with long-term changes, with the suggestion that there may be a tendency to some bunching of such changes at roughly hundred year intervals, it is not intended seriously to propound this as a theory. The intention is rather to stimulate consideration of the hypothesis that human evolution may be influenced in its surface manifestations by rhythms or cycles, conditioned by time lags and by the duration of slow processes of response or reaction to social impacts or stimuli.

If such secular pulses or cultural shock waves prove to be a reality they will evidently have a particular significance for those countries, led by Japan, which have in recent decades undergone drastic and rapid westernization. This may be expected to produce some backlash and to result in special stresses and problems for several ensuing generations. The noosphere, like a forest or an animal, may be subject to a norm of growth rate which governs the crystalization of new ideas and inventions and the acceptance of new intellectual concepts or aesthetic styles. By learning more about these processes, both in individuals and in society, we may hope both to advance our exploration of the noosphere and to monitor human progress toward achieving new standards and remedying weaknesses and faults in society.

Although it is customary and simpler to refer to nations as a whole, it is obvious that within nations certain strata, such as peasants, are relatively impervious to time-linked changes in attitudes, while others, such as intellectuals and communicators, may be hypersensitive to them. This can create severe internal stresses within society, and can lead to oscillations through the adoption of new measures or forms for which too many people are still unprepared and may result in insistence upon a reversal. This factor of social conductivity is of the utmost significance to human evolution, and it calls for close study.

In primitive societies tabus and dogmas, lack of education, and restricted capabilities and instruments make for low social conductivity. There is often a conscious restriction to ruling and priestly castes of the function of evaluating the new and the unfamiliar.

In theory such castes are better able to interpret, digest, and pass on new ideas and practices, but in fact they often tend simply to block them in the effort to hold intact a social pattern which is much to their own advantage. Rebellions and dissident movements have sprung from attempts to break such a priestly or kingly monopoly and to become informed and able to reach an independent judgment upon neglected or suppressed knowledge. The history of translations of the Bible, and of school teaching of science, provide examples. It is only very lately that major human societies have emerged in which no area of knowledge is subject to formal monopoly or censorship.

Now, over most of the world, we are faced with an opposite problem. Large unsophisticated masses are confronted with so much complex and baffling or alarming information, on so many matters, that they are tempted to turn for guidance and reassurance to some strange and unreliable quarters. Honest and trustworthy interpretation is concentrated on day-to-day events and short-term trends, leaving people more and more troubled about where it is all leading. Conventional and traditional loyalties and habits no longer suffice to prevent breakaway movements of disturbing scale and temper. The failure to modernize and reinterpret the idea-systems which are the cement of society reduces some regions, or even whole nations, to the verge of ungovernability. At the same time countless individuals are tempted to give up in despair the effort to reconcile irreconcilable demands and pressures upon them, and to relapse into apathy, inertia, and escapism, or to break out in pointless violence or exaggerated unconformity.

As rational beings we must cease shrugging our shoulders and turning our backs on these supposedly inexplicable and senseless developments of our time. They are in fact natural and inevitable consequences of clearly discernible gross defects in the adaptation of our culture to changing circumstances, for which our cultural and political leaders bear entire responsibility. While preaching the responsibilities of the led they have signally defaulted on carrying out their own.

Ordinary men and women cannot be expected to directly face and adapt themselves to so many vast new challenges, striking them in such raw and chaotic form. They are entitled to expect the leaders of their culture and their polity to sort these things out for them and to provide them with a buffer against their impact and a framework within which to maintain a footing. Instead they are being left defenseless against the new pressures of change, while most of their leaders remain obsessed with irrelevances and trivialities.

What has been left undone cannot now be done; time has passed on, and its heirs have reluctantly taken their legacy. It is nevertheless not too late to recognize and proclaim the mistakes and defaults which have been committed, and to give credible assurances that they will no longer be continued. That, however, must involve the willingness of many politicians, administrators, and leaders of our contemporary culture to go back to school again, and to learn just where they went wrong in permitting our present perilous and almost unmanageable situation to arise.

Those who are too stubborn, too worn out, or too unresourceful to face this personal readaptation have no business to continue in roles carrying social responsibility. It is a paradox of today that while international and national industry is ruthlessly eliminating executives who cannot match the exacting standards of the current ratrace, their counterpart figures in activities much more decisive for the survival of mankind are so often permitted to carry on complacently with the mischief which the results show them to be doing.

Just as conservationists have learned the hard way that the planetary environment forms an indissoluble whole, and must be treated as such, so the managers of the nomosphere and the technosphere, and in fact all the leaders of mankind, must learn to think and act in terms of global human potentialities and requirements over a much more adequate time scale than the brief moments in evolution which they have hitherto been content to consider. This is not a matter of taste or preference; it is a question of human survival.

Only in this way can the cohesion of society be restored, and a new pattern established which will enable institutions and programs to keep in step with all the changes which time so quickly brings. Broad and long-term adaptations cannot be achieved by leaders incapable of seeing beyond the ends of their noses. Under such sluggardly and visionless guidance mankind will only slip farther into chaos, until soon the point of no return is passed. Unless more voices are raised more loudly and persistently in fundamental criticism of our current style of government it will soon be too late.

Fortunately we are witnessing a rapid wearing down of the edges and barriers between national, multinational, and global administrations, and domestically between central and local government and all sorts of paragovernmental or nongovernmental organizations. Indeed the growing currency of the unpleasing term "N.G.O.s" (meaning nongovernmental organizations) is a straw in the wind. Not so long ago it would never have occurred to officials to consider them. Here again it has been the process of preparing for the 1972 United Nations Stockholm Conference on the Human Environment which has set new standards of open-ended consultation and removed some barriers between international and national bureaucracies and the rest. We owe the improvement, however, not to a change of heart but to the undeniable incapacity of the officials to cope with much of the subject matter.

From an ecological standpoint this must be regarded as a significant and constructive change. Rigid hierarchies and hard divisions between different parts of an ecosystem are not favored at the higher levels of living animals and plants. Man's addiction to such practices during the past few thousand years may have been temporarily justifiable, but it is unlikely to prove in harmony with his future path of evolution.

A particularly unfortunate trend, now happily showing signs of reversal, has been the dominant status usurped by national central government over regional and local government, even on matters of local concern and origin. The undesirable results of this trend have now been officially conceded in the U.S.A., France, and other leading western countries, as well as in Britain. Government is not a thing apart or above, but one of several essential threads in a living pattern of society, which must function as, when and where the life and the action is, in a healthy and self-regulating mutual relationship with other activities. Only along these lines can the corruption of power be held within bounds, and a social environment created which permits and brings out the exercise of constructive and cooperative human talents, instead of blocking and diverting them into violent or negative channels, as our modern social structure has so conspicuously managed to do.

It is, however, perfectly clear that neither the elected representatives of the people nor their salaried administrators are going to go this way unless they are continually reminded that it is the way the electorate expect and require them to go. Virtually all governments at both these levels have a record of neglecting and brushing off obligations to consult opinion outside the government unless they are either looking for an alibi over some unpopular decision or are hopelessly out of their depth on some technical or intimate problem, or have been compelled at least to go through the motions of consultation by some powerful pressure group. Rather than idly misquote "the price of freedom is eternal vigilance" it is well to recall precisely what John Philpot Curran said in the significant year 1790:

> The condition upon which God hath given liberty to man is eternal vigilance; which condition if he break, servitude is at once the consequence of his crime, and the punishment of his guilt.

By repenting of their crime, and reviving their vigilance, conservationists have shown that their servitude, which resulted from earlier defaults, can be brought to an end. The victory, however, cannot endure unless far wider circles of citizens take the same path.

Study of the successful conduct under Maurice Strong of the "Stockholm process" reveals four gross structural failures underlying the present miserable performance of international institutions and policies. These are:

(1) Failure by member states to coordinate at domestic level their own national interest groups, aims, and policies, to enable and require their spokesmen internationally to express a comprehensive and thought-out national view rather than a half-baked departmental brief.

(2) Failure of like-minded governments to develop, on such a basis, a coherent and acceptable series of policy goals for which their representatives are prepared to work together responsibly and consistently within the United Nations, both in the General Assembly and its satellites, and on the governing bodies of the Special Agencies, so that the officials of these agencies are not left so largely to devise their own policies.

(3) Failure to counter separatist empire-building tendencies

among the administrators of the various international bureaucracies, and to insist upon adoption of a modern coordinated structure, on the lines so well stated in the Jackson Report, as a complement to the point made immediately above.

(4) A complete overhaul of the list of recognized nongovernmental organizations having consultative status with the U.N., and adoption of new procedures for insuring that those organizations which are genuinely international in effective membership, and genuinely doing constructive study and experiment in their fields, are brought into fuller and more regular consultation, while mere pressure groups (especially all those tied to one country, such as the United States) should be transferred to the appropriate national cooperating body, and should have no direct access to the U.N. level.

Reform on these lines would greatly assist in converting into regular practice, right across the board, the admirable but still highly precarious gains achieved by the Stockholm process.

It is too early to be optimistic that anything of the sort will happen, but at least there are certain encouraging signs. The United Kingdom government, which has a shockingly retrograde past record in these matters, has lately begun to adopt a more positive line, as have the United States, Sweden, and other countries. After years of stultification over population policy due to the pressure of reactionary interests the United Nations seems to have hit on a successful formula for getting round such inhibitions in the shape of the United Nations Fund for Population Activities (UNFPA). This has quickly grown, on a basis of voluntary contributions, to thirty-two million dollars a year—still a grossly inadequate level, but far better than the laughable resources made available through the fifties and sixties.

A number of the specialized international bodies—such as the World Bank (IBRD) under Robert McNamara, the Organization for Economic Cooperation and Development in Paris, and even, under its new regime, the Intergovernmental Maritime Consultative Organisation in London—have very lately shown encouraging responsiveness to neglected world needs. Some of the regional bodies, such as the Council of Europe and the Economic Commission for Europe in Geneva, are also showing substantial constructive activity. The expansion and reorientation of the European Economic Community give additional grounds for hope of a transformation in the atmosphere and the effectiveness of supranational organizations, and of an increasingly close contact between them and the democratic institutions, at citizen and representative levels, in the various countries. It may be no coincidence that these signs of adaptation in global institutions are coming simultaneously with signs of an awakening and a revived capability for constructive outgoing effort on the part of Europe.

If such progress is to be sustained and steadily strengthened in the climate of the seventies it can only be on the basis of more lively and practical participation by far more citizens and voluntary groups. All major streams of common interest, of collective study and thought, and of shared aspirations not only need to be suitably voiced but to be accorded adequate constitutional status, for which the best of the N.G.O.s form a feeble prototype. The precedent is not by any means a happy one but such a constitutional status has been accorded in Great Britain since World War II to the Trades Union Congress. Had that worthy body been able to rise to its contemporary opportunities and responsibilities the relationship might by now have been demonstrated as a useful model.

In *The System* I put forward the proposal "to marry the citizen's unsatisfied hunger for status and participation with Parliament's unsatisfied hunger for information and support." I pointed out that during World War II successful prototypes to fill these functions were operated in Britain. Supply of suitable material could be organized without difficulty and at reasonable cost. The more demanding tasks would be the creation of a Bureau of Current Affairs to distribute and supplement the material and to help to organize local citizens groups in areas of sufficient vitality. A national council of citizens groups would lay down ground rules and would have in the last resort power of intervention to check serious abuses.

Examples were given of possible kinds of activity, appropriate to such citizen groups. One obvious one would be a series of open occasions at which the local Member of Parliament would give a brief report of his parliamentary activities relating to the constituency, followed by open discussion. The long gap in time between elections, and the lack of a direct continuing personal communication between electors, of whatever political views, and their representative, might thus be narrowed. Another promising area for regular discussions would be the problems and achievements of local educational institutions at all levels, and relations between parents, teachers, students, and the community. Whenever some project or development aroused local criticism its promoters could be invited to expound and defend it, and to hear and try to meet criticism. Comparison of American and European experience in this area could be fruitful.

Where it appears that decision-making might be assisted by a clear expression of local opinion the citizens groups could organize an opinion poll and discuss its results and limitations with local elected representatives. Professional help in formulating, securing completion of, and analyzing the results of questionnaires should be made available freely through the Current Affairs central organization, which would guarantee the objectivity of the poll. Citizens groups might form a channel for providing television and radio networks and local stations with an enlarged range of suitable material and speakers. Interesting visitors from other places or countries might be given a forum to speak on topics of mutual concern and to help in comparing experiences.

It would be too much to hope that such a pattern would become universal or even general at any early date. But even if something over ten percent of local communities could successfully sustain live citizen groups on these lines they would alter the context of democratic politics and would help to bring about a softening of the excessively hard line now drawn between government and governed.

It will no doubt be said that various (half-hearted and half-baked) attempts in this direction have shown by their failure that it cannot be done. The answer is that, like many other things, it cannot be done by people who do not really believe in its aims and are unwilling to make an adequate effort to achieve them. Both politicians and administrators have had a strong vested interest in seeing that nothing of the sort starts or, if started, is allowed to succeed. This attitude must be smoked out by publicity and open criticism, in order to provide a genuine opportunity for a fair trial of the potential and to satisfy busy and able people that they will not be wasting their time in helping to realize in such ways an authentic pattern of democracy.

Mention was made in the previous chapter of the neglect by adults of the varied and pressing needs of teenagers, and the problems of facilitating their rapid transit from a childish to an adult role. One obvious approach would be to match the proposed local citizen groups with twin groups of junior citizens within, say, the age group of fourteen to nineteen. It would be the task of the older group to find premises and resources, to provide personally suitable liaison officers, and, on request, to insure that material and speakers were made available on specific topics into which the junior citizens wished to inquire. Basically the junior citizens should be able to decide their own scope, programs, and ways of operating, in the knowledge that they could expect understanding and support from the main local citizen group, for which they would in due course provide recruits and leaders.

Such a channel would encourage and assist young people who were ready to take an interest in public affairs, however unconventional and however critical, to tap the necessary basic resources in terms of a place to meet and to make themselves at home (preferably not shared with others), and of access to information and know-how on request, through the medium of sympathetic and understanding adult collaborators. Where local matters specifically affecting young people arise, the junior citizens should always be provided with the facts, and invited to comment and report, with the assurance that their contribution would be fully considered in the presence of their representative by the appropriate formal or informal body. Through such channels young people desirous of having a say in affairs would be enabled to do so, even before reaching voting age as individuals.

In places where the local age structure so demands, it might also be valuable to create senior citizens groups, probably within the ambit of the normal local group, to handle the special problems and to mobilize the special potential of people who have retired from fulltime work.

While it is not argued that the framework and pattern above indicated is the only right way it presents a coherent and comprehensive means of correcting the chaotic fragmentation and the crippling loss of identity and contact which is one of the most conspicuous achievements of modern progress. As a first step we need to secure widespread public recognition of the scale and character of this vast social vacuum, and to bring home to all, and not least to politicians and administrators, the urgent need to fill it if countless grave social evils resulting from it are to be successfully handled. It is indeed ludicrous and tragic to see so many well-meaning people running around vainly trying to remedy what are merely symptoms, oblivious to the immense tear in the fabric of human relations which has been made, and which is still being enlarged by modern blindness and neglect of essentials.

A lively and continuous interchange between family and family centers, between both and local citizens groups, including junior groups, between voluntary bodies and local and central government, and between national and international bodies, would create the new style of government, and of relations between government and governed, which our age plainly requires. Playing down the hard lines of hierarchy, exclusivity, and legalism, and playing up responsibility, openness, consultation, and informality, we might in more senses than one learn to succeed, and to increase happiness by learning to cease handling our affairs the hard way.

11

A WAY TO HUMAN SURVIVAL?

One of the most valuable of recently created idea systems is that which enables people generally to grasp the plight of threatened species of wild animals living far away in unfamiliar surroundings and to express effectively a will to assist their survival. Although in some ways comparable with the nineteenth-century humanitarian movement against cruelty to animals this new enlightened and cooperative sympathy contrasts with it in being global rather than localized, in focusing on the whole species rather than the stricken individual, and in seeking to maintain a valuable and healthy heritage, rather than to combat specific human abuses and cruelties after they have happened. Perhaps most important of all, it combines scientific inquiry with the furtherance of fundamental values—a combination which is urgently needed in so many other fields.

Millions of conservationists follow alertly reports of the annual journeys of the few dozen surviving whooping cranes as they run the gauntlet of so many perils on their migratory journeys between Wood Buffalo Park and their winter home at Aransas, or the rescue measures for the orangutans of Southeast Asia, or the eleventh-hour attempts to salvage the stock of Arabian oryx both in Arabia and at their emergency adoptive home in Arizona.

Such is the skill, the vividness, and the emotional appeal of these exercises in communication that the situations and problems they portray have become more real and familiar to many than the plight of numerous fellow members of their own species. Those, and they are plenty, who criticize this contrast should rather ask themselves how it is that with so much money and goodwill as they have long had at their disposal they should have permitted it to come about. Who but themselves are standing in the way of a comparably successful approach to the plight of mankind?

After two world wars and countless other fatal mass catastrophes it should by now be plain that while a humanitarian appeal can successfully deal with smallish numbers of cases on a sustained basis, or much larger numbers during occasional short-term emergencies, it is not adaptable to handling the chronic and unending flow of pitiable consequences of mistaken general practices and policies where these are continuing indefinitely. To try to make it do so is to risk blunting the response and spoiling the role for charitable appeals generally. There are already indications that sections of the public are becoming immunized against such an approach. They are unready to support continuing efforts to palliate, by official or voluntary aid, distress which is manifestly being manufactured on an ever-increasing scale by stubborn failure to face and deal with, for example, the population explosion.

Indeed, there is a substantial overlap in membership between the groups which are most active in promoting an illusory charitable treatment of such evils, and those who most persistently block reasonable attempts to remedy them at the source. To say this is not to criticize the high motives and excellent work of those who rightly obey their consciences in seeking to minister to those in distress wherever they may be. It is rather addressed to the mistaken social preference for ad hoc rescue measures afterwards, rather than for comprehensive and scientifically based preventive programs in advance.

It is here that the example of wild life conservation and its successful popular appeal is relevant. Are we right to be moving toward a situation where the most soundly based and widely backed methods for conserving threatened species are being used in the case of every animal except man? Apart from the many well-tried techniques and patterns of organization which have been mentioned earlier there is the immensely potent opportunity, waiting to be seized, of translating and applying for the benefit of man the dynamic and persuasive new idea-system concerning the watch over, and constructive aid for, a species whose survival needs to be assured.

What would this approach involve? To follow out the parallel we would require an objective appraisal of the present status on the planet of this species Man, and of the nature, scale, and whereabouts of the factors which are judged to amount to a threat to his survival. Evidently these would include the lack, unique in the animal world, of an effective means of adjusting population to resources, and of keeping this adjustment in operation. Studies of the nature and treatment of this lack and practical experiments would need to be matched by a continuous monitoring of progress both toward evolving a means and toward correcting the menacing consequences of having left it so late—a situation which is only too familiar in conservation of wild life, although not on such an awe-inspiring scale.

They would include also the growing failure to comprehend and channel Man's natural aggressiveness, and to prevent it from being so damagingly turned against his own species both on the collective and the individual plane—another immense area where Man is the most backward of animals.

A third factor would be the peculiar and puzzling human record of opening up exciting new potentialities of immense promise, such as access to the noosphere, and then choosing to go off on a tangent into some evolutionary blind alley. Among the oddest of man's peculiar endowments is wrongheadedness.

A fourth would be the complacency and defeatism with which modern man has permitted modern technology to undermine and wreck not only his natural environment but some of the social structures and practices essential to the orderly and peaceful development of domestic living, without even observing what is happening, still less making any effort at remedy. Man alone among animals lacks a comprehensive series of safety devices to contain his activities within limits essential for survival. Individual farsightedness can avail little until mankind develops a corresponding social organ. What social evolutionary mutation can bring that about?

The recent spread and transformation of idea systems, especially in the realm of conservation, suggests that it should not be unduly difficult to win widespread acceptance for the concept of regarding and treating man as a threatened species. By doing so it might be possible to bypass and surmount many deeply embedded resistances and inhibitions which would block or delay a more conventional approach.

One clear lesson from the successes of conservation is never to rely on conventional political channels and methods until a position of real strength has been built up freshly outside them. A second is the critical importance of presenting a big plain understandable target for effort, support by plenty of unarguable facts and evocative pictures, balanced between the extremes of horror and of a promised land. We deplore the confusions and frustrations of our times, but the way we go about handling our affairs and envisaging our own identity and situation is incapable of producing any other result. If we genuinely desire something different, we must take the trouble to learn different ways of pursuing it.

Hamlet long since anticipated our predicament in the familiar words:

> ... this goodly frame, the earth, seems to me a sterile promontory; this most excellent canopy, the air, look you, this brave o'erhanging firmament, this majestical roof fretted with golden fire, why, it appears no other thing to me but a foul and pestilent congregation of vapours. What a piece of work is a man! how noble in reason! how infinite in faculty! in form and moving how express and admirable! in action how like an angel! in apprehension how like a god! the beauty of the world! the paragon of animals!

His gloomy conceits about the earth have now become so far realized as to gain scientific confirmation, especially for his suspicions on air pollution. It is equally discouraging to find how far betrayals and cynicism have taken us from the human ideal which, even in Shakespeare's day, could be voiced only in ironic terms.

One of the unhappiest features of contemporary culture is the extent to which disillusionment and fragmentation have taken possession of artistic and literary expression. In place of a response to challenge and a bold handling of the way to fulfillment, we find at the highest level little except morbid introspection and the analysis and display of splinters and negations. It is doubtful whether in the whole history of human culture a parallel phase can be found in which the arts and literature as a whole had so little positive and worthwhile to contribute. Evidently one of the reasons for the meteoric and almost absurd cult of ecology at the present time is desperation to find something to fill the role from which the leaders of art and literature have temporarily chosen to abdicate. Nature abhors a vacuum and appropriately moves to fill it through nature study.

How and when will the arts pull themselves together again and begin to resume their customary function? How will they view and picture the new world, brave or otherwise, which will result from the impact of biological principles on a bankrupt and otherwise leaderless culture? How long will it take to get the trauma of the earlier twentieth century out of their system? How will they make terms with the larger and more critical audience arising from expanded higher education? Although such questions are peripheral to the present book, and no basis seems yet to exist for attempting to answer them, there should be no mistaking their significance for the future.

A fresh creative wave, fully adapted to the Big Change, cannot indefinitely remain wanting. When it comes it may prove decisive in setting that new style and new harmony between thought and feeling which meanwhile we so badly miss. Perhaps under its benign influence the idea-systems and new values which we now must struggle clumsily to express and define in bald prose may become clothed with a new grace and beauty, capable of permeating and giving renewed strength to the jangled and bewildered human consciousness.

To be able to stand back far enough and to use enough of our new technical resources to view man and his situation in perspective is the key to all other progress. Thanks to the animals we now have the capability to achieve this. By looking steadily at them we may regain our human self-respect. Ecology, moreover, brings a further essential gift to the study of human affairs. The absurdly brief time spans which have been accepted as normal and adequate for the study and conduct of human affairs make no sense at all to an ecologist, who has to think in terms not only of decades but of centuries, as we all should do. Such a refocusing of our vision would spontaneously and instantly correct the astigmatism which so often makes folly seem like reason. If our schools make any serious attempt to teach ecological principles the students themselves will carry over these enlightening perspectives to other studies, and these will soon permeate public attitudes. Our contemporary culture is too preoccupied with distance and too negligent of time. Enhanced time consciousness can do much to prevent the aggravation of many of our problems, and to promote the gradual alleviation of others.

There is indeed a particular pleasure in the possession of a lively sensibility to the passage and associations of time. Each period, each decade, each year, and each season subtly changes everybody and everything in it. A connoisseur can usually sense remarkably closely the date of some work of art or design from its style and execution. Unless it is a fake, or a legitimate imitation, the time of its conception is plainly stamped upon it. As the Gothic revival shows, once the period to which a style genuinely belongs has passed even the most skilled and thorough efforts to return to it prove lacking in some essential.

It is the same with literary expression, with colloquial language and even with machines and everyday structures. With the conspicuous exception of sentimental revivals of past collective experiences and their memories our contemporary culture is uneasy, clumsy, and ignorant where time is concerned. This defect, however, is now tending to be corrected by the intense and widening interest in history and landscape, in antiques and fashions, and in other kinds of knowledge which call for some awareness of the significance of time in human affairs. Such tendencies can do much to enrich people's lives and to spread sophistication.

One area where a better perspective and more down-to-earth attitudes are much needed is the treatment of death. The more we accept the fact of evolution the more we are bound to accept death as a natural and essential corollary to it. As Professor Laski wryly pointed out in contemplating the aging leaders of the prewar Labour Party, "While there's death there's hope!" Whatever may be the validity of religious beliefs in an afterlife, and in supernatural intervention, it is unfortunate that the indirect consequence of their exercise has been to surround the physical fact of death with so much morbid and unhealthy emotionalism. Unfortunately the influential circles which have compelled the churches and their allies to accept the permissiveness of modern society in matters of personal conduct, especially those of most concern to the young, are at one with the most bigoted religious groups in being fully content to maintain old tabus about death. Sooner or later the influence of the Big Change must be felt here too. The subject will be thrown open, if in no other way, by the delicate and difficult decisions, which cannot long be postponed, on the ethics of applying modern medical techniques to the artificial prolongation of life, in various circumstances not covered by traditional medical codes.

In this sphere of ethics we can expect no direct guidance from biological principles. Indirectly, however, they furnish two valuable leads. First, since the individual is the agent through whom evolution actually functions, while the species is an abstract generalization, it follows that the individual needs to be cherished and protected to whatever extent may be necessary in order to enable him to make his contributions, by selection, and by adding to the common stock of transmitted knowledge and experience. Any repression or distortion of the individual's self-fulfillment, which may contribute to social evolution, cannot be justified. To find otherwise would imply conceding to the state, or some other entity, a higher role than that of the evolution of the species, which biologically would be nonsense. Indirectly therefore a biologically oriented society is under obligation to function as a free society.

In modern times, however, the well-meant efforts of lawyers and reformers to safeguard liberties and good causes have led to a proliferation of "rights" and "charters" purporting to assure certain absolute guarantees against interference with certain kinds of freedom of action or expression, certain kinds of environmental protection and so forth. This has given rise to a good deal of muddle-headedness of the kind enshrined in the legal title "Tree Preservation Order." It may not be true that only God can make a tree (from which it might follow that only God can preserve one), but it is certain that no legal order can do more than prohibit certain specific interferences, with an ax or other instrument, and then provide suitable punishment if the prohibition is flouted. Preservation may still prove impossible for physical reasons over which the law has no power. Broadly speaking the same applies to human "rights" generally. If they run counter to strong natural, social, or economic forces they are unlikely to prove worth very much.

It follows, therefore, that a clearer distinction should be drawn between legal provisions calculated to provide legal defense and remedy against other individuals or corporate bodies infringing them, and desired access, for instance, to natural resources. Declarations of intent are not practically enforceable. We should worry less about rights and more about learning to conduct ourselves so that what we desire comes about. Obviously legal measures must fall within what is physically possible but cannot fully cover it. The human ecological background is highly significant to the framing and enforcement of rights. These processes must leave over an important residue to be taken care of, if at all, by administration and management.

Unfortunately legal definitions and doctrine concerning "natural" rights grew up at a period before the character and limits of what is genuinely "natural" began to be recognized. Indeed few words are so often so ignorantly misused by educated people as this word "natural." This is one of many areas in which revision and redefinition will be needed if law is to be harmonized with what we now understand from science. The legal citizen and the biological individual are not quite the same person. Do deterrents deter? What makes a criminal, and who is a criminal? What are the limits of reasonable interferences with environment and its common values? What are the "rights" of children as against their parents? These and many other issues will need reviewing in any movement to bring the law into harmony with people as science shows them to be, and with society as it can or should function.

Closely allied problems arise in considering the relation of a biologically oriented community to the state and to supranational authorities. The latter tend to be functional bodies constituted for well-defined practical and generally agreed purposes, without any undisclosed or mystical underlying reservoir of purported authority. So far as that applies they are in principle compatible with a biologically oriented society, but unfortunately there are two snags. First, they are largely staffed by administrators molded by and then transferred from the public services of sovereign states, which do claim a mystical and indefinite range of basic authority over their citizens. Second, they are often governed by Councils representative of these sovereign states.

It seems accordingly that, if the jungle law of conflicting nation-states is to be replaced by a more civilized international order, sovereign states will eventually have to make some formal renunciation of their claims to be entitled to do more than to administer and operate such laws, programs, policies, and finances as are from time to time entrusted to them constitutionally by citizens to whom they are responsible. This is going to mean amending a whole lot of constitutional textbooks. The long-cherished power to declare war on a neighbor is evidently among those which will have to go. Like dehorned cattle on a modern farm the states of the world will become much much less touchy and neurotic when they are humanely relieved of their aggressive paraphernalia, and the mumbo-jumbo which goes with it.

There may however consequentially be a need to strengthen internal police forces, at any rate for a time, in order to give assurance against subversion and planned minority violence. Ceremonial units and technical specialist corps, such as engineers and military transport available for emergencies, should also be kept in being, possibly linked with some form of compulsory civilian service for common purposes of benefit to the community.

Adaptation of the social structure to conform to the principles which have been proved to work in the biosphere means moving away from artificially externalized, segregated hierarchical institutions and developing in their place a pattern of organically linked networks of control and driving force. These should coincide as nearly as possible with the distribution of capability for decision-making, and for input of energy, at all levels, and over the entire extent of a diverse and spontaneously self-adapting and self-renewing system. In other words we should cease trying to concentrate and centralize power at some artificially misconceived "summit" level, and seek to link power and decision-making with all the activities which can generate power and which require decisions to be made, all the way down the line and across the board.

It is doubtless some glimmering of this truth which makes "grassroots" a favorite word among politicians. They, however, are united in confining their contacts with the human grassroots to flattery and to gathering better hints for building up their own personal power and keeping the grassroots where they belong, ever ready to be trodden underfoot.

It is interesting to find that some of the latest studies in business management have come up with similar conclusions, involving a thorough definition of each job responsibility, and the placing of this responsibility within the organization as close as possible to the point where the information and contacts involved in it are located. Here it can be performed with the maximum of personal communication, face to face, and the minimum of paperwork and remote control. Unfortunately this approach is so diametrically opposed to recent attitudes and teaching, and to the whole complex of conventional organization and methods, that not even its basic simplicity and commonsense can enable it to be readily understood and followed through in administration and in business, even where the will exists.

Although fundamental ideas and attitudes are all-important in constructive treatment of the Big Change their very situation as fundamental makes it all the more difficult to reach back to the semiconscious layers of the mind and of the culture in which they lurk. Individuals and society are at one in their dogged resolution to defend this cluttered and cobwebbed inner sanctuary of their being from outside inspection or intervention. They will bravely admit a new machine into their homes, or parade the streets in a new fashion. They will even crudely advertise their differentness by growing long hair or adopting unconventional ways. Yet under the surface we still find the good old neolithic type basically unchanged, having learned nothing and forgotten nothing. The platitude that human nature does not change rests on this. Yet it is only a half-truth, reflecting the general reluctance and incapacity to tackle problems of adaptation below the surface, and the still inadequate psychological and anthropological equipment for doing so.

Modern politics, left, right, or center, represent a tacit conspiracy to pretend that this problem does not exist. They assume that all necessary or desired changes, whatever these may be, are attainable by externalized institutional and material manipulations, involving a minimum of deeper understanding or adaptation, and a maximum of voting and similar rituals, sanctifying the operations of political parties and of government agencies.

Far from tackling the more profound levels of innate human barbarism, politicians do not scruple to pander to them and to exploit their dark powers. Almost up to this day the proceedings of the great party conventions in the United States for choosing the two protagonists for the most powerful post in the world have exhibited ceremonial rites and antics of a nature which might well have been pronounced too crude and barbaric to be acceptable in the conduct of neolithic affairs.

The savage beast, at once collective and individual, which hides so close beneath the veneer of our civilization has not only been tolerated but has been continuously nurtured and kept as a pet by party politicians. They find it a readily available source of aid and response for the type of appeal on which the power of even the highest-minded of them must rest. Underlying countless debates, and issues appearing in abstract or in practical shape, is the question of whether mankind is to tacitly go on agreeing to keep and nourish this monstrous pet, or whether to set about in earnest the long and difficult job of getting rid of it as a major force in society. Until that job is squarely faced, and until its implications are fully probed and weighed, the evolution of Man and the fulfillment of his potential will continue to be largely nullified. Given the will and the resources it seems not improbable that the back of the task could be broken within, say, the next three hundred years.

Strategically such progress as has hitherto been made has been rather by means of tackling and bringing under civilized guidance particular excrescences of human activity than by an all-out frontal attack. Such attacks have principally been launched by the great religions, especially Christianity, but in historical perspective they are seen in many respects to have compromised away their essential principles in exchange for superficial acceptance, rather than to have genuinely transformed deeper motivations and attitudes in accord with their announced beliefs. Certainly within living memory hardly any religious group except the Society of Friends is on the record as having carried through a serious and effective continuous campaign of public witness to its ostensible beliefs, or as having even attempted realistically and wholeheartedly to combat the often unbridled aggression, violence, and materialism of our times.

Nevertheless, without fully deserving to be called a civilization, our culture has achieved during the past few centuries some notable and apparently enduring advances, in the direction of mitigating barbarous tendencies. One of the most interesting was the largely feminine success during late medieval times in establishing courtly politeness and true consideration for the weak and in creating the refinement of sexual relations which came to be called love. Here is a large realm of human living, of intimate personal significance, in which far-reaching advances were achieved without initiative from church or state. They are to this day only upheld by a prolonged and intense struggle on the part of the mothers, and to a lesser extent the fathers, of each new generation.

No aspect of our culture gives more encouragement for the prospect of strengthening and extending it, yet none shows more clearly the difficulties and demands involved. None, moreover, so vividly demonstrates in every home the perennial upwelling of primitive brutish barbarism, and the millennial nature of the task of replacing repeated environmental conditioning by an eventual evolution through the selection of human types more inherently adapted to civilized living.

To cite one other example, the fairly rapid and widespread acceptance of the rule of law (in some communities as universal practice and in others at least as an intermittently or partially realized ideal) demonstrates the possibility of using psychological, political, and legal means with sufficient resolution, dedication, and consistency to achieve far-reaching results. Indeed the universality of the demand for justice, and of the readiness to make big sacrifices for it, is among the most essential human traits without which any aspiration to become civilized would be no more than an empty vision.

After the defeat and collapse of the Pax Romana the western world took around a millennium to return seriously to the task of making a reality of the rule of law. Since then we have reached the present degree of progress, such as it is, after around four hundred years of organized struggle. Thanks to this success many other advances can be regarded as possible within a much shorter timespan.

The main interest through whose agency the rule of law was worked out in theory and practice was that of the lawyers, forming a corporate profession autonomous within but essential to the state, which was biased the other way. By a curious modern illusion many members of the public have recently come to regard the state as an agency of progress, and to demand the creation of some new ministry for every problem that occurs. Even if departments of central government were much more intelligent and efficient than they usually are they would be miscast in such a pathfinding role. It is a legacy of the neglect to find other means of tackling so many social and economic problems, and of the excessive politicization of modern society, that such solutions have come to be thought of as making sense.

Only during the last couple of decades in Britain has there been a substantial growth of organizations designed to develop some broad field of collective activity with the necessary financial resources and the essential minimum freedom from political and central bureaucratic interference in their operations. The first, and also the most successful and influential throughout, has been the British Broadcasting Corporation. The BBC has played a vastly significant role in raising standards of public appreciation and taste, and in giving the new more educated public access to its own cultural inheritance, and an assured awareness of its identity and its abilities. Entering so many homes, and communicating so intimately and continuously with so many dawning personalities and budding minds, the BBC has come creditably close to realizing its full potential as a service of public information and education on the grand scale.

Less directly, but also significantly as a source of public patronage to creative artists, the Arts Council has given backing and encouragement to the expanding national effort in music and ballet, opera and drama, painting, sculpture, and to a lesser extent literature. Whatever complaints they may still have, those who practice in these fields are immeasurably better taken care of and appreciated than they were before World War II.

In sport and physical recreation, in tourism and in other fields, similar bodies are growing up to set higher standards and to develop new facilities and activities. Particularly relevant here are the growth points in science and in higher education. If the arrears and the gaps in structure indicated in this book are to begin to be made good there will be a major continuing commitment for research and higher instruction and training. In both these areas the past two decades have seen a vast build-up in personnel and resources, which may be expected to tip the balance in favor of long-term reconstruction, and to provide more adequate means for its pursuance concurrently with the satisfaction of current manpower demands. At the time of writing, both in the United States and in Britain and elsewhere, surpluses of graduates and postgraduates unable to find specialized jobs requiring qualifications up to their level are building up.

Here is evidence of a disequilibrium over the matching of expanded university-trained personnel and enlarged research resources by adequate deployment of effort in the use of this new manpower and knowledge for correcting structural deficiencies in society, and for catching up with the backlog of neglected tasks. For example, the success of the conservation movement in concentrating public concern upon pollution and other environmental shortcomings has led to reinforcement of many agencies and activities concerned.

Corresponding reinforcements have, however, not yet begun in many other neglected areas, where no effective group of citizens has yet persuaded politicians, administrators, and managers to pay heed. At any rate it is comforting to find that when the message gets through in these other fields it will not always be necessary to wait for one or more decades before manpower at graduate level can be provided. Indeed the existence and threatened growth of this pool of unemployed graduates should make it politically easier to develop additional services in which they can usefully be absorbed. There are dangers, as Ivan Illich has emphasized, in permitting the renewal of "conviviality" between ordinary men and women to be inhibited by the encroachment of professionalism, but the problem is mainly one of providing the right structure and conditions to enable professionals to form the essential core of a broad amateur effort.

In this great new fraternity of graduates and postgraduates, partially emancipated from inherited social mythology, and partially equipped to work out and apply new approaches to social as well as technical problems, we find one of the most solid and substantial grounds for expecting some constructive response to the challenge of the Big Change. So far, it must be freely admitted, the yield has been disappointing. The universities of the western world, from Berkeley to the Sorbonne and the London School of Economics, have certainly built up a new and intense interest in current affairs. They have, nevertheless, largely permitted it to be diverted by thinly disguised old-fashioned types of campus politicians into simplistic or counterproductively violent channels, unworthy of ostensibly educated young men and women and exerting a predominantly negative and unconstructive influence on the urgent problems of our time. We need not, however, take too seriously this false start by the previous generation of students. The year 1968, like the year 1848, may prove to have been more significant as a portent and a social thermometer than for anything it actually did.

Probably the main relevance of these events is the emergence of the universities as a new estate in the body politic, dynamic, uncommitted, potentially well-informed, and surprisingly strong in numbers and resources, compared with earlier major organized interests who have been accustomed to call the tune. Already there are promising indications that the initial splits between faculty and undergraduates, and between political activists and the mugwump majority, are gradually healing. The academic estate, even when it cannot speak with one voice on public affairs, will at least speak the same language and exert a steady influence toward the same kind of new approach. If it can do this, nothing can prevent it from rapidly assuming a dominant role in the handling of the Big Change.

Until quite recently western universities had mostly either remained under a suffocating ecclesiastical tutelage, like Oxford, or been forced by economic stringency to conciliate largely conservative potential donors, like many leading American universities and the red-brick group in England. Even now, most of the universities of continental Europe, not excluding free Switzerland, are subject to continuous and damaging state interference behind the scenes. They look with envy on the buffer afforded to their British brethren by the ingenious and successful device of the University Grants Committee—another significant illustration of the principle of devolution from immediate state control. As has been shown in other fields, the success of that principle vindicates the kind of pattern of institutions to which ecological principles point, as against the monolithic and dogmatic alternative.

At best, however, the emerging academic giant must and should remain fundamentally an independent estate, within which scholarship can consider, test, and develop new ideas and new interpretations, without closing the door to others as they come along. Universities like to think of themselves as the vanguard of advancing civilization, but their record gives only limited support to that claim. There is accordingly a need for a counterpart series of institutions of higher study and experiment which can boldly concentrate upon pathfinding in particular fields, using particular moral hypotheses and particular methods and techniques in order to minimize for the future the number and extent of neglected social and economic problems, and to serve in the front rank as organs for human evolution.

This need has long been appreciated by, for example, leading foundations based on private benevolence, such as the Smithsonian, the Carnegie, the Rockefeller, the Max Planck, the Nuffield, the Ford, the Nobel, the Leverhulme, the Wenner-Gren, and others. Each has found its own fruitful field of specialization. For example the Smithsonian, the earliest prototype, and the closest to government, has concentrated upon supporting programed scientific research and exploration, and the maintenance of first-rate study collections. The Carnegie Foundation has had a mission to stimulate new growth throughout wide circles of the population by such means as public libraries and promising new local initiatives in recreation, the arts, and education. The Rockefeller Foundation has had a remarkable far-reaching effect through picking and backing promising young men of many nationalities to fulfill their projects, and to acquire mature experience early in life. The Green Revolution, based on brilliant research in genetics and related agricultural science, is also largely a feather in the Rockefeller cap, even if its sustained contribution poses to disappoint the more optimistic of the forecasters. Nobel has gone to the extreme of offering rewards of the highest value and prestige to scientists, writers, statesmen, and others for new contributions of the utmost international significance.

Such examples amply testify to the fruitfulness of this comparatively new approach which, let it once again be noted, owes nothing to governments, unless the grudging acceptance by Congress in 1846 of James Smithson's imaginative bequest is accorded a measure of credit on the ground that it might easily have been declined. All these great foundations regularly issue admirable and informative reports, and each has its band of eager clients avid for clues on how to win new grants for their pet projects. It is remarkable all the same that even informed public opinion still has little interest in or understanding of their significance as a group, to the evolution of modern civilization. I was lately able to buy a new copy of an excellent illustrated history of the Rockefeller Foundation at one seventh of its published price. No type of organization has done more to promote and sustain the function of social evolution, yet few have themselves attracted so little discriminating appreciation on that account. This fact is both symptomatic of the blind-spots which have already been identified in contemporary attitudes to social evolution, but at the same time encouraging as showing what a useful basis already exists, almost unheeded, for the kind of development which is here argued to be urgently necessary.

While foundations commonly exercise choice and influence by the judicious grant-aiding of suitable projects, there are also many bodies which directly undertake operations within their chosen field. Some of these are scientific, such as the Charles Darwin Foundation for Galapagos, the famous center of higher ecological studies at Montpellier in France, or the Serengeti Research Station in Tanzania. Others, like Resources for the Future, Inc., in Washington, or the National Institute for Social and Economic Research, PEP and Chatham House (the Royal Institute of International Affairs) in London are national in form, even though they often occupy themselves with wider issues.

Other pioneering international bodies such as the Swiss-based Red Cross, and outward-oriented national organizations such as the British Voluntary Service Overseas, and the American Peace Corps, provide particular forms of altruistic service. By making a tally of such bodies one arrives at a surprising range and scale of disinterested effort, often maintained against great difficulties, at times with very slender resources. Undoubtedly the potential and the experience exists to multiply their contribution, if ever public opinion gets round to recognizing the obligation to do so, and the many benefits which would result.

A distinct kind of international initiative in the scientific field was successfully demonstrated by the International Geophysical Year and has since been repeated in the International Biological Programme. The concept here has been to select a complex of problems the understanding of which can be advanced by simultaneous programed research and survey in different continents, and to organize such a program under the International Council of Scientific Unions (ICSU) through the various national Academies of Science and scientific institutions. While IGY attracted massive logistic and financial support from leading governments, especially for its research in Antarctica, IBP has had to struggle through as a poor relation, only saved from collapse in its earlier phases by the provision of free facilities and considerable grant aid from the United Kingdom through the Royal Society. If, as now seems likely, the IBP comes through as a success, there is much to be learned from its experience.

Perhaps the most important need is to do something about the disparity between the vast potential and responsibilities of ICSU and its microscopic resources and consequently ineffective organs. A former General Secretary, taking office with extreme reluctance, ruefully observed to me that he knew his acceptance would cost him two bitter losses—one would be his science and the other his family.

In a world which benefits so much from science, and depends so much on science for its future, it is highly discreditable that those eminent scientists who strive hardest to maintain the global interscientific organization should be handicapped, penalized, harassed, and frustrated in their efforts, as they so often are. Few investments for the human future could be more rewarding than a massive endowment of ICSU and of the specialist scientific unions which compose it.

The experience of the International Union for Conservation of Nature and Natural Resources, as one of the very few which owns its own office and can employ a permanent staff, shows how much the world is missing in terms of international scientific cooperation through this policy of penury. If a human presence in the noosphere is to be effectively maintained on an international basis, here is one of the most urgent points of action.

Mention has been made earlier of the outstanding contribution from the United States toward international teaching of science in schools, notably through the Biological Sciences Curriculum Study. It is disturbing to reflect that but for the brilliant initiative and massive follow-through of a very small group of people within a single country, and their enlightened awareness of the needs of other nations, the students of the world might well have been condemned to learn their science on an obsolete basis for at least a couple more decades. Why, when we have a United Nations Educational and Scientific Organization, should the great advances now being made in worldwide scientific teaching not have been promoted as a world task? Why is there still so little effective international work on the learning process, and on its application to different teaching problems in different lands? A well-led and well-backed world effort in the study and application of improved methods of education could give very great dividends, even indirectly, in enabling many nations to create the basis of informed opinion for tackling such problems as the population explosion. What is already being done is far below one thousandth of the requirement.

Going back to the first Renaissance we can now see that it came to birth through three intimately interrelated stimuli. First, following the Crusades, came the influx of Moslem/Arab learning and of Byzantine scholars, returning to the West the lost intellectual and artistic legacy of Greece and Rome. Without these dramatic cultural impacts there could have been no Renaissance. But they had to be welcomed within already mature and talented centers of learning, able to absorb, digest, and disseminate the essentials for their own time.

Fortunately enough of these existed, or were promptly created, to perform this digestive and interpretive task. It would, however, have still proved of no avail had not the spirit of the times, and the openhandedness of patrons, provided the necessary encouragement, resources, and communications to spread and follow up the good news quickly and widely.

In our day we do not have to await a great intellectual stimulus from outside, still less from the past; it springs with vigor from the challenge of our own advances and the resulting stresses and demands. Poor as we are in intellectual and artistic institutions, no previous generation has disposed of so strong and numerous an array of them, and similarly with the media. However badly we have degraded and misused them, we have at our service an overwhelming capability for communication. In terms of fundamental requirements for the constructive transformation of our world culture and society we are not in bad shape. The obstacles and shortcomings, although immense and depressing, are essentially secondary. Our civilization is passively adaptable, but it has yet to adapt itself to actively adapting. The will, the energy, the imagination, the perspective, the creative sympathy, the scholarly reassessment of attitudes and values underlying events, the readiness for teamwork, the capacity to convert ideas into action—these are the things that are in short supply. A main reason why they are short is that so much of current resources and energies is misdirected into obsolete and sterile channels, political, religious, philosophic, and artistic.

Many people sense this critical set of defects without being able to particularize or to convert them into a diagnosis supporting remedial action. The malaise, or even revulsion, which builds up against each successive conference, where so much has to be said in order to get so little done, is a clear illustration. The aim of this book has been to try to show more clearly the flow processes generated from the stresses between current social evolution and the resulting emotional reactions. Alienation, ideological reappraisal, the absorption of new knowledge about man and his environment, the improvement of education and communication, the restructuring of government and of social institutions, the emergence of new men in new roles are among the signs of these pressures and tensions. Properly handled they can assist toward the framing and execution of programs, each of which may contribute to harmonizing the sum of current human effort with the total human predicament. This is no small task, but no smaller concept has much chance of succeeding. That it will stretch our minds, extend our perspectives, and challenge us to grope our way down to the very roots of our humanity are to be viewed not as burdens but as benefits. If we are not here on earth for such business we have no business to be here at all. The planet may well need an animal such as Man could become, but it would be well rid of a creature such as he now is.

12

CONCLUSION

Man has run out of environment. This is true in three distinct senses. The most obvious, and currently the most discussed, is that he has poisoned, injured, or destroyed so much of his physical habitat that it threatens to become uninhabitable for coming generations. The second, no less ominous, is that he has allowed and is still encouraging his numbers and density to outrun its capacity, even if it had stayed healthy and sound. But beyond these is the yet more disturbing fact that, in discarding and outgrowing his inherited physical and social environment, Man has hitherto failed to create around him anything that can take its place and cover his nakedness, psychically as well as socially. Man has become that hitherto inconceivable ecological monstrosity—an animal without a habitat. The biological peril and instability of such a predicament can hardly be exaggerated.

For all living things the essence of a habitat is that it must be total, enduring and sustaining. In other words, a habitat must be habitable, not only in terms of food intake and reproduction but as an enfolding, protective, and satisfying world. It must offer resources and present challenges to which the species is capable of adapting its physiological and behavioral patterns in a meaningful and rewarding way. Insofar as the habitat itself is in course of change, such change must be compatible, in its rate and direction, with that of which its users are capable.

Modern man has committed the crime and the blunder of breaking away from his well-tried natural environment without having had the wit to perceive, the resourcefulness to measure, or the resolution to tackle the need for creating in its place a new and viable sociobiological environment. Those who have worked themselves up into a state of panic over the threat of pollution are still preoccupying themselves with early symptoms rather than the fundamental problem. They should not, however, be discouraged, since there is good reason to suppose that, in our contemporary culture, the best way to order may lead through ordure. Those who have been temporarily seduced by the sweet smell of success must be sobered up by the foul stink of failure. The more deeply they inhale it the better they will prepare themselves for the intensely demanding adaptations which are the price of survival.

Our environment, both inner and outer, simply mirrors who and what we are. The mess that the world is in is entirely of our making, and it has not happened by mistake. We have willed it to be just as it is, while stubbornly deceiving ourselves that we were willing it quite differently. Let us cease excusing ourselves with such lies as that the squalid chaos which is closing in upon us is the Will of God, or that we have lacked the resources to do better, or that natural constraints and hazards have been too strong for us. We stand in the dock without an alibi, and it would be best to be honest about it, for that way we will find ourselves so much sooner on the road out of our predicament, if it is not by then already closed.

If we believe that mankind should have a future it is time for us to insure that it is a future which we can bequeath to our descendants without feeling shame and guilt. We need in fact to reorient our attitude to time, absorbing more from the past, fussing less about the present and reaching out toward the future in a friendly and helpful way. We should try to perceive the nature of its promise, and to assist it to emerge without having to struggle unnecessarily against arbitrary handicaps perpetuated or created for it by our lack of courteous consideration for its predicament. In blunt terms, let us stop being beastly to the future, if we are to dare to hope that the future may not be beastly to us.

We can best show courtesy toward the future by adopting a pattern of living in which its hopes and its problems are daily in our minds. But this requires a vigorous effort of mind-stretching. In every human activity we should make sure that there are doors leading to the future and that they are kept open, or always ready to be opened, like the escape doors in places of public assembly. The kind of culture which locks its doors against the future has had its day. To keep these doors open takes courage, but above all it means making sure that when we peer through them it will be with pride rather than with a consciousness of betrayal.

Perhaps the writing of this book will prove to have been a mere futility. Even if it is not much too late for its message to prove of service, it could still be too early for the message to be acceptable. Although the message is consistent with many others which have lately been issued by other writers, too much time could be lost in a confused and confusing debate making too much of points of difference and losing sight of the large elements of agreement.

Be that as it may, no one in these days can think such

thoughts as these and be content to leave them unsaid. Vigorous currents are converging toward a far more integrated and whole view of human life and its meaning, and of human affairs and their conduct, than ever before. Perhaps the Big Change will assume a more positive and constructive shape than has so far seemed likely, and the healing forces which are so desperately needed by mankind will begin to work faster. Perhaps, if the worst comes to the worst, catastrophe may be less than total, and those who survive it may be in a frame of mind to make a fresh start. To attempt prophecy is pointless, but to do everything possible to avert what current prophecy often predicts is still worthwhile.

Index

active change (*see* classifications of change)
adventure playgrounds, 135
advertisements, effect on living style, 194, 197
  suggested restrictions, 199
agriculture
  damage to environment, 41
  statistics on number of people engaged in, 62–63
anthropology
  and Book of Man, 93
  repercussions of recent progress in, 9, 61
antibiotics, misuse of, 71–72
archaeology
  and Book of Man, 93
  increased knowledge in, 12, 41, 61
Arctic Research Laboratory, 186–187
arts and literature, disillusion of in contemporary culture, 256–257
Arts Council, 266
Auden, W. H., quoted, 131

Bangla Desh catastrophe, 151
Bates, Marston, 96
Bauhaus, 133
Biological Sciences Curriculum Study, 96, 221, 272
biology
  importance in education, 94, 96
  study of, in *Green Version*, 96–97
Biology: An Environmental Approach, 97
biomass
  described, 17
  expanded, 170
biome stations, 185–187
biosphere
  described, 16–17
  and evolution, 21, 94
  and pollution, 169, 181, 183
  and harmonious relations among spheres, 22–23, 82–83
  repercussions of population explosion on, 168
Book of Man, 90–93, 96–101, 105
  compared with Bible, 92
  contents
    biology in, 94, 96–97
    Part One, 93–94
    Part Two (discoveries), 97–98
    Part Three (history of earth's peoples), 98–99
    Part Four (culture and art), 100
    Part Five (capabilities and limitations), 100–101
    Part Six (review of recent progress), 101
  distribution of, 90–91
  in education, 92–93
  function, 91–92
  importance of self-knowledge, 105
  outline, 101
Borlaug, Norman, 169
breeding patterns, 59, 64, 76–77
  breeding groups, 156–157
  changing groups, 157–159, 229–230
  inbreeding and outbreeding, 41–42, 74–75
  and intelligence reserves, 74, 78–79
  large families, 158, 217
  and physical unfitness, 71
  state intervention, 158–159
  nature of, 160

breeding patterns (*cont.*)
  state intervention (*cont.*)
    undesirable intervention, 160–161
  and young people, 72, 159
  (*See also* gene flow)
British Broadcasting Corporation, 100, 201, 266
British Trust for Ornithology, 182
British Voluntary Service Overseas, 271
Brookings Institute, 132
Bureau of Current Affairs (proposed), 139–141, 247–248
  opinion poll organized, 248

Carnegie Foundation, 269
Carr-Saunders, 41
Charlemagne, 44
Charles Darwin Foundation for Galapagos, Montpellier, France, 270–271
Charles II, 107
Chatham House (the Royal Institute of International Affairs), London, 132, 271
churches (*see* religion)
citizens, 138
  definition, 231
  groups suggested, 139–141, 247–251
    for senior citizens, 250
    for teenagers, 249–250
  citizens' information bureau (proposed), 139–141
  (*See also* Bureau of Current Affairs)
Civilisation, Kenneth Clark, 100
Clark, Kenneth, 100
classifications of change
  defined, 36
  examples of active changes
    mass media of communication, 48
    meritocracy, 42–43
    population explosion, 38–39
  examples of hard changes
    liberalization of laws, 51
    popularity of world travel, 58
    supranational organizations, 43
    welfare state, 37
  examples of negative changes
    permissive society, 51
    student opposition to war, 58–59
  examples of positive changes
    mass media of communication, 48
    meritocracy, 42–43
    population explosion, 38–39
    student support of supranationalism, 58–59
  examples of soft changes
    mass media of communication, 48
    meritocracy, 42–43
    permissive society, 37, 51
    population explosion, 38–39
Clausewitz, Karl von, 192
Club of Rome, 202
College of Parenthood (proposed), 214–215
Commoner, Barry, 202–203
communication media (*see* media, mass)
computers facilitating change, 81
Concorde, 50, 225
conservation
  charting destruction and damage of resources, 172, 181
  popularity of appeal of wildlife conservation, 253–254
conservationists
  awareness of components of today's problems, 202
  and leadership, 119, 126, 141, 179
  new frontiersmen, 94
  revived vigilance towards liberty, 245
  view of planet as indissoluble whole, 243
  view of policies of economic growth, 49–50
conservation movement, international
  building a supporters' movement, 138
  catalyst for new cultures, 113
  experience in success drawn upon, 8–9, 70, 109, 119–122, 124, 127, 129, 255, 267

INDEX 281

Second International Congress of the World Wildlife Fund, 121
United States movement, 119
viewed as visionary, 141
consumer demands in Britain reviewed, 79–80
Consumer Protection, Inc., 201
Council of Europe, 128, 247
Curran, John Philpot, 245 (quoted)

Darlington, C. D., *Evolution of Man and Society*, 10, 40, 42 (quoted)
Dartington Hall, 133
Darwin, Charles, 40, 111
death control, 71, 258–259
  death rate statistics, 144, 150
  ethics and artificial prolongation of life, 45, 72, 259
dehumanization, 206–207
  population explosion effects on, 208
  stage of evolution, 236
Demographic Yearbook, 176
Diaghilev Ballet, 133
disarmament, 52, 56, 57, 192–193
Duke of Edinburgh's awards, 135

Earth Day, 1970, New York, 123
ecology
  as base for social evolution, 14, 93, 111, 210
  contributions of, 13–14
  expanded time span for study, 257
  ecological approach to biology in *Green Version*, 96
  ecological factors in prehistory understood, 98
  ecological illiteracy, 90, 110
  ecological studies and alternative philosophies to man over nature, 112
  ecological view of the state, 233–235
ecologists
  breakdown of isolationism among, 187
  increasingly listened to, 2, 10
  as healers, 115
  as new frontiersmen, 94
  probe of virgin land, 170
  of the future, 9
  replacing artistic and literary culture, 11, 256
  strategic task of combining with ethology, 13
  state view of, 234
  views and principles of, 110, 191, 236
Economic and Social Council, 176
Economic Commission for Europe, Geneva, 247
economy
  in Britain since 1918 reviewed, 80
  complication of problems, 123
  comsumptionist, 201
  indiscriminate growth criticism, 49–50
  instability of, 193
ecosystems, 244
  substitution of one for another, 179
  of today, 110, 235
education
  and arts and literature, 257
  criticized, 98, 197
  curricula and Book of Man, 92
  effect on consumer demand, 79
  expansion of
    in history, 44
    recently, 43
  future, 78, 266–267
  of girls reappraised, 221–222
  graduates, 267–268
  importance of biology in, 94, 96
  institutions
    discrimination in access to, 237
    held back by conciliation towards donors, 268
    inheritors of role of church, 45
    as missions of exploration in noosphere, 24
  state interference in, 269
  and mass media, 47–48
  and myths, 88
  need to improve methods, 83, 196, 272
  for parenthood, 213–214

education (*cont.*)
  of politicians and leaders, 242
  on problem of population explosion, 146
  resistance to learning, 215
Environmental Protection Act, 180–181
Environmental Revolution: A Guide for the New Masters of the World, The, Max Nicholson, 8–9 (quoted), 110, 121, 180
ethology
  basic to human society, 11, 14, 93
  defined, 12
  and ecology, 13, 112
  ethological factors in prehistory, 98
  repercussions of recent progress in, 9
eugenics, 132–133
European Economic Community, 247
evolution
  acceleration of, 86
  aiding man's progress, 7, 121
  breeding patterns and, 40–41, 210
  caused by response to challenge, 195
  and individuals, 41, 68
  ecological-ethological view of, 112, 210
  evolutionary *vs.* counter-evolutionary criteria for judging political strategy, 236
  future, 67, 117
  and intelligence, 40–41
  intervention questioned, 32–33
  and need for conscious effort, 69, 82
  peaceful transition likely in Britain, 81
  reviewed in
    Book of Man, 97–98
    History of Mankind, 90
  Evolution of Man and Society, C. D. Darlington, 10, 40, 42 (quoted)
extremists profit by change, 109

Fabian socialism, 161

Food and Agriculture Organization, 132, 177
Ford Foundation, 269
Forester, Jay, 81, 202
funding
  conservation and, 127, 179
  education stultification by potential donors, 268
  expense of family centers justified, 224, 225
  for ICSU, 271–272
  overfunding for technology criticized, 45, 47, 78
  of monitoring indicator species, 184–185
  suggested increase for social sciences, 134
  UN Fund for Population Activity, 128, 130, 246
Future Shock, Alvin Toffler, 117

Galbraith, J. K., 10, 50–51
Galileo Galilei, 46
gene flow
  changing pattern of, 40
  new sources of, 45
generation gap, 226–227
genetics, 41, 132, 270
grant-giving bodies, 134, 269–271
Great Debate, the, 232–233, 237
Green Revolution, 169, 270
Green Version, 96–97 (quoted)
G.N.P. (Gross National Product)
  leveling off, 28–29
  pursuit of, criticized, 25, 45, 73
  statistics on, by country, 29, 63–64

Hansard Society, 139
hard changes (*see* classifications of change)
health, 77, 130
  progress reviewed, 70–71
  requirements in, 71–72
  (*See also* medical techniques)
higher learning (*see* education)
History of Mankind: Scientific and cultural Development, 90
Hitler, Adolf, 132
humanist movement, 125
Huxley, Julian, *Science of Life,* 90

idea systems, 49, 254–255
  current weaknesses in, 117, 241–242
  of future, 35, 102, 257
  and plight of wild animals, 252, 254
  and population explosion, 162
Illich, Ivan, 267
illiteracy, 24, 62, 77
immortality, 21, 142
inflation, 60
intelligence
  evolution of, 40–41, 74
  and world noosphere program, 130
Intergovernmental Maritime Consultative Organisation, London, 246–247
International Biological Programme, 110, 271
  biome stations, 185–187
  Varna General Assembly, 184
International Council of Scientific Unions (ICSU), 128, 130, 184–186, 271
International Geophysical Year, 130, 271
international institutions (*see* supranational institutions)
International Noosphere Program (proposed), 130
International Union for Conservation of Nature and Natural Resources (IUCN), 129, 187, 272
International Union for Evolution of Mankind (INTUNEMAN) (proposed), 127–128, 132, 188
  administration of, 128
  studies, 128–129
Invisible College, 133
ITV programs, 201

Jackson Report, 246
Jung, C. G., 73
juvenile delinquence as pollution, 73

Laski, Harold, 258 (quoted)
law, rule of, 265–266

leadership, 11, 14, 243
  in conservation movement, 120, 126
  criticized, 7, 15, 226
  and education, 180, 242
  importance of, 124–127, 141
  meritocracy, 42–43
  and new men, 34, 47, 80, 119, 180
  personnel selection, 34–35
  of student population, 58, 59
legal measures for environmental protection, 259–261
Leverhulme Foundation, 269
living patterns
  adaptation of women to new, 221
  experiments in, 137–138
  imbalance or harmony with nature, 48
  leading to physical unfitness, 71
leisure
  enforcement and deprivation of, 203–204, 220
  hour-by-hour analysis of, 204–205
  and MIT studies, 202
  and population explosion, 77, 78, 208
  quality of
    capability for, developed, 198–199
    criticized, 197, 201, 219
    defined, 191
    ecological principles and, 191
    higher, urged, 30, 76–78, 199, 202, 203
    lack of elegance in, 105
    politics and, 191–192
    war-making effect on, 192–193
Lorenz, Konrad, 10

McNamara, Robert, 246
Man the tool-maker, 22, 98, 196
  as problem needing feminine influence, 194–195
  and technosphere, 21, 107, 118
marriage, 210, 211
materialism, 14, 50, 51, 161
Marxism, 4, 55, 104, 161
Max Planck Foundation, 269

Meadows, Dennis L., 81, 202
media, mass
  disaster reports aid to conservationists, 122
  effect on change, 4, 5, 47–49
  potential, 273
  example of soft, positive, active change, 48
  humanist movement vs. religious propaganda, 125
  T.V.
    aid in international link, 100
    effect on culture, 100, 201, 266
Medical Research Council's center for studying the common cold, 135
medical techniques of artificial prolongation of life, 45, 72, 259
mental health, 26, 73
meritocracy, 44, 47–48, 49, 60
  described, 42–43
military-industrial complex, 56
military-political establishment, 52–53
myths
  criticized, 26
  eroded by world travel, 58
  function described, 87–88
  usage, 89–90
  value, 88–89

Nader, Ralph, 201–202
National Institute of Social and Economic Research, 132, 271
nationalism, 57–58
National Planning Association, 132
Nature Conservancy, the, 182–184
negative change (see classifications of change)
Neill, A. S., 133
N.G.O.s (nongovernmental organizations), 243–244, 246, 247
Nicholson, Max
  The Environmental Revolution, 8–9 (quoted)
  The System, 139
Nobel Foundation, 269, 270
Nobel Prize, 136

nomosphere
  absence of recognition of, 118, 133–134
  and ancient Greece, 232
  criticized, 19, 21–22
  and cultural scene, 110
  defined, 17–18
  described, 107–108, 235–236
  relation to other spheres, 21, 82–83
  suggested programs for, 131
noosphere
  absence of public appreciation of, 133–134
  and ancient Greece, 232
  and cultural scene, 110
  defined, 16, 17
  described, 107–108, 235–236
  evolution of, 69
  exploration of, 23–24
  man's heritage in, 86, 255
  norm of growth rate, 240
  relation to other spheres, 21–23, 82–83
  suggested world programs for, 130
Northcliffe press, 79
nuclear weapons, 52
Nuffield Foundation, 269

Organization of American States, 128
Organization for Economic Cooperation and Development, Paris, 246
ornithology
  example of peregrine poisoning, 181–184
  study in relation to man, 12
Orwell, George, 55
Outline of History, H. G. Wells, 90
Owen, Robert, 133

palaeontology, 12, 93
parenthood
  pledges of prior claim of children proposed, 212–213, 216–218
  responsibilities, 75–76
  fathers denied by ratrace, 219

INDEX

minimum standards for
  fathers suggested, 220
  role filled by society, 25
  and "wanted child," 143, 75–76
passive change (*see* classifications of change)
Pathfinder status, 136–137
Peace Corps (American), 271
peasants, urban subculture of, 62
Peckham Pioneer Health Centre, 135, 222–225
permissive society
  described, 51
  effect on laws, 209
  example of soft change, 37, 51
  mass reaction toward, 15
Pentagon Papers, The, 53
PEP, 132, 176, 271
Pestalozzi, Johann Heinrich, 133
Phenomenon of Man, The, Pierre Teilhard de Chardin, 15–16 (quoted)
Philippa of Hainauet, 202
police forces, internal, 261
politics
  criteria for judging strategy, evolution-counterrevolution, 236–237
  criticized, 112, 232, 263–264
  decentralization recommended, 191–192, 244–245, 262
  and pollution of culture, 26, 113
  struggles among doctrines, 110–111
  and student population, 58–59, 268
  suggestions for future, 117–118, 130
  (*See also* Marxism)
political zones of instability, 53–54
pollution
  criminality as, 73
  deliberate, unrecognized, 181
  by expansion of G.N.P., 28
  and synthetic materials, 169, 203
  threat of, 109, 122, 174, 256, 275–276

pollution control
  by changing living patterns to higher quality, 29, 202
  by monitoring indicator species, 184–188
  by tracing products and users, 199
  example of warning of peregrine poisoning, 181–184
  new enthusiasm for, 50, 77
  danger of dealing with symptoms, 27
  possibility of, 188–189
population explosion
  acceptable levels, 77, 147
  causes of, 151, 162
  as example of soft, positive, active change, 38–39
  example of animal regulation of, 155–156
  effect of pledged parenthood on, 217–218
  possibility of reduction, 153–154, 155
  principle threat to mankind, 122, 167
  problem described, 39–40, 146–147, 151–152
  and public response, 42, 253
  and reclaimed virgin land, 170–171
  solutions
    family planning policies, 124, 162
    short-sighted, 27, 76, 162
    UN handling of, 246
    and world study of education, 273
  statistics on
    birth rates, 149–150
    by country, 144
    by year, 143–145
  Zero Population Growth, 147–148
  women's role and, 162–165
  (*See also* breeding patterns; Zero Population Growth)
positive change (*see* classifications of change)
primitive peoples, 61–62
prophecy, 38

prophecy (cont.)
  justification for doomsday
    prophets, 168, 175
  methods of, 66–68

racial friction and stress of
    inflation, 60
ratrace, the, 30
  effect on parenthood, 219
  and Pathfinder award, 137
  women and, 163, 164
Red Cross, Swiss-based, 271
religion
  beliefs criticized, 10, 41, 259
  and Book of Man, 92–93
  breaks with, 10–11, 51
  freedom of, urged, 105–106
  history, 10–11, 103–104, 264
  mass media coverage of, 125
  need for, in man, 83
  need for changes in churches,
    83–84, 106–107
Renaissance, 10–11, 273
resources
  allocation of, 26–30, 226
  available living space, 171
  conservation of, lacking,
    172–175
  failure of synthetics as solution,
    169
  failure of virgin lands as
    solution, 170–171
  minerals, 172, 178
  nonrenewable, 168–169, 175–
    177
  suggested agency of evaluation,
    175–177
  and population explosion, 146,
    170–171
  prejudgments urged, 178–179
Resources for the Future, Inc.,
    Washington, D.C., 132, 271
Rockefeller Foundation, 269–270
Royal Court Theatre of Chelsea,
    133
Royal Society, 239, 271
  birth of, 133
rule of law, 265–266

Salisbury, Robert Arthur, 79
science in decline, 45–47

Science of Life, Huxley, Wells, 90
Second International Congress of
    the World Wildlife Fund,
    London, 1970, 121
Serengeti Research Station,
    Tansania, 271
Shakespeare, William, 239
  Hamlet, 256 (quoted)
Simon Population Trust, 160–161
Six-Day War, 54
Smithson, James, 270
Smithsonian Foundation, 269
social sciences, 11, 134, 135
Social Science Development
    Council, 134
Social Science Research Council,
    134
Society of Friends, 264
soft changes (*see* classifications
    of change)
Soil Conservation Districts, 177
sovereign state
  concept of, reconsidered,
    232–233
  curbing of, 53, 139, 261
  and splinter nationalism, 57–58
  war-making
    and confrontation with new
      social forces, 52
    disarmament, 57, 192–193
    tension and stress from, 192
Sputnik, 97
state intervention
  in breeding patterns, 218, 237
  and permissive society, 51
  in Universities, 269
Stockholm process, 245–246
stress
  advertisement and, 193–194
  atlas of, 194
  from conflict of early and
    late changers, 6
  of inflation, causing racial
    friction, 60
  of war-making, 192–193
Strong, Maurice, 188, 245
Study of Instinct, The, Niko
    Tinbergen, 10
Suez crises, 1956, 52, 56
  example of counterevolutionary
    strategy, 237

supranational institutions
  as example of hard change, 43
  failures analyzed, 245–246
  growth of, 57
  listing of specific organizations, 246–247
  and opportunities for meritocracy, 43
supernationalism among students, 59
system, the, 7, 210
  crumbling, 3–4, 11
  and Darwin, 111
  support for, 6, 232
System, The, M. Nicholson, 139, 247

Teacher's Guide to the Green Version, 96
technology
  domination of
    created during WWII, 134
    criticized, 103, 134, 196, 232
    in future, 67
    impact on culture, 59, 113, 255
      enforced leisure, 203–204, 220
    questioned by sources of investment funds, 45
    questioned by public, 47, 50
    in Western world, 49, 98
  methods used for mankind's benefit, 30, 132
technosphere
  defined, 16
  described, 17–18
  destructiveness of, 22–23, 181
  pollution as byproduct of, 174
  in relation to other spheres, 21–23, 82–83, 107–108, 118
  and strata of discarded thought, 235–236
teenagers (*see* young people)
Teilhard de Chardin, Pierre, 17, 107
  The Phenomenon of Man, 15–16 (quoted)
television (*see* media, mass)

time lag between impacts and repercussions
  illustrated, 238–240
  strata impervious to, 241
time span and future views, 5, 6, 257
Tinbergen, Niko, *The Study of Instinct,* 10
Toffler, Alvin, *Future Shock,* 117
Trades Union Congress, 247
"Tree Preservation Order," 260
Trust for Ornithology, 182
Tundra Biome, 186–187

UNESCO, 128
  and *History of Mankind,* 90
United Nations
  and Book of Man, 90–91
  concern over National Parks, 176–177
  and failure of international institutions, 84, 245–246
  and INTUNEMAN, 128, 132
  and opportunities for meritocracy, 43
  population statistics, 144–145, 153
  and program funding, 127, 130
United Nations Educational and Scientific Organization, 272
United Nations Environmental Fund, 175
United Nations Fund for Population Activities (UNFPA), 128, 130, 246
United Nations Population Commission report of 1969, 149
United Nations Population Division publication, 176
United Nations Stockholm Conference on the Human Environment, 188, 243–244
University Grants Committee, 269
unwanted children, 217–218

Varna General Assembly of International Biological Programme, 184
Vietnam War, 52–53, 196
Voluntary Service Overseas (British), 271

war-making
  beginning to be questioned, 53
  lebensraum argument, 55
  legacies that cripple
    evolution, 195
  man-oriented, 194–195
  psychological release by, 56
welfare state, 75, 84
  as example of hard change, 37
Wells, H. G., 90
Wennr-Gren Foundation, 269
Women's Lib, 164, 195
Wordsworth, William, 113 (quoted)
World Bank (IBRD), 246
World Fund for Human Fulfillment, 127, 128
World Health Organization, 128, 132
World Land Bank, 177
World Meteorological Organization, 131–132
World Population and Resources (PEP), 176
World Weather Watch, 131
women
  in age of chivalry, 164, 264–265
  education and employment of reappraised, 221–222
  future envisioned, 229
  mothers in Peckham Pioneer Health Centre, 223
  needs for, 73, 86–87, 195
  politics and dominance of man over, 112
  and ratrace, 30, 163
  status of, and population explosion, 162–163
  and style of living, 197, 220–221
  viewpoint on man-oriented problems urged, 59, 194–195

Young, Michael, 42
young people
  and appeal of parenthood education, 215
  demands of the future on, 83
  doubts and criticisms of, 45, 50, 53, 99, 112
  problems of huge numbers of, 146–147
  and ratrace society, 30, 163
  teenagers, 226–228
    junior citizen groups suggested, 249–250

zero economic growth, 29
Zero Population Growth
  demonstration areas, 149, 154
  need for, 230
  probability of, 147, 153
  statistics on, 148
zones of political instability, 53–54

DATE DUE

GAYLORD   PRINTED IN U.S.A.